The Politics of Federal Prosecution

CHRISTINA L. BOYD, MICHAEL J. NELSON,
IAN OSTRANDER, AND ETHAN D. BOLDT

OXFORD
UNIVERSITY PRESS

OXFORD
UNIVERSITY PRESS

Oxford University Press is a department of the University of Oxford. It furthers the University's objective of excellence in research, scholarship, and education by publishing worldwide. Oxford is a registered trade mark of Oxford University Press in the UK and certain other countries.

Published in the United States of America by Oxford University Press
198 Madison Avenue, New York, NY 10016, United States of America.

Library of Congress Cataloging-in-Publication Data

Names: Boyd, Christina L., author. | Nelson, Michael J. (Political scientist) author. | Ostrander, Ian, author. | Boldt, Ethan D., author.
Title: The politics of federal prosecution / Christina L. Boyd, Michael J. Nelson, Ian Ostrander, and Ethan D. Boldt.
Description: New York, NY : Oxford University Press, [2021] | Includes bibliographical references and index.
Identifiers: LCCN 2020036339 | ISBN 9780197554685 (hardback) | ISBN 9780197554708 (epub) | ISBN 9780197554692 (updf) | ISBN 9780197554715 (online)
Subjects: LCSH: Prosecution—United States. | Public prosecutors—United States. | Prosecution—Political aspects—United States
Classification: LCC KF9640 .B69 2021 | DDC 345.73/05042—dc23
LC record available at https://lccn.loc.gov/2020036339

DOI: 10.1093/oso/9780197554685.001.0001

1 3 5 7 9 8 6 4 2

Printed by Integrated Books International, United States of America

Contents

Acknowledgments

We owe a debt of gratitude to our colleagues, in our home institutions and beyond, who have read and commented on parts of this work, patiently listened as we have discussed exciting things like the history of asset forfeiture or Rod Rosenstein's remarkable DOJ longevity, and supported our research efforts. Thank you to Scott Ainsworth, Ryan Black, Charles Bullock, Roberto Carlos, Jamie Carson, Paul Collins, Amanda Driscoll, Tracey George, Susan Haire, Morgan Hazelton, Erin Heidt-Forsythe, Rachael Hinkle, George Krause, David Lewis, Michael Lynch, Anthony Madonna, John Maltese, Alyx Mark, Keith Schnakenberg, Kevin Scott, Alicia Uribe, Richard Vining, Teena Wilhelm, Margaret Williams, Jeffrey Yates, and Albert Yoon. Various pieces of this work were presented at the Midwest Political Science Association and Southern Political Science Association annual meetings, and the project was strengthened by our smart discussants and audience members.

This project has benefited greatly from the assistance of graduate and undergraduate researchers who helped with data collection, researching federal prosecutors, the DOJ, federal criminal laws, and editing. We thank them immensely! This includes Ruth Ann Bailey, Matt Baker, Andrew Bernstein, Bryan Black, Emma Brunner, Michael Burnham, Alex Corluyan, Nicholas Duffey, Caitlyn Kinard, John Kirby, Peter McAndrews, Steven Morgan, Rebekah Phelps, Reid Powell, Charles Ryan, Taran Samrath, Cullen Threlkeld, and Andrew Tyner. We are also grateful to Jamie Berezin, David Lipp, Karen Jameson, and the full team at Oxford University Press for their guidance and support of this book.

To Andrew Martin, Lee Epstein, Jim Gibson, Mike Gizzi, Jim Spriggs, Susan Haire, Bill Lowry, Margaret Taylor, and Steve Smith, we thank you for being the wonderful mentors who trained us to be social scientists and inspired us to ask research questions about our legal and political systems that matter.

Christy Boyd thanks the University of Georgia's Research Foundation, Department of Political Science, and School of Public and International Affairs for supporting this research. Christy dedicates this book to her loving parents, Jack and Cathy Boyd, who passed away eight days apart from one another in late 2018 and early 2019. Christy attributes all that is good about her, from hard work, to warmth, to humor, to her parents.

Michael Nelson thanks Penn State's Department of Political Science, the Political Science department's Board of Visitors, McCourtney Institute for Democracy (and its director Michael Berkman), and College of the Liberal Arts for supporting this research. He dedicates this book to Rachel Paine Caufield who convinced him to become a political science major and then to go to graduate school. She continues to be a role model, mentor, and friend. He also owes a special debt of gratitude to Matt and Ellen Schill. The very first data for this book was collected on the day that Matt and Ellen were engaged, and the book got to the finish line while he was quarantining with Matt, Ellen, and their one-year-old son during the COVID-19 pandemic almost a decade later. He is lucky to have such great friends.

Ian Ostrander dedicates this book to his spouse, Mariana Medina, and their son, Evan Ostrander. Mariana has long been a source of professional and personal support while their two-year-old son has never failed to make life more interesting during what have been especially interesting times. He would also like to thank Michigan State University and the Department of Political Science for supporting this research. Ian is also grateful to his colleagues and students who have over time patiently endured ironically long discussions of Senate procedures and delay.

Ethan Boldt is grateful to the Department of Political Science and Public Policy and the College of Arts, Humanities and Social Sciences at North Dakota State University and his Ph.D.-granting institution, the University of Georgia, for supporting this research. Ethan dedicates this book to the friends who supported him through graduate school: Doug Atkinson, Jason Byers, Allison Cuttner, Josh Jackson, and George Williford. Thanks for everything and then some. Ethan gives special thanks to his brother Evan for allowing him to work endlessly in his home office during holiday breaks and for being his first best friend.

C.L.B. Athens, Georgia, USA
M.J.N. State College, Pennsylvania, USA
I.O. East Lansing, Michigan, USA
E.D.B. Fargo, North Dakota, USA

1
Introduction

In February 2016, while testifying in a House Appropriations Subcommittee hearing, U.S. Attorney General Loretta Lynch, a Barack Obama appointee, promised that her department would act with independence in investigating Hillary Clinton's usage of a personal email server during her tenure as Secretary of State. During that hearing, Congressman John Carter (R-TX) asked Lynch:

> If the FBI makes the case that Hillary Clinton mishandled classified information and put America's security at risk, will you prosecute the case? . . . [P]lease look the American people in the eye and tell us what your position is as you are the chief prosecutor of the United States.

In response to this questioning, Lynch asserted that:

> [The matter] is being handled by . . . independent attorneys in the Department of Justice. They follow the evidence, they look at the law and they'll make a recommendation to me when the time is appropriate. . . This will be conducted as every other case. We will review all the facts and all the evidence and come to an independent conclusion as how to best handle it. And I am also aware of no efforts to undermine our review or investigation into this matter at all. (Goldman 2016)

Despite strong claims of prosecutorial independence, many Republicans complained that a Department of Justice (DOJ) run by Obama appointees could not impartially pass legal judgment on the Hillary Clinton-emails matter. A June 27, 2016, meeting between Lynch and former U.S. President Bill Clinton would not help matters. The two privately talked for approximately 20 minutes on a plane sitting on the Phoenix Sky Harbor airport tarmac in a meeting described as unplanned and "primarily social." Despite the meeting's claimed innocuous content,

The Politics of Federal Prosecution. Christina L. Boyd, Michael J. Nelson, Ian Ostrander, and Ethan D. Boldt, Oxford University Press (2021).
DOI: 10.1093/oso/9780197554685.003.0001

it "caused a cascading political storm" for Hillary Clinton's presidential campaign and "provided fodder for Republicans who have accused the Justice Department of bias in its inquiry into Secretary Clinton's use of a private email server at the State Department" (Chozick 2016). Even Democrats expressed concerns about the meeting; Senator Chris Coons (D-DE) remarked that the meeting sent "the wrong signal . . . I think she should have steered clear, even of a brief, casual social meeting with the former president" (Chozick 2016).

The drama surrounding Attorney General Lynch and the Clintons reflects a persistent concern about the potential effects of politics on the Department of Justice's prosecutorial decision-making. And while highly salient, it is by no means an isolated case. Recent accounts of political factors interplaying with prosecutors and potential prosecutions abound:

- Prosecutors' decisions whether to charge police officers and protesters in race-police crises in Minneapolis, Ferguson, Cleveland, Baltimore, Louisville, and New York City.
- President Trump's March 2017 order that all Obama-era federal prosecutors immediately tender their resignations.
- Federal government disputes with General David Petraeus regarding the protection of classified political materials.
- The firing of Republican-appointed U.S. Attorney David Iglesias for allegedly refusing to prosecute Democrats on voter fraud charges just prior to the 2006 election.
- The Attorney General, at the behest of the Trump Administration, withdrawing a harsh sentence recommendation and replacing it with a significantly reduced one for Trump political ally Roger Stone.

These are but a handful of recent events that have firmly placed the U.S. criminal justice system—and specifically prosecutors within that system—in the spotlight. And in each high-profile case, political factors appear to influence the decisions made by and regarding prosecutors. But are these salient events and decisions representative of what happens with prosecutors in the criminal justice system more generally? In other words, *do politics and political factors regularly affect federal prosecutors' selection and decision-making?* This book tackles this very question.

1.1 Political Tensions for Federal Prosecutors

The U.S. Department of Justice (DOJ) is charged with federal law enforcement and criminal justice administration including enforcing federal law, providing "federal leadership in preventing and controlling crime," seeking "just punishment for those guilty of unlawful behavior," and "fair and impartial administration of justice" (U.S. Department of Justice 2020b). The job of carrying out much of this DOJ mission rests with 93 federal prosecutors—the U.S. Attorneys—and their staff in their geographically dispersed offices around the country. Federal prosecutors argue that they are guided by the principle of seeking and accomplishing justice in their work (Melilli 1992). Or, as Justice Sutherland put it in 1935 U.S. Supreme Court opinion in *Berger v. United States*, 295 U.S. 78, a federal prosecutor's interest "in criminal prosecution is not that it shall win a case, but that justice shall be done" (88).

An aspirational view of justice is one that operates within a framework of due process, neutrality, and independence. Embedded in this view is "a belief in governmental limitation, of barriers to whimsical authority by political officials. It suggests an adherence to the old adage that ours 'is a government of laws, not of men'; that our system of justice is premised upon rules and upon structure, not upon the personal idiosyncrasies of public officials" or mass appeal (Atkins and Pogrebin 1982, 3). Many believe that federal prosecutors pursue justice by following these principles, arguing that a prosecutor's duty is "to make reflective and independent judgments that conform with the evidence" and law rather than external factors (DiBiagio 2000, 66).

This emphasis on independence and due process in prosecutorial decision-making, rather than being mindful of outside forces, dates back to at least Thomas Jefferson. Jefferson famously wrote in 1816 that "[t]he most sacred of the duties of government [is] to do equal and impartial justice to all its citizens" (Jefferson 1816). Modern rhetoric continues to reinforce this point, with President Obama stating in 2016 that "I guarantee that there is no political influence in any investigation conducted by the Justice Department, or the FBI . . . in any case" (Fox News Sunday 2016). Seymour (1975) went so far as to say that U.S. Attorneys operate in "splendid isolation." Eisenstein (1978, 11) further asserted that U.S. Attorneys hold "a degree of autonomy and independence from the department perhaps unmatched by any other field service in the federal government." In other words, Attorney General Lynch isn't the only one who thinks the DOJ's "independent attorneys" reach "independent conclusions."

Despite working in an ostensibly "isolated" and "unfettered" environment (Seymour 1975; Whitford and Yates 2009, 116) and numerous promises of commitments to independence, the potential for political factors to affect prosecutors and their decisions looms large. Federal prosecutors make decisions regarding criminal offenses that are often highly political and controversial in nature or consequence. They hold enormous grants of discretion or latitude in how they seek justice in the criminal matters in their districts meaning that "unlike the symbolic idea of due process," factors other than "rules may guide decision-making within the administration of criminal justice" in the federal system (Atkins and Pogrebin 1982, 3). And, of course, U.S. Attorneys' prosecuted cases are decided and reviewed by a judiciary that is itself frequently political (Epstein and Knight 1998; Hettinger, Lindquist, and Martinek 2006, 2004).

At the national level, the president and Congress are powerful political principals that can influence the behavior of U.S. Attorneys, their agents. As we explore in much more detail to come, U.S. Attorneys are selected and removed through a politically driven process (Nelson and Ostrander 2016; Scott 2007). They operate within the purview of the DOJ, an executive branch agency, and are led by the Attorney General, himself a presidential appointee and high-ranking member of the president's cabinet. U.S. Attorneys receive their funding from Congress and their authority to prosecute many crimes through laws and regulations passed by Congress and the executive branch. These and other mechanisms within principal-agency theory work together to allow the president and Congress to constrain the policy priorities of U.S. Attorneys and incentivize prosecutorial decision-making outcomes that are desirable by the national principals.

Federal prosecutors are also members of the local community in which they work. As such, they likely value community priorities and share beliefs with that local population on important public issues (Whitford and Yates 2009) and often plan to return to work (or run for office) in that district when their tenure as U.S. Attorney is completed. What is good or politically palatable prosecutorial policy for the Eastern District of Virginia or the Southern District of New York simply may not sit well in places like Oregon, Montana, and Texas. As such, federal prosecutors can find themselves torn between the DOJ's national policy objectives and their district's localized needs and preferences.

We thus suspect that the work of federal prosecutors is often just as much about "politics" as it is about some neutral and objective version of "justice." This can put U.S. Attorneys in a very tough position—effectively caught in a battle between the neutral, impartial demands of due process and the law and political pressure from a national administration or local forces that may push for more aggressive prosecutions for certain offenses (Perry 1998).

1.2 Politics and Prosecution: Does It Matter?

There may be no better time than the present to examine federal prosecutors and the political tensions that they face in carrying out their work. The influence of federal prosecutors in the American criminal justice system is, arguably, at an all-time high today. The prosecutor is "the real arbiter of what laws shall be enforced and against whom" (National Commission on Law Observance and Enforcement 1931, 19). U.S. Attorneys "sit at the center of the federal prosecutorial machine" (Whitford 2002, 11) and are responsible for making many pivotal and highly discretionary decisions. These include, for example, whether to argue against bail, whether to prosecute or decline prosecution, what charges to bring, whether to offer a plea bargain, and what sentence to recommend to the trial judge (e.g., Howard et al. 2000). Because of the well-documented decline of trials and uptick in settled outcomes in American courts, federal prosecutors are no longer "merely law enforcers. They are the final adjudicators in the vast majority of cases" (Barkow 2009, 871).

The past century has also seen notable changes to criminal law that directly affect federal prosecutors. One of these is an increase in the federalization of criminal law. As evidence of this, Barkow (2009) reports that over 40% of criminal laws enacted at the federal level since the Civil War were passed after 1970. One important result of this federalization of criminal law has been to shift a number of offenses into the jurisdiction of U.S. Attorneys (Clymer 1997; Heller 1997). The adoption of advisory and mandatory sentencing guidelines has also directly impacted federal prosecutors. Sentencing guidelines "confined the discretion of judges but increased the sentencing power of prosecutors" (Alschuler 1991, 903). Today, there are "currently no effective legal checks in place to police the manner in which prosecutors exercise their discretion" (Barkow 2009, 869).

In an era where gridlock and a perpetual partisan messaging campaign have paralyzed the legislative branch's ability to pass major bipartisan policies (Lee 2016), legislative solutions for societal ills like mass incarceration seem distant. If federal prosecutors are under Washington's tight control, prospects for reform could nonetheless be attainable through an administrative strategy (Nathan 1983). The executive branch itself could implement explicit guidance for federal prosecutors that would change which cases are prosecuted and brought to trial and what sentences are pursued. At the same time, any such reforms would be feeble: they could be singlehandedly and swiftly reversed by a new administration. At the other end of the spectrum, if federal prosecutors act subject to the whims of their localities, acting independently of Washington's direction, the predictability and uniformity that supposedly lies at the heart of the criminal justice system would be called into question. As a result, clarifying the relationship between political considerations and the exercise of prosecutorial discretion is critical for our full understanding of how the federal judicial process works (or does not work).

Similarly, decisions made by prosecutors that are seen as being driven by political factors, and not the law or objective rules, can undermine the public's essential confidence in government. A large literature on the public's support for governmental institutions has established that decisions based on *politics* rather than on *principle* undermine public support (Gibson and Caldeira 2009; Gibson and Nelson 2017; Hibbing and Theiss-Morse 1995). Were it the case that prosecutorial decisions were based on the prosecutor's self-interest rather than on an objective review of the facts, the very public support that is essential to maintain the judiciary's unique role in the political system could tumble (Gibson and Nelson 2014).

There is already empirical evidence that judges are geographically biased in their decision-making (Epstein et al. 2008); were prosecutors similarly subject to strong local considerations, it would only exacerbate an already looming growing legitimacy deficit facing the criminal justice system (Gibson and Nelson 2018; Rocque 2011). Critical ongoing issues in the system include race, punitiveness, drugs, criminal sentencing, overcrowding in prisons, and beyond (Gibson 1978; Hurwitz and Peffley 2005; Nelson 2014; Peffley and Hurwitz 2010; Tiede 2009). Many of these issues are themselves politically controversial, and the presence of systematic political influence on prosecutorial staffing and decision-making may do little to quell concerns about the health and fairness of the U.S. criminal justice system.

Finally, we note that the apparent interplay between federal prosecution and politics shows no signs of disappearing or diminishing in importance.

As the pages of this book will highlight, no recent presidential administration has been spared from significant, politically tinged controversies involving selection, retention, and decision-making of federal prosecutors. Our insights in this book are thus not likely to be time bound and may prove informative on the politics of federal prosecution for many years to come.

1.3 Structure of the Book

The Politics of Federal Prosecution aims to provide a comprehensive examination of how and when political factors affect federal prosecutors' staffing and decision-making. Throughout the book, we utilize a combination of original, newly compiled, and hard-to-access data to investigate the relationship between prosecutors and politics. We introduce the data in the chapters that follow. Where possible, we utilize graphics in the text to communicate information about data and statistical results.

Chapter 2 provides an overview and broad introduction to federal prosecutors and the U.S. DOJ. The chapter follows the historical evolution of the DOJ (and its predecessors). We provide evidence that politics and the administration of federal justice have always been tightly intertwined. Moreover, enlargement of the federal law since the Civil War has brought with it enlargement of the federal prosecutorial machine, the DOJ, and the role of the U.S. Attorney General. Using data from the DOJ, we illustrate the growth of the federal prosecutorial machine and discuss its ramifications for the role of the U.S. Attorney in the modern political system.

Chapters 3 and 4 explore the political nature of staffing federal prosecutorial positions, broadly defined. Chapter 3 focuses specifically on the selection and appointment of federal prosecutors. It overviews the political nomination and confirmation process for U.S. Attorneys, revealing that U.S. Attorneys are the rare federal office in which all three branches of government play a role in the staffing process. We then turn to an empirical examination of how politics play an important role in determining whether U.S. Attorney nominations are confirmed by the Senate as well as how long it takes to receive confirmation. As our results reveal, presidents nearly always succeed in their nominations of U.S. Attorneys; however, the Senate can and does check the president by delaying confirmation votes—sometimes "to death"—for overtly political nominees for U.S. Attorney.

Chapter 4 presents the politics relating to the retention, departure, or removal of federal prosecutors. As we fully detail, U.S. Attorneys serve at the pleasure of the president and can be dismissed. This power allows presidents to wield ongoing power over the application of federal law beyond simply choosing the U.S. Attorneys. However, aside from a routine turnover of U.S. Attorney positions at the beginning of a new administration, presidents rarely use this power. When presidents remove U.S. Attorneys in the middle of their term, they can pay great political costs to do so. In the most prominent recent example, President George W. Bush faced heated blowback for firing a handful of U.S. Attorneys in late 2006, a case we review in detail. We further follow U.S. Attorneys' careers—to Congress, the bench, and the statehouse—after they leave office, illustrating that U.S. Attorney positions serve as a springboard for many ambitious politicians to seek higher office. In this way, presidential selections of U.S. Attorneys have long-lasting effects on American politics.

Chapters 5 through 8 explore the decisions federal prosecutors make and how political factors are likely to cabin those decisions. In Chapter 5, we explore the theory for why we should expect the priorities and preferences of the president, Congress, and a U.S. Attorney's local public to serve as important checks on the prosecutorial agendas of these federal prosecutors. As we argue in the chapter, prosecutors hold vast discretion that extends to nearly all of their decisions, from before criminal cases are filed through offender sentencing. Via principal-agency theory, we can understand how political principals like the president and Congress can influence the behavior and policy priorities of local federal prosecutors and incentivize U.S. Attorney decision-making and prosecutorial outcomes that are desirable by the principals. We expect that presidential rhetoric and congressional hearings on crime-fighting priorities will provide important, meaningful signals regarding these principals' priorities and how they should translate to responsive prosecutorial behavior. In addition to congressional and presidential effects on prosecutors, we also anticipate that U.S. Attorneys will be mindful of the preferences of their local public since even appointed prosecutors, like U.S. Attorneys, have good reason to pay heed to their local public and its views toward crime (something that can vary considerably depending on one's region of the country). Chapter 5 also introduces the empirical measures used to capture political superiors' communication to federal prosecutors via presidential rhetoric, congressional hearings, and local factors like local public opinion on crime, punitiveness levels, and crime rates.

Chapter 6 centers on the highly discretionary decision of prosecutors to bring or decline to bring prosecutions in individual criminal matters. This is a critical agenda-setting decision for the criminal justice system: when a prosecutor declines to bring a prosecution, no case results. After examining the descriptive data and underlying policies on federal declinations, Chapter 6 then provides an empirical test of how presidential, congressional, and local public political factors affect the decision to prosecute or decline to prosecute federal criminal matters. To do so, we analyze data containing nearly 200,000 federal criminal matters from 1996 to 2011 involving violent crime. Our results reveal sizable political effects on whether federal prosecutors bring violent crime prosecutions.

In Chapter 7, we examine another area of discretionary prosecutorial decision-making of great importance in the criminal justice system: the charging and bargaining process. Based on Chapter 5's theoretical story on political responsiveness in prosecutorial decisions, we expect that prosecutors will be less likely to demonstrate leniency in providing charge reductions and offering substantial assistance downward sentencing departures when their political principals and local public send strong signals regarding their prosecutorial priorities for a given area of crime. To empirically test this, we rely on DOJ and U.S. Sentencing Commission data of individual federal violent crime criminal matters. We find evidence that political responsiveness helps drive prosecutorial charging and bargaining behavior.

Chapter 8 explores how prosecutorial aggressiveness in fighting the tools and instrumentalities of crime can be affected by the political winds of the moment. To do this, we focus on how federal prosecutors use their criminal asset forfeiture powers to creatively battle crime when it is politically important to do so. After introducing federal criminal asset forfeiture, the chapter details the close connection between criminal forfeiture and political motivations and tracks the evolution of forfeiture policy in federal laws and Supreme Court opinions. For Chapter 8's empirical test, we analyze annual forfeiture for 89 federal districts from 1996 to 2013. Our results indicate that, as was the case with other prosecutorial decisions, criminal forfeiture serves as another key way that U.S. Attorneys respond to political signals from political superiors on the importance of prioritizing the fight of federal crime. Chapter 8 concludes by reflecting and providing descriptive evidence on how it appears that federal prosecutors and the DOJ have largely replaced controversy-prone civil asset forfeitures with their less controversial cousin, criminal forfeitures.

Finally, in Chapter 9, we conclude by summarizing our key analysis and findings and tying our various inquiries together. In doing so, we reflect on the broad conclusions about how political factors affect federal prosecutorial staffing and decision-making. Chapter 9 provides an opportunity to reflect on our findings' broader implications for the work of prosecutors in the United States, the criminal justice system, and public perceptions of that system. We also ponder about the criminal justice issues and strategies that we have seen emerge during the first years of the Trump Administration for the DOJ and federal prosecutors and discuss what is likely to come in these areas for the remaining years of the Trump Administration and in the years that follow.

In short, this book provides a tour of the political influences that shape U.S. Attorneys from their nomination, into their workplaces, and into the broader political system. While these individuals may try to limit the influence of partisan politics on their decision-making, they are political appointees, confirmed through a political process, who are charged with enforcing the president's law enforcement priorities. As a result, politics is inextricably linked to every aspect of that behavior. That fact is the central theme of this book.

2

Federal Prosecution Yesterday and Today

> [R]epublican attorneys . . . being the doors of entrance into the courts, are indispensably necessary as a shield to the republican part of our fellow-citizens.
>
> —Thomas Jefferson, March 1801[1]

> I want the American people to have a Justice Department and United States Attorneys' Offices that enforce the law without regard to political influence and partisanship. I want that today, but I want to set the standard so that whoever is President 2 years from now, whether it is a Democratic or Republican administration, we have an independent prosecutor system that will prosecute without fear or favor.
>
> —Sen. Patrick Leahy, March 2007[2]

Made more than two hundred years apart, these two statements by prominent U.S. political leaders illustrate two very different conceptions about the role of U.S. Attorneys in the American political system. When he became president in 1801, Thomas Jefferson faced a judiciary packed *entirely* with Federalist judges (Knudson 1970). Jefferson argued that the appointment of U.S. Attorneys who shared his Democratic-Republican partisan leanings was essential to mitigate the partisan leanings of an unfriendly judiciary. As a modern-day chairman of the powerful Senate Judiciary Committee, Vermont Senator Patrick Leahy presented a starkly different ideal for federal prosecutors: one insulated from partisan preferences. Speaking in response to George W. Bush Administration's decision to fire several U.S. Attorneys, Leahy suggested that U.S. Attorneys should be freed to work independently of political pressures. As the juxtaposition of these two statements suggests,

[1] Quoted in Cummings and McFarland (1937, 53).
[2] Quoted in Senate Judiciary Committee (2007, 74).

The Politics of Federal Prosecution. Christina L. Boyd, Michael J. Nelson, Ian Ostrander, and Ethan D. Boldt, Oxford University Press (2021).
DOI: 10.1093/oso/9780197554685.003.0002

the relationship between federal prosecutors and the political process has been a never-ending conversation in the United States.

Our task in this chapter is to explain how the country has evolved on this spectrum, with Jefferson openly hoping U.S. Attorneys would perform their work in a partisan fashion and Leahy providing a paean to prosecutorial independence. As we will see, one major theme in the development of federal prosecution has been a gradually increasing centralization of authority over U.S. Attorneys by federal law enforcement agencies. While U.S. Attorneys were once entirely free from federal supervision, today their authority is increasingly defined and overseen from Washington, D.C. In this chapter, we demonstrate that the administration of federal justice has always been politically tinged. Moreover, this relationship has magnified as the size of the federal government and the role of the federal prosecutorial machine have increased.

To this end, we discuss the changing relationship between U.S. Attorneys and the Department of Justice (DOJ), an agency that was not created until after the Civil War. We explain the evolution of the design, structure, and responsibilities of the DOJ from its inception to today and review the organization of the modern DOJ. We distinguish between the agency's law enforcement activities and its more traditional prosecutorial arm. We explain the different types of federal prosecutorial positions, including the U.S. Attorney General, the Deputy Attorney General, the Associate Attorney General, the Solicitor General, and the Assistant U.S. Attorneys. Lastly, we show that, despite the broad authority of the DOJ to shape the administration of federal justice, much of the prosecutorial decision-making takes place within the 93 U.S. Attorneys offices around the country.

2.1 The Historical Development of United States Attorneys

We begin by reviewing the history of federal prosecutorial power in the United States since the Colonial Era. This history helps highlight how the authority of federal prosecution has been inextricably linked to politics since the very beginning of America's founding. It also demonstrates the federal government's ever-changing role in supervising U.S. Attorneys. U.S. Attorneys have always been local political officials. But, the level of federal oversight they have experienced (and who conducts that oversight) has changed dramatically throughout American history.

2.1.1 Federal Prosecution in Early American History

Even before independence, prosecutors played an important role in America. Legal matters in Colonial America were handled by an Attorney General in each colony. The colonial Attorneys General were, in essence, agents of the English Attorney General and were charged with enforcing English law (Key 1938). The prosecutorial powers wielded by these early prosecutors were rarely defined formally in statute; instead, they were "possessed with the common law powers and duties of [their] prototype in England, except as changed by specific statute or charter" (Key 1938, 169). The lack of statutory restrictions on their power gave prosecutors a broad grant of authority in early America.

When the colonies banded together to form a unified political system, they rejected the need for a centralized, national prosecutorial office. While the Continental Congress discussed creating an Attorney General "to prosecute all suits on behalf of the United States," it ultimately rejected the idea. And, when the states first formed a national government under the Articles of Confederation, that weak federal government did not include a federal prosecutorial position. Instead, the federal government appointed a "procurator" in individual states to prosecute crimes on behalf of the national government (Key 1938).

The ratification of the U.S. Constitution brought with it a stronger and more centralized federal government. However, the framers specified no procedure to enforce or prosecute violations of federal law. While the Constitution carefully explains the structure of Congress and the presidency in its text, the document is relatively silent about the structure and function of the federal judicial branch. Article III of the Constitution creates the federal judiciary in just a few short paragraphs; the U.S. Supreme Court is the only judicial body it explicitly creates. The Constitution gives Congress the authority to create and dictate the structure of lower federal courts as it sees fit.

Congress—in the first session of the first Congress—quickly seized that opportunity, expanding the size of the federal judiciary when it passed the Judiciary Act of 1789. The law created 13 judicial districts in the 11 states with a district court and a circuit court in each district.[3] Supreme Court justices "rode circuit" to help staff the circuit courts, physically traveling from one location to the next to sit as judges on the local circuit courts (Stras 2007).

With the creation of a relatively strong federal government came an obvious problem: someone had to represent the United States in lawsuits in which the federal government was a litigant.[4] The Judiciary Act of 1789 attempted to solve this problem by creating the position of Attorney General, a person "learned in the law" who was given the responsibility

> to prosecute and conduct all suits in the Supreme Court in which the United States shall be concerned, and to give his advice and opinion upon questions of law when required by the President of the United States, or when requested by the heads of any of the departments, touching any matters that may concern their departments. (1 Stat. 92)

This relatively vague grant of authority provided the Attorney General broad power to represent the federal government in legal matters before the Supreme Court. But, the Act also decentralized the federal prosecutorial power, denying the Attorney General the ability to represent the federal government in the lower courts.

The authority to represent the federal government in the lower courts was given to another group of people, called "district attorneys." Borrowing language from a 1704 Connecticut law, the Judiciary Act of 1789 provided for the appointment of "a meet person learned in the law to act as an attorney for the United States" in each judicial district (National Commission on Law Observance and Enforcement 1931). These district attorneys were the first United States Attorneys.[5] These early federal prosecutors had the duty

[3] Virginia and Massachusetts had two judicial districts. Virginia was divided into the District of Virginia and the District of Kentucky; Massachusetts was divided into the District of Maine and the District of Massachusetts.

[4] The prosecutorial function in early America was even more diffuse than one might expect. Private citizens at this point in history could directly start a prosecution, could request a warrant from a judge to arrest a defendant, and could present evidence directly to grand juries (Dangel 1990). Because there was no federal law enforcement authority at this point in history and the resources of the district attorneys were puny, the direct involvement of the public as prosecutors helped to police conduct in early America (Krent 1989).

[5] The "district attorney" label persisted for over 150 years. Congress did not formally codify the term "United States Attorney" until 1948 (Coats and Stephens 2015).

> to prosecute in such district all delinquents for crimes and offences, cognizable under the authority of the United States, and all civil actions in which the United States shall be concerned, except before the supreme court in the district in which that court shall be holden. (1 Stat. 92)

In other words, the district attorneys had full authority to decide when and how to represent the federal government within their geographic domain.

Who should choose the Attorney General and district attorneys? Congress went back and forth on this point. Early versions of the Judiciary Act of 1789 relied on *judicial* appointments, requiring the Supreme Court to appoint the Attorney General and the local district court to appoint the local district attorney (Warren 1923). Congress eventually opted against providing judges the ability to appoint the prosecutors who would practice before them. Instead, the final version of the law was silent on the question of who should appoint these officials. In response, President Washington stepped in, sending Congress a slate of justices, district judges, and U.S. Attorneys on September 24, 1789. Congress confirmed these nominations quickly, and the precedent for staffing these positions was created (Warren 1923).

While early U.S. Attorneys had a broad grant of power to prosecute violations of federal law in their geographic district, their power was curtailed by a practicality: the scope of federal law in early America was thin. State law, rather than federal law, was the source of most criminal law in early America (Beale 1996). As a result, U.S. Attorneys in pre-Civil War America were generally limited to prosecuting only those cases directly mentioned in the U.S. Constitution, such as piracy, counterfeiting, treason, felonies committed on the high seas, perjury, bribery, and extortion (Executive Office for U.S. Attorneys 1989).

That so many of these crimes were financial crimes is directly related to the compensation for federal prosecutors in the first few decades of American history. Early U.S. Attorneys did not have a set salary; rather, they received "such fees as shall be taxed therefor [*sic*] in the respective courts before which the suits or prosecutions shall be" (1 Stat. at L., p. 92–3, ch. 20). As a report by the (Executive Office for U.S. Attorneys 1989, 5) explains:

> Until 1896, United States Attorneys were paid on a fee system based on the cases they prosecuted. Those fees could amount to quite a substantial sum if the district was located on the coast. In those districts, maritime cases filled the docket with seizures and forfeitures involving substantial amounts of

> expensive cargo. One United States Attorney in such a district reportedly received an annual income of $100,000 as early as 1804, a substantial fortune for that time.[6] In contrast, when regulated salaries were introduced in 1896, they ranged from $2,500 to $5,000.

In other words, early U.S. Attorneys were (literally) able to profit directly from their prosecutions.

Though individual U.S. Attorneys could become quite wealthy if their prosecutions were profitable, the same was not true of the first Attorneys General. While the salaries of the Secretaries of State and the Treasury were set by Congress at $3,500 a year, the salary for the first Attorney General received only $1,500 per year because Congress did not believe the position was a full-time job (Easby-Smith 1904). Moreover, Congress provided the first Attorney General with no support staff or even office space in the nation's capitol. The Attorney General did not receive the help of a clerk for 27 years after the position was created and was not provided his "proper" rank in the cabinet order until 1886 (Easby-Smith 1904; Key 1938).

To compound the institutional weakness of early Attorneys General, the Judiciary Act of 1789 provided the Attorney General no legal authority to participate in lower court proceedings for cases he would eventually have to handle on appeal before the U.S. Supreme Court (Krent 1989). Because each district attorney could act freely, the Attorney General had no way to coordinate the legal arguments made by the United States before the federal courts. Instead, there was no way to ensure that different attorneys representing the federal government made arguments in their local courts that were compatible; instead, district attorneys routinely made legal arguments that contradicted each other, thereby ensuring that the federal government had no official legal position on many important matters (Spaulding 2008).[7]

Instead of allowing the Attorney General to coordinate the work of the district attorneys, Congress gave formal supervisory authority to the Secretary of State. In practice, though, the Secretary rarely interacted with the district attorneys (limiting his interactions mostly to cases implicating foreign policy). Federal prosecutors were not even required to file reports to the Secretary updating him on their work (Dangel 1990).

[6] This would be over $2 million in 2020 dollars.

[7] While it was not mandated, some district attorneys did voluntarily coordinate with the Attorney General, particularly in high profile cases (Bloch 1989). This, however, was the exception rather than the rule.

This lack of oversight immediately caused problems. The first Attorney General, Edmund Randolph, sent President Washington a letter after a year as Attorney General, asking for his position to be empowered. He wrote:

> [I]t may frequently arise that the United States may be deeply affected by various proceedings in the inferior courts, which no appeal can rectify. The peculiar duty of the Attorney General calls upon him to watch over these cases; and being, in the eye of the world, responsible for the final issue, to offer advice at the earliest stage of any business; and indeed, until repeated adjudications shall have settled a clear line of partition between the federal and State courts, his best exertions cannot be too often repeated to oppose the danger of a schism. For this purpose the attorneys of the districts ought, I conceive, to be under an obligation to transmit to him a state of every case in which the harmony of the two judiciaries may be hazarded, and to communicate to him those topics on which the subjects of foreign nations may complain in the administration of justice. Perhaps, too, in the review which the President takes of the affairs of the Union at the opening of each session of Congress, the judicial department will be comprehended. But the Attorney General, who ought to be able to represent the true situation of it, must be forever incompetent to the task until he may officially, and with the right of expecting an answer, propound his inquiries to the district attorneys. (quoted in Bloch 1989, 586–87)

Washington took Randolph's concerns to Congress. However, Congress did not increase the Attorney General's formal powers at that juncture nor did it give the Attorney General the authority to supervise the district attorneys.

Congress eventually did increase oversight of federal prosecutors in the early 1800s. However, it did not give that authority to the Attorney General. Instead, Congress moved control of federal prosecutors to the Treasury Department. These Treasury Department officials lacked the education and expertise necessary to supervise the federal prosecutors effectively. Indeed, at one point, Congress gave authority to supervise the district attorneys to "an accounting officer with a very small salary" and no legal background (Key 1938, 177).

It was not until 1830 that Congress gave supervisory control to a legal professional who also had the power to enforce uniform standards over federal prosecutions. That position, the Solicitor of the Treasury, was given control over the U.S. Attorneys, the U.S. Marshals, and the Clerks of Court (Act of May 29, 1830, ch. 153, 4 Stat. 414). The Solicitor was further given the authority to create uniform rules for district attorneys to follow. Congress's action in the creation of this position marked the first major federal attempt to centralize control over federal prosecution and to provide uniformity in the implementation of federal law across the country.[8]

In short, the early history of U.S. Attorneys is characterized by an immense freedom to do their jobs without consistent or centralized oversight by the federal government. In the words of one former United States Attorney, early U.S. Attorneys worked in "splendid isolation . . . Each was a king in his own domain, appointed by the President of the United States and directly answerable to him alone" due to the lack of effective federal government oversight (Executive Office for U.S. Attorneys 1989, 5). Until the federal government began to provide stricter oversight of federal prosecution, district attorneys were free to pursue whatever legal strategies they saw best even if they contradicted what the federal government would eventually argue before the U.S. Supreme Court. As a result, the enforcement of federal law was far from uniform or consistent across the country.

While it caused many practical problems, the decentralized nature of district attorneys' authority in early America also had benefits. For example, this decentralized system provided political cover for the Attorney General. According to one law professor:

> Whether intended or not, the resulting disarray may have worked to enhance the independence of each department, and certainly the district attorneys, from direct political accountability to the President. It also likely relieved the Attorney General from some of the political pressure that centralized authority entails. (Spaulding 2008, 1959)

[8] The creation of the Solicitor of the Treasury was offered as a proposal by Daniel Webster as an alternative to a request by President Andrew Jackson to place the Attorney General on equal position with other cabinet heads and to give the Attorney General supervisory authority over the district attorneys: essentially a request to create the Department of Justice 50 years before that agency was created (Key 1938). Though President Andrew Jackson signed the bill into law, he expressed his frustration with the disorganized structure of the federal government's legal matters that same year. In his second annual message to Congress, he stated, "I am convinced that the public interest would be greatly promoted by giving [the Attorney General] the general superintendence of the various law agents of the Government, and of all law proceedings, whether civil or criminal, in which the United States may be interested" (Jackson 1830).

In other words, while the Attorney General could not supervise the district attorneys' work, he also could not be blamed for any poor decisions they made. This pattern continued until the Civil War.

2.1.2 Civil War, Reconstruction, and the Emergence of the DOJ

After the Civil War, Congress finally centralized the country's legal apparatus by creating the Department of Justice. Congress formally passed the Act to Establish the Department of Justice (16 Stat. 162, Ch. 150) on April 28, 1870. In both houses, the Act passed by voice vote, so no formal statement of legislative opposition to the agency's creation exists. President Grant signed the bill on June 22, 1870, and the DOJ was formally established on July 1, 1870. Headed by the Attorney General, the DOJ was responsible for handling all criminal and civil legal matters in which the federal government played a part.

Historians have provided three major explanations for the creation of the DOJ (Shugerman 2014). First, historians have argued that the DOJ was created in response to the rise of litigation in the United States during and after the Civil War. To fund its war efforts, the federal government had levied taxes, which created an enormous number of legal disputes on topics as disparate as property disputes, customs, and taxation. Consequentially, the resolution of these conflicts required a substantial increase in governmental legal resources, which provided the justification for the creation of the DOJ (Shugerman 2014). The amount of litigation in federal courts greatly outpaced the ability of the Attorney General and federal prosecutors to manage it. As Key (1938) explains, "[n]o more than three or four months [of war] were necessary to bring glaringly to the public intention the incongruity of having district attorneys working individually, and at times divergently, without direction from a centralized head" (180). Individual agencies responded to this increase in litigation by hiring outside attorneys to litigate on behalf of the federal government and by creating chief legal officers, called Solicitors, for their department (Cummings and McFarland 1937).[9] The result was a patchwork legal infrastructure for the federal government.

[9] The federal government spent nearly a half-million dollars for legal services during a three-year period immediately after the Civil War (Key 1938).

Much litigation on behalf of the federal government—even before the U.S. Supreme Court—was carried out by private attorneys hired because of their political connections rather than their legal acumen and with no long-term connection to the government or its interests (Waxman 2000). These private attorneys made "ill-considered and inconsistent representations about the position of the United States with respect to interpretations of law" (Waxman 2000, 1300). Moreover, because each agency had its own chief legal officer, agencies were free to pursue conflicting and contradictory legal strategies in the courts. Further, the U.S. Attorneys had no single supervisory authority. By creating a single Department of Justice and empowering the Attorney General to supervise the legal officers of all other agencies, the creation of the DOJ provided a way for Congress to centralize the nation's legal affairs and handle the challenging legal environment the country faced during the Civil War and Reconstruction (Cummings and McFarland 1937). A unified DOJ could establish uniform legal positions for the federal government that local prosecutors could implement in their own caseloads.

Second, some historians have suggested that Congress established the DOJ in an effort to enforce Reconstruction and civil rights (Spaulding 2008). After the Civil War, the legal landscape of the United States changed dramatically as Congress passed the Reconstruction Amendments and their enabling legislation. These laws provided the federal government with legal tools to ensure the equal treatment of newly freed Blacks and required extensive coordination across jurisdictions. Federal law enforcement officials often had to intervene in the South to ensure compliance by recalcitrant political actors. All of these efforts exhausted an already stretched thin federal legal apparatus, and the creation of the DOJ offered the additional resources and coordinated power that the federal government needed to succeed in its efforts at Reconstruction (Spaulding 2008).

Finally, historians have suggested that Congress sought to professionalize and insulate the nation's legal apparatus from the politicized and patronage-driven executive branch. As both of the above accounts suggest, the DOJ was created during a time period when the government's legal needs were expanding. At the same time, the federal bureaucracy was embedded in a rich patronage tradition, where jobs were handed out to loyal party members and tended to turn over with the occupant of the Oval Office (Hoogenboom 1961). As a *New York Times* article announcing the creation of the Department explained:

> Under the old system, each of the Departments of the Government at Washington had a legal branch, presided over by a solicitor; and some of them had several of these officials. Of course they were appointed by the Secretary whose department they were connected, and their places were regarded as part of his legitimate patronage. They were, moreover, free from any outside control or interference, and were not always on the best terms with each other. The result was that the old system was discordant and expensive, and was radically opposed to any reform. (*New York Times* 1870, 4)

By removing the control of legal officers from this politicized environment and placing it under the control of the Attorney General, an office that—all things considered—was less politicized, Congress hoped to promote a nonpartisan and independent legal resource for the federal government (Shugerman 2014).

One consequence of the Attorney General's new responsibilities as head of an executive agency was that he could no longer be the government's point person before the U.S. Supreme Court. Therefore, Congress simultaneously created a new position, the Solicitor General. The Solicitor General was empowered to serve as the federal government's chief legal representative before the U.S. Supreme Court and to exercise the duties of the Attorney General when he was unable to do so (Easby-Smith 1904). The report accompanying the Act described the position as follows:

> We propose to create . . . a new officer, to be called the solicitor general of the United States, part of whose duty it shall be to try . . . cases in whatever courts they may arise. We propose to have a man of sufficient learning, ability, and experience that he can be sent to New Orleans or to New York, or into any court wherever the Government has any interest in litigation, and there present the case of the United States as it should be presented. (Congressional Globe, 41st Congress, 2d Sess. 3035 (1870))

The Act also authorized the creation of two Assistant Attorneys General to help the Attorney General and the Solicitor General carry out their work (Easby-Smith 1904).

However, control over the authority to supervise the district attorneys continued to be contested. Before the creation of the DOJ, Congress passed a bill on August 2, 1861, to give the Attorney General supervisory authority over the district attorneys. The Attorney General only retained this power for *four days* before Congress passed a second law "explaining" that laws affecting the authority of the Solicitor of the Treasury were not altered by the new bill (Key 1938). So, supervision of the U.S. Attorneys returned to the Treasury Department, whose hold on the U.S. Attorneys only strengthened during the Civil War and its immediate aftermath.[10]

After the DOJ was established, the Treasury Department continued to insist that it had the authority to direct the work of these the U.S. Attorneys, at least as their work pertained to cases involving taxation (Key 1938). This dispute was finally resolved in 1933 when President Franklin Roosevelt signed Executive Order 6166, which provided "The functions of prosecuting in the courts of the United States claims and demands by, and offenses against, the Government of the United States, and of defending claims and demands against the Government, and of supervising the work of United States attorneys . . . are transferred to the Department of Justice." Nearly 150 years after they were created, the country's chief prosecutors were finally supervised by the federal government's chief legal officer.

2.1.3 The Growth of Federal Law and Its Enforcement

During the first 50 years of the DOJ's history, the United States experienced an enormous growth in the size and complexity of federal law. One legal scholar has gone so far as to claim "[f]ederal criminal law barely existed prior to 1896," with the first federal penitentiary being built in that year (Barkow 2009, 884). For early American history, federal law dealt almost exclusively with injuries to the federal government, with laws against bribing federal officials, treason, perjury in federal court, or tax fraud (Beale 1996). Most crimes against individuals, such as murder, robbery, fraud, and assault, were outside of the reach of federal law and as such were handled by state prosecutors in state courts (Beale 1996). Because U.S. Attorneys prosecute federal crimes, not state crimes; and because federal criminal law was effectively nonexistent, the reach of U.S. Attorneys was limited for many decades.

The period after the Civil War was marked by a drastic increase in federal criminal law. Congress passed laws against mail fraud and other crimes relating to interstate commerce (e.g., criminalizing the interstate

[10] Congress made one other minor alteration to the supervision of the U.S. Attorneys during this period, giving the Commissioner of Internal Revenue the authority to establish regulations to guide the work of the district attorneys (Key 1938).

transportation of livestock that had contagious diseases or transporting lottery tickets across state lines) (Task Force on the Federalization of Criminal Law 1998; Beale 1996). With Prohibition and the adoption of the Eighteenth Amendment came a second major expansion in federal criminal law. Because local and state authorities were reluctant to prosecute violations of Prohibition, federal prosecutors had to step in. At the height of Prohibition, there were 65,960 Prohibition-related cases in the federal judicial system (Beale 1996).

The scope of federal criminal law continued to grow during the Great Depression and New Deal eras. When a congressional committee concluded that the state governments were incapable of controlling this growing criminal activity, Congress responded by creating new federal penalties for crimes like bank robbery, extortion and robbery, interstate transportation of stolen property, and flight to avoid prosecution (Beale 1996). This era also saw an increase in federal regulatory laws that carried criminal penalties (Barkow 2009). Indeed, by 1929, the director of the federal Bureau of Prisons noted the "great increase in Federal crime" caused in part by "a transference of many offenses from the states to the federal government" (quoted in Barkow 2009, 884).

As the scale of federal law has grown, so have the responsibilities of U.S. Attorneys and the DOJ.[11] According to a U.S. Task Force on the Federalization of Criminal Law,

> In the twentieth century, increasing federal programs also correspondingly multiplied the criminal sanctions that were attached to these programs, but other factors such as Prohibition ushered in further federal criminal lawmaking. In the 1960s and 1970s, however, concern with organized crime, drugs, street violence, and other social ills precipitated a particularly significant rise in federal legislation tending to criminalize activity involving more local conduct, conduct previously left to state regulation. With concern about crime mounting in the 1980s and 1990s, the trend to federalize crime has continued dramatically, covering more conduct formerly

[11] Surprisingly, until 1953, the position of U.S. Attorney was not necessarily a full-time one. Until that year, individuals who held this position were able to continue to work in private practice while simultaneously serving as a federal prosecutor. This could cause awkward courtroom confrontations when the United States Attorney found that he was prosecuting a defendant represented by one of his colleagues (Executive Office for U.S. Attorneys 1989).

> left exclusively to state prosecution. (Task Force on the Federalization of Criminal Law 1998, 7)

Indeed, that task force found that more than 40% of federal criminal laws created since the Civil War have been enacted since 1970 (Task Force on the Federalization of Criminal Law 1998, 7).

The increase in the scope of federal law has corresponded with an increase in the resources available to U.S. Attorneys offices. Since the mid-1970s, the amount of funds Congress has appropriated for federal prosecutions has greatly increased, and the number of federal prosecutors working in U.S. Attorneys offices similarly rose from about 3,000 attorneys in the 1970s to more than 8,000 in the 1990s (Beale 1996).

Figure 2.1 illustrates the dramatic growth of the Department of Justice over the past few decades according to the Fiscal Year 2021 federal budget (Office of Management and Budget 2020). The left-hand plot illustrates the growth of the DOJ's budget. The right-hand plot shows growth of the size of the DOJ's workforce. Both plots present the DOJ's statistics as a percentage of the total federal government. That both plots show a drastic upward trend over time is evidence of the large growth of the DOJ—even relative to the rest of the federal government—over time. These years have "witnessed a dramatic expansion of the power and prestige of prosecutors" (Ma 2002,

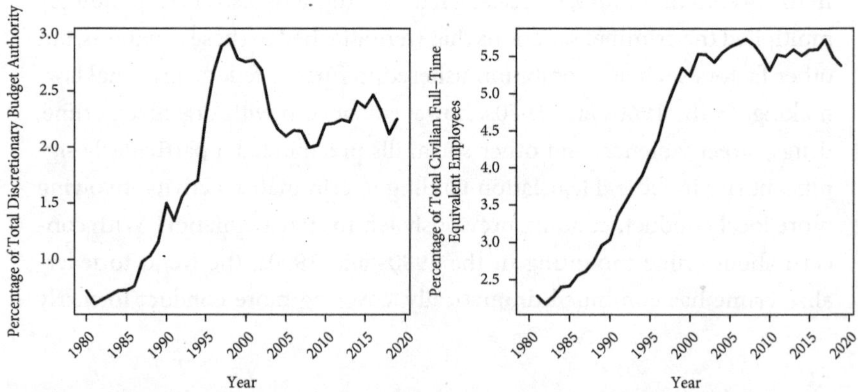

Figure 2.1 The Growth of the Department of Justice in the Modern Era. The left-hand panel shows the growth of the DOJ's budget. The right-hand plot shows growth of the size of the DOJ's workforce. Both plots present the DOJ's statistics as a percentage of the total federal government.

23) such that "[i]t is hard to overstate the power of federal prosecutors" (Barkow 2009, 870).

2.1.4 The Work of Assistant U.S. Attorneys

This expansion in federal law and the budget for U.S. Attorneys offices has been accompanied by a corresponding increase in the number of Assistant United States Attorneys (AUSAs). Assistant U.S. Attorneys are the staff attorneys who work under the U.S. Attorney in each local office. The AUSA position was first created by Congress in 1861 in an attempt to help the federal government deal with a war-related increase in the government's caseload (Shugerman 2014).[12] Initially, many judicial districts did not have an AUSA, and, of those that did, they were allowed to hire only a single assistant. (Shugerman 2014). Between 1871 and 1876, the number of AUSAs grew from 37 to 67 (Shugerman 2014).

That number has continued to grow. As of 2010, U.S. Attorneys' Offices were staffed by 6,075 attorneys, 54% of whom were Assistant U.S. Attorneys. Of those attorneys with prosecution or litigation responsibilities, 66% were Assistant U.S. Attorneys (Executive Office for U.S. Attorneys 2010).

In addition to the growth in raw numbers of AUSAs, the constitution of AUSAs in terms of professional experience has changed as well. As of 2009, the average Assistant U.S. Attorney had 11 years of experience in a U.S. Attorney's office in addition to some amount of prior legal experience (Executive Office for U.S. Attorneys 2009).

This high amount of experience, professionalization, and tenure length among Assistant United States Attorneys is a relatively new phenomenon.[13] As Eisenstein (2008) recounts:

> In the mid-1960s to early 1970s, the most serious problem in the representation of the federal government in U.S. district courts was the inexperience of AUSAs . . . AUSAs typically left about the time they gained the experience to do their jobs well; positions with local law firms seeking attorneys with

[12] See Act of Aug. 2, 186 1, ch. 37, §2, 12 Stat. 285, 285.

[13] Of course, increased tenure is not always a good thing. Some of Lochner's (2002) interviewees described colleagues who lacked the motivation to take on difficult tasks, knowing that their quasi-civil service status provided them with job security. The presence of these low-motivation AUSAs in an office may stymie an ambitious U.S. Attorney's ability to achieve her policy goals (Beale 2009).

> litigation experience in federal court paid far more than the modest salary AUSAs earned in government service. Even AUSAs who wished to stay typically had to leave when party control of the presidency changed. (236)

For much of our history, these Assistant U.S. Attorneys left office when party control of the presidency changed because it was common for these positions to be patronage appointments, filled at the beginning of each presidential term. As Attorney General Bell, in testimony to Congress in 1978, recounted,

> I remember going to the U.S. attorney's office in the courthouse in Atlanta once right after a new President had taken office, and the office was dark. The lights were off. I finally found one assistant. I said, "What are you doing here?" He said, "They let me stay on just to tell the new people what's happening around here." That's the way it used to be. It's a lot better now than it was then. (Subcommittee on Courts, Civil Liberties, and the Administration of Justice 1978, 41)

Indeed, in 1963, the first year of the Johnson Administration, 40% of the country's AUSAs resigned and had to be replaced. Seeking to professionalize these positions, the DOJ took steps to lengthen the amount of time individuals spent as Assistant U.S. Attorneys by increasing the average salary for an AUSA, which made the position more attractive to highly qualified individuals. Further, the positions were provided with quasi-civil service protections, providing AUSAs additional job security, thereby limiting their need to resign at the end of a presidential term (Beale 2009; Lochner 2002).[14] Together, these two reforms made the positions desirable to highly competent legal professionals and also helped protect those people from standard political turnover. By 1977, the first year of Jimmy Carter's presidency, the turnover rate was reduced to 21% in 1977 (Subcommittee on Courts, Civil Liberties, and the Administration of Justice 1978, 41).

The professionalization of Assistant U.S. Attorneys has changed the way local offices function. As turnover in local offices decreased and the size of the typical office increased, Assistant U.S. Attorneys became more likely to specialize in particular types of cases. This specialization, in turn, weakened

[14] While AUSAs have never been provided explicit civil service protections, the Merit Systems Protection Board ruled in 2002 that AUSAs fired for misconduct are entitled to the protections given to civil service employees (Eisenstein 2008; *Hamlett v. Dep't of Justice*, 20 M.S.P.R. 674 (2002)).

the control that the DOJ headquarters had over local offices. Experienced attorneys with a deep knowledge of their particular field are more likely to be comfortable litigating their cases without assistance from the career attorneys in Washington, D.C., thereby lessening the control that those attorneys can exert over the operations of local offices (Eisenstein 2008).

Another consequence of increased tenure and professionalization among U.S. Attorneys over the past half-century has been the establishment of deep communication networks across U.S. Attorneys' offices (Eisenstein 2008). A rise in multidistrict litigation led the DOJ to host conferences for U.S. Attorneys with supervisory authority and those who prosecute particular types of crimes like terrorism (Eisenstein 2008). Rather than needing to seek the advice of Main Justice on a tricky case, many career prosecutors know their colleagues at other district offices and can seek advice through those channels. As Eisenstein (2008, 239–40) explains, "The presence of career attorneys who take pride in their skills, regard themselves as at least as knowledgeable and experienced as attorneys at Main Justice, and adhere to their offices' traditions of independence, all promote autonomy from DOJ control."

2.2 U.S. Attorneys and the Modern DOJ

Far from its humble origins in the late 1800s, "the Department of Justice has evolved into the world's largest law office and the chief enforcer of federal laws" in the United States (U.S. Department of Justice 2020a). The modern DOJ plays an important role in both the investigation of federal crimes and the prosecution of those crimes. Today, the Department's attorneys represent the federal government at all levels of the federal judicial hierarchy, and its law enforcement officials investigate federal crimes from the mundane to the extraordinary.

2.2.1 The Organization of the DOJ

The contemporary Department of Justice is a complex organization that blends law enforcement and prosecutorial activities. To give a sense of the agency's structure, Figure 2.2 displays the DOJ's official organizational chart as of 2018.

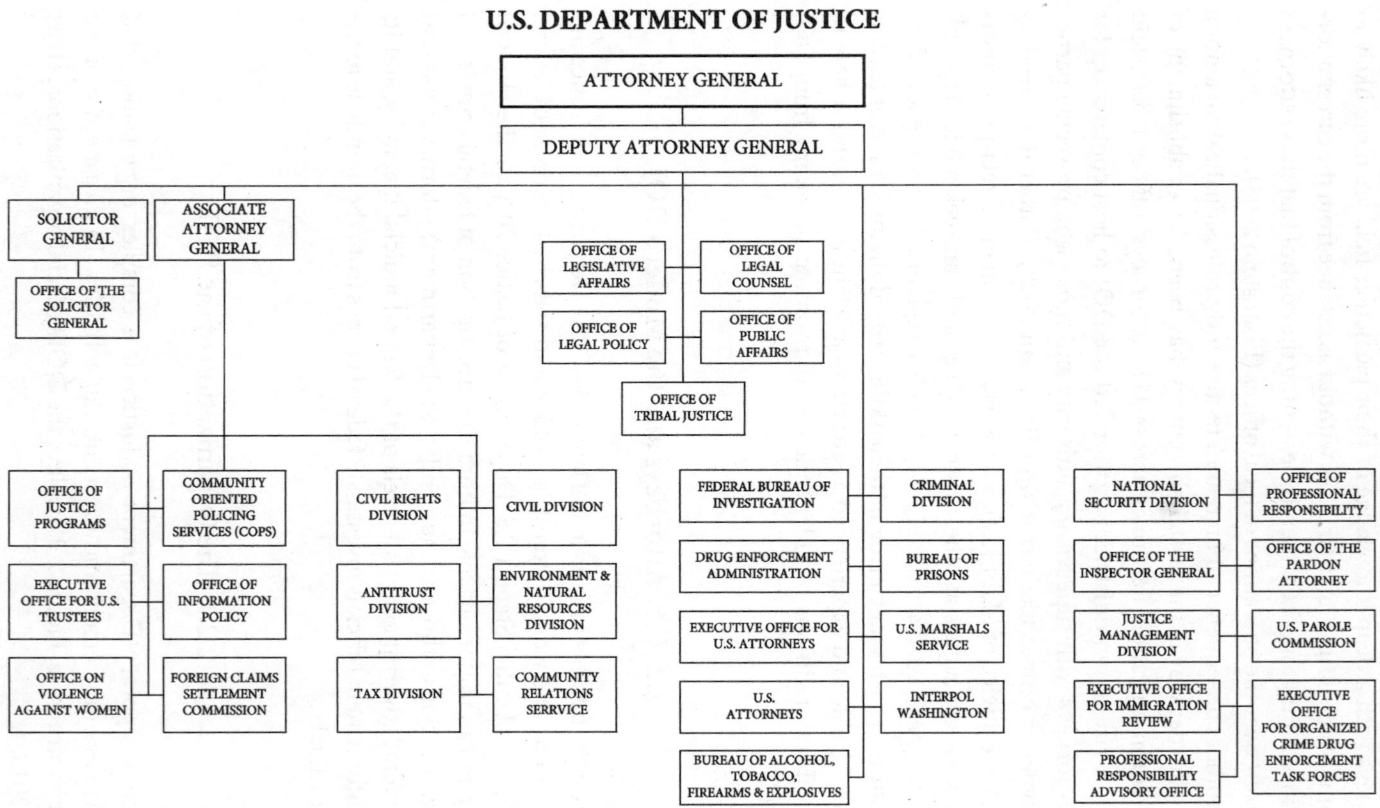

Figure 2.2 U.S. Department of Justice Organizational Chart, 2018 (U.S. Department of Justice 2018a).

The legal work of the Department is managed by a series of divisions, separated by the type of case. Today, the Department has eight divisions: Antitrust, Civil, Civil Rights, Criminal, Environmental and Natural Resources, Justice Management, National Security, and Tax.

Other portions of the DOJ investigate potential criminal activity. These agencies include the United States Marshals Service; the Federal Bureau of Investigation (FBI); the Bureau of Alcohol, Tobacco, Firearms and Explosives (ATF); and the Drug Enforcement Administration (DEA). These law enforcement agencies investigate federal crimes and refer suspected criminal activity to the U.S. Attorneys for potential prosecution.

2.2.2 DOJ Leadership

The management of the 113,000 DOJ employees and the agency's $29.2 billion budget falls to four officials who serve at the agency's apex (U.S. Department of Justice 2019c). Today, the Department's affairs are managed by the Attorney General, a Deputy Attorney General, an Associate Attorney General, and the U.S. Solicitor General. Each of these individuals is nominated by the president, confirmed by the Senate, and serves at the pleasure of the president.

The responsibilities of the U.S. Attorney General have grown far beyond the relatively small scope of power granted to the office in the Judiciary Act of 1789. Today, the Attorney General is responsible for supervising the entire DOJ, including the Federal Bureau of Investigation; the Drug Enforcement Administration; the Bureau of Alcohol, Tobacco, Firearms and Explosives; the Bureau of Prisons; the U.S. Attorneys; and the U.S. Marshals. In addition to her oversight responsibilities, the Attorney General is formally responsible for representing the United States in court, providing legal advice to the president and the cabinet, and making recommendations for federal judicial appointments (U.S. Department of Justice 2014).

The Attorney General's chief assistant is the Deputy Attorney General, a position created in 1950. The Deputy Attorney General acts as an intermediary between the White House and the DOJ on criminal matters, by providing advice on pardons and decisions about whether to seek the death penalty in criminal cases, and the executive's foreign policy apparatus. For example, the Deputy Attorney General is responsible for representing the DOJ in National Security Council and Homeland Security Council meetings and authorizing searches and surveillance under the Foreign Intelligence Surveillance Act (FISA). Like the Attorney General, the Deputy Attorney General is nominated by the president and confirmed by the Senate (U.S. Department of Justice 2014).

The third-ranking official in the DOJ is the Associate Attorney General, a position created in 1977. Whereas the Deputy Attorney General's portfolio focuses on criminal matters, the Associate Attorney General is responsible for supervising the Department's Civil, Civil Rights, Antitrust, Tax, and Environmental and Natural Resources divisions (U.S. Department of Justice 2014).

The other major figure at the DOJ is the U.S. Solicitor General, who is in charge of representing the U.S. federal government before the United States Supreme Court. The Solicitor General and the Deputy Solicitors General frequently appear in oral argument before the U.S. Supreme Court, and the Court regularly asks the Solicitor General's office to weigh in about whether or not a particular case is worthy of the Court's time and attention. Perhaps because of the Office of the Solicitor General's historically nonpartisan and highly professionalized reputation, the Court often follows the office's recommendations, and the office's attorneys enjoy very high rates of success when their cases come before the Supreme Court (see, e.g., Bailey, Kamoie, and Maltzman 2005; Black and Owens 2012).

2.2.3 The DOJ and U.S. Attorneys Today

The bureaucratization of the DOJ has helped to centralize oversight of U.S. Attorneys and to ensure consistent practices across districts. The process of centralization began in the late 1930s with the first USA Attorneys Conference in 1939, which provided an opportunity for geographically dispersed officials to meet and discuss their work.

However, it was not until the early 1950s that centralization took hold. Another major centralization mechanism, the Executive Office for United States Attorneys (EOUSA), was created on April 6, 1953. The EOUSA was created in order to "provide general executive assistance and supervision to the offices of the United States Attorneys" and to "serve as liaison, coordinator and expediter with respect to the Offices of the United States Attorneys, and between those offices and other elements of the Department [of Justice]" (Executive Office for U.S. Attorneys 1989, 6). Today, the

EOUSA's function falls more on the side of coordination, providing support to local U.S. Attorney staff, publishing a policy guide called the *United States Attorneys' Manual*, and administering continuing legal education for U.S. Attorneys and their assistants (U.S. Department of Justice 2018b).

But perhaps the greatest consequence of the centralization of authority over the U.S. Attorneys has been the ability of the DOJ to set national prosecution priorities, communicating to local U.S. Attorneys what types of crimes should be prioritized and which crimes should receive less attention. This puts U.S. Attorneys in a difficult position. As Eisenstein (1978, 197) explains:

> [U.S. Attorneys] belong to a national administration and carry out policies established by the president and his attorney general, who represent a national constituency. But they also represent their locality, and the interests and policy preferences of important segments of the local community sometimes conflict sharply with those of the national administration.

The Department's level of control also varies across offices. Eisenstein (1978) demonstrates that the Department's level of oversight varies with the size of the U.S. Attorney's office. Smaller offices are likely to receive higher levels of oversight than are larger offices. As Eisenstein (2008, 236) explains: "The size of an office, more than anything, determine[s] the ability of a USAO to resist domination by Main Justice. Other things being equal, the larger the office, the more robust its ability to develop the expertise to handle complex litigation itself rather than relying on career attorneys dispatched from Washington."

The Attorney General communicates the Department's policy priorities to local U.S. attorneys through policy memoranda. These memos constitute one way that the political priorities of the administration are expressed through the administration of justice. They provide guidance to local offices about the crimes they should prioritize and, in some cases, how particular types of cases should be handled. These memos are not binding on local offices, and they can (and often are) rescinded by a new Attorney General after a presidential transition. These memos therefore do not have the force of law, but rather guide local prosecutors as they use their discretion.

Policy memos surrounding criminal charging provide an excellent example of the sort of policy pronouncements (with major political consequences) these memos provide. Consider, for example, the back-and-forth between the policy positions of the DOJ over the past two decades.

In 2003, Attorney General John Ashcroft instructed that U.S. Attorneys "must" charge and pursue "the most serious, readily provable offense" in a given case (Ashcroft 2003). These guidelines relaxed under the Obama Administration, when Attorney General Eric Holder wrote in a 2010 memo that prosecutors "should ordinarily" (not "must") charge "the most serious offense that is likely to result in a sustainable conviction" and explicitly provided prosecutors the discretion to conduct an "individualized assessment" of the case to determine what the charge should be, backtracking from a specific list of exceptions provided in the Ashcroft memo (Holder 2010). And, in a 2013 memo, Holder authorized prosecutors to not pursue mandatory minimum charges in cases involving nonviolent minor drug offenses (Holder 2013). Under the Trump Administration, Attorney General Jeff Sessions steered prosecutors back toward stricter enforcement, writing:

> it is a core principle that prosecutors should charge and pursue the most serious, readily provable offense. This policy affirms our responsibility to enforce the law, is moral and just, and produces consistency. This policy fully utilizes the tools Congress has given us. By definition, the most serious offenses are those that carry the most substantial guidelines sentence, including mandatory minimum sentences. (Sessions 2017)

Thus, the Sessions memo moved federal prosecutors explicitly away from the Holder-era mandatory minimum policy. The practice of Attorneys General providing guidance on how prosecutors should charge offenses through the issuance of policy memoranda dates back to the 1980s. However, while all administrations issue guidance telling prosecutors they should only charge offenses that are likely to "stick," Democratic Administrations tend to provide more leeway to prosecutors about which charges to pursue while Republican Administrations tend to promote harsh application of existing laws (Freed and Miller 1994; Vinegrad 2017).

Aside from the bread-and-butter issue of charging criminals, the DOJ has used policy memos to direct the work of U.S. Attorneys on nearly every important issue—from immigration, to COVID-19, to elections. For example, in a policy memo that sparked widespread debate, Attorney General Barr issued a memorandum in the middle of the 2020 presidential primary season stating that no investigation of a candidate for president or vice president (or any senior campaign staff member) could be conducted without the Attorney General's written approval (Barr 2020a).

Democratic Administrations have used these memos, as well. For example, the Obama-era DOJ issued a memo in 2013 directing U.S. Attorneys to only prosecute marijuana-related offenses when they presented a threat to the administration's federal law enforcement priorities (Cole 2013). And, in another major policy memo, the Obama DOJ issued a memo encouraging prosecutors to target not only corporations that commit crimes but also the executives in charge of those companies at the time the alleged crime was committed (Yates 2015).

2.3 What Have We Learned?

Our goal in this chapter was to try to understand how the position of U.S. Attorney has evolved since its inception. To this end, we began in Colonial America and moved through U.S. history, charting the ever-changing position U.S. Attorneys have had in the U.S. political system over time. Through this trek, two major themes have emerged.

First, and perhaps most importantly, we have seen how closely interwoven with politics the administration of federal justice has always been. This linkage has only expanded as the federal government has increased in size and authority. As the scope of federal law has grown, it has created new opportunities for U.S. Attorneys to play an important role in the American political system. At every major turn in U.S. history—from the Civil War to Prohibition to the Civil Rights Movement—Congress has passed laws regulating the conduct of the American people, and the U.S. Attorneys have exercised their power to implement and enforce these laws. As a result, U.S. Attorneys have put their stamp on nearly every major moment in American history.

Second, the extent to which U.S. Attorneys are subject to meaningful control by the federal government has drastically changed over time. Though they have existed for nearly all of American history, U.S. Attorneys were not supervised by the Attorney General for the first century of the republic. Instead, the federal government relied on a decentralized supervisory structure led by principals as diverse as the Secretary of State and a non-attorney Treasury Department bureaucrat. Though the DOJ has increased its centralized supervisory authority over the past 50 years, much of the prosecutorial decision-making takes place within the 93 U.S. Attorney Offices around the country. Still, there is ample room for centralized political signals from the

DOJ, the Attorney General, and other national and local forces. This creates a potential problem: "Consistency is absolutely necessary in the field of litigation, for when the United States appears in court it appears as a single entity, even though internally it is made up of many autonomous units. A decision in a case brought at the instance of one bureau may effect many or all of the other branches of the government" (Key 1938, 198–99, original spelling retained). As we move through the rest of this book, this question of consistency is a driving force: If you may have violated federal criminal law, how much does your fate depend on *who* the local U.S. Attorney is and under what political circumstances she is operating? As a first step to address that question, we move in Chapter 3 toward an understanding of the sort of people who become U.S. Attorneys, testing what factors make nominees more or less likely to be successful in the U.S. Senate confirmation process.

3

Confirming U.S. Attorneys

On September 17, 2009, almost nine months to the day that he took the oath of office as president, Barack Obama nominated three people to serve as U.S. Attorneys: Carmen Milagros Ortiz for the District of Massachusetts, Michael J. Moore for the Middle District of Georgia, and Edward J. Tarver for the Southern District of Georgia (The White House 2009). Before these three individuals could assume their roles, federal law required the U.S. Senate to confirm their nominations.

And it (eventually) did. Five weeks later, the Senate Judiciary Committee passed Tarver and Ortiz's nominations to the full Senate for a final vote. That same day, Tarver and Ortiz's nominations were placed on the Senate Executive Calendar. The next week, on November 5, the Senate confirmed Tarver and Ortiz as new U.S. Attorneys by a voice vote.[1]

Moore would have a much more drawn-out path. Months went by before the Senate Judiciary Committee took any action on Moore's nomination. Eventually, one day shy of the one-year anniversary of President Obama forwarding his name, the Senate Judiciary Committee formally considered Moore's nomination. Later that day, the Committee voted in favor of Moore and forwarded him to the full Senate for its final consideration. Finally, on September 29, 2010—377 days after Obama originally nominated Moore to the post—the Senate confirmed him by voice vote with no formal opposition. Moore waited over a year to be confirmed for his position, yet at no stage of this year-long process was any dissent against Moore's nomination noted in the *Congressional Record*.

Moore's predecessor in office, Maxwell Wood, served as U.S. Attorney through almost all of the George W. Bush Administration. Wood continued to serve into the first few months of the Obama Administration before resigning in July 2009 in order to pursue a run for Georgia Attorney General (Wagner

[1] Voice votes, in which members orally state their preferences as a group (yea or nay) while the chair determines which side has the majority, are a quick way for the Senate to vote on a bill or nomination. Voice votes indicate general agreement among senators; any member can ask for a recorded vote if the majority is unclear or if the issue is contentious enough to merit a record.

The Politics of Federal Prosecution. Christina L. Boyd, Michael J. Nelson, Ian Ostrander, and Ethan D. Boldt, Oxford University Press (2021).
DOI: 10.1093/oso/9780197554685.003.0003

2009). Though he and Moore sought the exact same position, Wood waited only 62 days from the time that Bush sent his nomination to the Senate until he was confirmed to serve. After Wood resigned, Obama waited two full months before nominating Moore as a permanent U.S. Attorney for that district.

Of course, even though the office lacked a full-time U.S. Attorney, the work of the U.S. Attorney's Office of the Middle District of Georgia continued in the 14-month period between Wood's resignation and Moore's confirmation. Throughout this period, G.F. "Pete" Peterman III, Wood's First Assistant U.S. Attorney, served as Acting U.S. Attorney (Ramati 2009). Despite never receiving Senate confirmation for his role, Peterman was responsible for supervising the district's 69 employees and directing their prosecutions for that 14-month period (Womack 2011).[2] By forcing Moore to wait over a year for his confirmation, the Senate's inaction enabled Peterman to direct the office's activities. By the time Moore took office, Peterman had been given over a year to put his stamp on the office's work.

These short anecdotes raise seemingly troubling questions about the process by which U.S. Attorneys reach office. Why are some nominees—like Ortiz, Tarver, and Wood—so quickly confirmed while others, like Moore, languish before the Senate for a year or more? Why would the Senate allow a federal law enforcement office to be run by an acting U.S. Attorney for over a year, especially when it had in its hands a nominee for that office from a copartisan president? And why would the Senate delay Moore's confirmation for so long when it would eventually confirm him without any noted opposition?

The answers to these questions lie at the heart of understanding the political process through which U.S. Attorneys get their jobs. Presidents sit at the apex of the executive branch, but they must rely on others to make sure that their policy goals are prioritized, passed into law, and eventually implemented. Staffing an administration with like-minded officials is critical to ensure that a president's agenda is realized. In this way, "personnel is policy."

U.S. Attorneys are no exception to this general rule. Because these officials have an immense amount of discretion once they are confirmed, putting the "right" person in office is very important. To this end, presidents have increasingly sought to appoint loyal copartisans as U.S. Attorneys. For example, the Administration of George W. Bush made an "unprecedented, determined, and multi-faceted" push toward appointing only nominees who

[2] Though less important from the standpoint of federal prosecutorial policy, no staff openings could be filled while the U.S. Attorney vacancy remained open nor could anyone who worked in that office receive a promotion until the Senate finally confirmed a U.S. Attorney (Womack 2011).

shared the administration's goals (Eisenstein 2008, 242). In another show of the importance of these positions to presidents, Donald Trump broke with tradition and personally interviewed some candidates to serve as U.S. Attorneys for the nation's busiest offices (Broach 2017; Kim and Bresnahan 2017). Thus, presidents view the selection process for these offices as extremely important.

Presidents cannot staff their administration unilaterally, however. The Constitution provides presidents with the power to nominate individuals to key offices, but it requires the "advice and consent" of the Senate for these nominees to be confirmed and take office. Overall, about 1,200 of the posts that a new president must fill, including federal judges, cabinet members, U.S. Attorneys, and high-ranking executive branch officials, require Senate confirmation. As a result, the Senate's priorities—which may align or conflict with the president's goals—can constrain a president's ability to staff his or her administration with like-minded officials. Just as senators may disapprove of a president's policies, they often oppose a president's proposed personnel. And, even if the Senate does eventually confirm a president's nominee, some nominees languish months—if not years—before they finally achieve confirmation.

In this chapter, we explore the politics surrounding the selection, nomination, and confirmation of U.S. Attorneys. First, we explain the Senate confirmation process for U.S. Attorneys, a unique ordeal that involves all three branches of the federal government and is structured to encourage timely confirmation. Second, we examine the demographic and professional background of U.S. Attorney nominees, demonstrating wide variation in the backgrounds of people who are nominated by different presidents. Finally, we combine our original data on U.S. Attorney nominees since the 100th Congress with congressional records on the outcomes of their nominations to explore how federal and/or local political considerations affect the outcomes of U.S. Attorney nominations.

3.1 Politics and Selecting U.S. Attorneys Since the Founding

Since their creation in the Judiciary Act of 1789, U.S. Attorneys have been nominated by the president and confirmed by the Senate before they take office. The historical development of the confirmation process illuminates the importance of two major issues—the professionalism of the nominee and the role of the home state senator—on the eventual fate of a U.S. Attorney nominee before the Senate.

Despite their formally nonpartisan law enforcement role, the selection of U.S. Attorneys has always been political. From the very beginning of U.S. history, U.S. Attorney positions were understood as "political plums" offered as rewards to loyal members of the president's party:

> Support of a candidate for federal office frequently was rewarded by appointment to law enforcement posts, and incumbents usually were men of stature and political influence in their districts. Almost invariably, they were stalwarts of the party in power. (Huston 1967, 64)

This pattern has continued throughout American history, with presidents using these positions to fill the ranks of U.S. Attorneys with loyal partisans.

Proposals to change this norm have frequently popped up throughout American history. In both the 1920s and the 1950s, proposals emerged to increase the role of merit in presidential selection of U.S. Attorney nominees or even to place U.S. Attorneys under the country's civil service system, thereby moving these posts away from presidential and congressional politics (Beale 2009, 410). These calls have not translated into action.

Even presidents who promise to emphasize merit over partisanship have fallen short. Jimmy Carter promised that "[a]ll federal judges and prosecutors should be appointed strictly on the basis of merit, without any consideration of political aspect or influence" in his administration (Gashko 1977). To this end, the Carter Administration proposed a formal commission-based merit selection plan for these positions; after the Senate rejected that plan, the Carter Administration encouraged senators to create commissions in their states to vet candidates for U.S. Attorney positions in an attempt to limit the influence of patronage in these nominations (Bell 1977). While some senators did set up these commissions, not all did so. And, despite his protestation, 67 of the first 68 Carter-nominated U.S. Attorneys were Democrats (Subcommittee on Courts, Civil Liberties, and the Administration of Justice 1978).

Carter's desire to use a merit-based procedure to constrain the ability of senators to use these positions as political plums put him directly in conflict with the other major theme in the development of the U.S. Attorney selection procedure: the special role of the home state senator. Historically, home state senators from the president's party are given the power to help choose the individual(s) who will serve as U.S. Attorney in their state. This process is called *senatorial courtesy*. As part of this process, home state senators receive a blue slip of paper (the "blue slip") to provide feedback on the nominee. In practice, this blue slip procedure ensures that senators are able to influence politics and patronage within their own state. Historically, nominees with unfavorable blue slips have not been advanced through the Senate (McMillion 2017; Sollenberger 2003), giving home state senators an "effective veto" over U.S. Attorney nominees (Cummings and McFarland 1937, 499). In practice, the blue slip process encourages presidents to consult with home state senators *before they nominate someone* to ensure that their eventual nominees are acceptable to those senators and will receive Senate consideration.

This practice has raised problems. Former Attorney General Wickersham's National Commission on Law Observance and Enforcement concluded:

> [A]n obstacle to effective control and efficient prosecution has been found in the power of the Senate with respect to appointments. The claim of the Senate not merely to exercise a collective power of rejecting unfit nominations but to dictate appointments as the patronage of the Senators of the State in which the district lies has often had a bad effect upon the personnel and conduct of the office. Also in States where the Senators are in opposition to the administration it happens too often that local political organizations insist on treating the office as political patronage, and thus deprive the President of the information and support he should have in order to make suitable appointments. (National Commission on Law Observance and Enforcement 1931, 9)

Or, to put it more bluntly, Luther Huston (1967), the Director of Public Information for the Department of Justice from 1957–61 recalled that *it was sometimes more difficult to satisfy a senator with a U.S. Attorney nominee than a U.S. Supreme Court nominee*.

Once confirmed, U.S. Attorneys acknowledge their debt to their senators. Take, for example, a colorful anecdote that Attorney General Bell shared with the Senate Judiciary Committee in 1978:

> The most poignant reference example I can give the committee of this business of U.S. attorneys owing their—at least some of their allegiance to persons other than the Attorney General and the President—I witnessed recently. I was in a U.S. attorney's office, a new one, and I was talking with him. I just happened to be in the city. He had a picture on the wall of one Senator from the State, who was a Democrat, and who had recommended him.
>
> He didn't have a picture of the President on the wall, nor the Attorney General. That's not required, that they have a picture of the Attorney General, or the president; but I thought it was interesting that he did have a picture of the Senator on the wall. It tells you a lot about the system. (Subcommittee on Courts, Civil Liberties, and the Administration of Justice 1978, 3708)

Indeed, the role of the home state senator is so powerful that, in practice "the Senate proposes and the President advises and consents" (Bell 1977, 3), flipping the traditional model of Senate confirmation on its head (Bell and Meador 1993).[3]

3.2 The Senate Confirmation Process

After a potential candidate is located, the administration must ensure that she can survive the Senate confirmation process. To maximize this chance, administrations vet nominees for quality, loyalty, scandal, and any other potential disqualifications before submitting the nomination to the Senate. The 1987 failed U.S. Supreme Court nomination of Judge Robert Bork marked a watershed change in the politics of Senate confirmation. Ever since that event, the Senate confirmation process has become increasingly and overtly politicized. In this environment, nominees face scrutiny not only over their qualifications but also a host of other issues related to their character and fitness for office (Carter 1994). As a result, the administration typically devotes a substantial amount of time and energy to vetting an individual before formally forwarding the nomination to the Senate.

[3] When there are no home state senators from the president's party, the administration typically coordinates with the most senior member of the state's U.S. House of Representatives delegation from the president's party and, where they share a party affiliation, the state's governor (Bell and Meador 1993; McCaffrey 2001; Shapiro 2009).

Once a nominee is chosen and vetted, the norms and procedure of the Senate dictate the nominee's fate. The president formally submits the nomination to the Senate, and the nomination is assigned to the appropriate committee for consideration. U.S. Attorney nominations are reviewed by the Senate Judiciary Committee, which also vets federal judges and considers legislation related to the U.S. justice system. The Committee, under the direction of its chairperson, often (but not always) holds public hearings on nominees, asking prospective U.S. Attorneys questions about their prosecutorial philosophy and how they plan to carry out the duties of their office once confirmed. There is no timetable for the Committee to decide whether to hold a hearing or as to when (or even if) they move the nomination to the full Senate for a vote. Most nominations that fail do so at the committee stage either through lack of sufficient support or because scrutiny uncovered issues concerning the nominee (Krutz, Fleisher, and Bond 1998).

Once the nomination has passed the Senate Judiciary Committee, it is placed on the Senate's executive calendar for future action. This calendar, however, is not deterministic. Placement of a nomination on the calendar provides no guarantee that a nominee will receive a vote. Because the Senate lacks a simple and quick means of ending debate, scheduling floor time in the Senate is often done through Unanimous Consent Agreements (UCA). Even if the nominee is supported by the rest of the Senate, a single senator who is unhappy with a nomination can stop the full chamber from considering that nominee. In fact, such "hostage taking" is a common feature of the nominations process generally.

In this difficult environment, Senate Majority Leaders heavily influence the speed of the process as they exercise significant influence over the chamber's agenda. First, a Majority Leader may simply schedule a vote through a UCA for noncontroversial nominees. Second, Majority Leaders can overcome minority opposition by calling a cloture vote on a nomination and ending a filibuster. This tactic became much easier after a 2013 rules change lowered the cloture threshold from 60 votes to a simple majority of 51 (Ostrander 2017). Third, a Majority Leader opposed to a nominee may simply block the nomination from full floor consideration thereby ensuring that the nomination fails at the end of the Congress. If the Senate does not vote on a nominee by the end of a Congress, a president must renominate that individual at the start of the following Congress in order for the Senate to consider the nomination again.

3.3 Filling Interim Vacancies

While the administration is vetting the new nominee and the Senate is considering whether or not to confirm her, the work of the local U.S. Attorney's office continues. One of the most unique features of the selection process for U.S. Attorneys is how their vacancies are filled on a temporary basis. Two statutes jointly govern what individual will serve as the leader of a local U.S. Attorney's office when a vacancy arises (Hauser 2018; Whelan 2003). In many circumstances, per the Vacancies Reform Act, the office will be led by an Acting U.S. Attorney. This individual is usually a career prosecutor, generally the First Assistant U.S. Attorney in that office. However, the president can name a different person as Acting U.S. Attorney by changing the order of succession through a presidential declaration. An Acting U.S. Attorney can only serve for a set period of time—currently 300 days—before an Interim U.S. Attorney must be appointed (Whelan 2003).

A different statute authorizes the Attorney General to appoint an Interim U.S. Attorney (28 U.S.C.A. §546(d)). Though the Attorney General must appoint an interim appointee at the expiration of an Acting U.S. Attorney's tenure, nothing in U.S. law prohibits the Attorney General from appointing an Interim U.S. Attorney at an earlier stage in the process (Whelan 2003). An interim appointee serves until the confirmation of a new U.S. Attorney.[4] If, after 120 days, the Senate has not confirmed a permanent replacement, the local district court can select their own individual to serve until a new nominee is confirmed.[5] If the administration chooses not to put forward a nominee for the position, the U.S. Attorney will serve indefinitely, as Geoffrey Berman did in the Southern District of New York for the first three years of Donald Trump's presidency (Weiser 2018; U.S. Department of Justice 2020c) and Paula Silsby did in Maine throughout the George W. Bush presidency (Jansen and Keisch 2007).

An anecdote from 2020 provides an example of the important role the district court plays in U.S. Attorney selection. The district court indicated to the interim U.S. Attorney for the District of Columbia, Tim Shea, that it would not appoint him to the position after his 120-day statutory term

[4] The Attorney General may appoint an Acting U.S. Attorney as an Interim U.S. Attorney, or the Attorney General may appoint a different individual as an Interim U.S. Attorney (Dienst and Connor 2018).

[5] District courts handle the selection of an Interim U.S. Attorney differently. Some courts make the appointment by a vote of the judges (e.g., Associated Press 2008); others allow a single judge to choose (e.g., Associated Press 2006).

expired (Shortell and Perez 2020). The court's actions came in response to a series of controversial decisions made under Shea's watch while his office was prosecuting Michael Flynn and Roger Stone, two allies of Donald Trump; Shea sided with DOJ officials over his office's career prosecutors to reduce a sentencing recommendation for Stone, and he filed a controversial motion to dismiss charges against Flynn even though Flynn had pled guilty to the charges (Alexander, Hsu, and Zapotosky 2020). In response, Shea left his position and Trump nominated Justin Herdman, an Ohio U.S. Attorney, to take over the D.C. office.

The Constitution and tradition also provide the president with the ability to temporarily but unilaterally fill vacant positions that happen to exist during a congressional recess of more than three days. In the past, recess appointments have been a significant presidential tool allowing executives to fill positions that would have otherwise remained vacant in the face of congressional opposition (Black et al. 2007). Such appointments are not ideal as they are more limited in life span than a confirmed appointee, but they have been used to fill U.S. Attorney positions. For example, President George W. Bush used a recess appointment to make Steven K. Mullins the U.S. Attorney for the District of South Dakota in January 2006. Recess appointments, however, may no longer be a viable option for future presidents. Under the Obama Administration, Congress began to block presidents from making recess appointments by ensuring the Congress never formally agreed to recess for more than three days at a time (Ostrander 2015). Given this impediment and the potential for Attorneys General to appoint interim U.S. Attorneys for up to 120 days at any point during a vacancy, it is unlikely that recess appointments will continue to be a common or viable pathway to U.S. Attorney offices.

3.4 Who Is Nominated to Be a U.S. Attorney?

What sorts of people do presidents nominate to be U.S. Attorneys? We argued that presidents want to put forward nominees who are likely to implement their priorities faithfully. But, aside from these policy-based considerations, presidents may vary in the extent to which they use these positions to advance the diversity of the executive branch by nominating individuals from historically underrepresented backgrounds. Additionally, presidents may seek to fill the ranks of U.S. Attorneys with graduates of elite law schools to

Table 3.1 Backgrounds of U.S. Attorney Nominees, 1989–2018. The data include each U.S. Attorney Nominee formally submitted to the Senate during these years according to congressional records.

President	Racial Minority	Female	In-State J.D.	Elite J.D.	Former AUSA	N
G. H.W. Bush	5%	10%	58%	12%	38%	60
Clinton	20%	23%	61%	13%	47%	132
G. W. Bush	13%	14%	58%	8%	54%	180
Obama	25%	24%	50%	18%	64%	117
Trump	9%	9%	59%	21%	61%	78
Total	16%	17%	57%	13%	54%	567

lend the positions an aura of prestige or, alternatively, administrations might favor graduates of local law schools to placate home state senators whose positive judgments of a nominee could be a prerequisite for a successful and speedy confirmation.

To investigate these presidential priorities, we collected original data on the professional and demographic backgrounds of every individual nominated to serve as a U.S. Attorney between the years 1989 and 2018. This time span enables us to examine the nominations made by George H.W. Bush, Bill Clinton, George W. Bush, and Barack Obama along with those made by Donald Trump in the first two years of his presidency.[6]

Table 3.1 shows the background of U.S. Attorney nominees by the president who nominated them. Perhaps the most striking information in the table comes in the first two columns, which record the percentage of female and minority nominees. Democratic presidents have been overwhelmingly more likely to nominate individuals from backgrounds historically underrepresented in the legal profession. While nearly one-in-four U.S. Attorneys nominated by Barack Obama were minorities or women, only one-in-ten of the nominees put forward by George H.W. Bush or Donald Trump in our data were women. Similarly, both of those Republican presidents nominated nine men for each female nominee they submitted to the Senate. While George W. Bush's nominees were more diverse than Donald Trump's, his

[6] Because so many presidential nominations happen at the beginning of a president's tenure, we exclude Reagan from our discussion in this section but include data from the early Trump Administration.

nominees were substantially less diverse than those put forward by either of the Democratic presidents in our data.

Conversely, there is more similarity across presidents in terms of the professional backgrounds of the nominees they put forward to the Senate. Consider nominees' educational backgrounds. Given that U.S. Attorneys are geographically dispersed across the country and often have the support of their home state senators, one might think these nominees are particularly likely to have completed their education in the state in which they plan to serve. Such an educational background might indicate a rich professional network that a potential nominee could exploit when she sought a Senator's support to serve as a U.S. Attorney. There is some evidence this is the case. The majority of the nominees put forward by each president graduated from law school in the state in which they are nominated to serve. There are some notable differences, though. Barack Obama was comparatively less likely to favor nominees who graduated from an in-state law school.

Other types of professional backgrounds are also important. While attending an in-state law school could give a potential nominee an edge, another type of legal background that could be potentially useful is a degree from an elite law school. Fourteen schools have long been recognized as highly ranked in the *U.S. News and World Report* rankings of law schools.[7] Table 3.1 shows that recent presidents have been slightly more likely to prioritize this type of elite legal education in their nominees. Compared to other the other presidents in our sample, George W. Bush was comparatively less likely to put forward nominees who had attended elite law schools.

Finally, U.S. Attorneys are charged with managing an office and leading a team of Assistant U.S. Attorneys (AUSAs). Prior service as a U.S. Attorney might give a nominee an edge in the selection process, as this experience could provide them with important background information (and a public track record) that could make them an attractive selection for potential presidents. Again, there is heterogeneity in presidents' tendencies to rely on this background characteristic. Only about one-in-three nominees put forward by George H.W. Bush had previously served as an AUSA; nearly two-thirds of Barack Obama's had done the same.

[7] The "T14" law schools are Berkeley, Columbia, Cornell, Duke, Georgetown, Harvard, NYU, Northwestern, Stanford, Chicago, Michigan, Pennsylvania, Virginia, and Yale. These law schools are routinely used as measures of "elite" law school status (e.g., Hinkle et al. 2012; Sen 2014).

What conclusions can we draw from this discussion? Aside from the clear partisan differences with respect to the demographic diversity of the nominees, there are few clear partisan or temporal trends with respect to the professional backgrounds of the nominees put forward to serve as U.S. Attorneys by the past five presidents. The general stability we observe in the professional backgrounds of U.S. Attorney nominees likely reflects a continuity of incentives that emphasize enduring features of the job. The consistent preference for U.S. Attorneys with in-state degrees demonstrates the local connection of these federal posts. Furthermore, the preference for former AUSAs, while only recently a majority of selections, demonstrates the technical expertise required of the job. Were presidential nominations consistently made with these professional incentives in mind, we would expect that the professional background of U.S. Attorneys will remain stable despite changes in partisan control of the presidency. And, indeed, this seems to be the case.

3.5 What Are the Outcomes of the Confirmation Process?

While winning a final vote is the only path to successful Senate confirmation, there are several different ways that a U.S. Attorney nomination can fail. To start, a nominee may be rejected by a direct vote in either the Judiciary Committee or on the floor of the Senate. Such failures are very rare for any kind of nomination and U.S. Attorney nominations are unlikely to ever fail in such a manner. If a nominee runs into trouble during the confirmation process, a president may withdraw that nomination and nominate another candidate. Withdrawal occurs when there is a credible threat of failure or, sometimes, when a nominee no longer wishes to wait out the process. Finally, all nominations not confirmed by the end of a Congress are automatically returned to the president. While a president may choose to renominate the individual, it is often the case that a nominee will be no more viable after an election than before.

Despite the many ways that a nomination may go awry, presidents are overwhelmingly successful with these nominations. Indeed, only four nominations between 1987 and 2018 failed outright.[8] Each of these

[8] For the remainder of this chapter, we include the final two years of the Reagan presidency in our dataset so that we are able to analyze the entire post-Bork period. The final two years of the Reagan Administration were not included in Table 3.1 to limit erroneous conclusions that might come from comparing the nominations at the end of one presidency to those made throughout other presidencies.

nominations failed before the Senate Judiciary Committee was able to hold hearings about or take a vote on the nomination. When presidents are not successful at placing their nominees at the helm of a local U.S. Attorney's office, the nomination's failure almost always results from Senate inaction, especially at the committee stage. Usually, these failures happen because the Senate does not confirm a nominee before the end of the Congress; in these circumstances, the nomination fails and must be resubmitted in the next Congress for reconsideration.

However, these high confirmation rates mask lengthy delays in the confirmation process. The average nominee waits 82 days from the day their nomination is submitted until the Senate eventually confirms her. However, there is wide variation in the speed at which the Senate acts. Indeed, the range of delay in our data is vast, ranging from nominees who were confirmed on the day they were nominated to another who waited 717 days for the Senate to act. In fact, the standard deviation of delay is larger than the average amount of delay: 83.6 days. This large number suggests an extremely broad variation in the amount of time a nominee waits for the Senate to act on her nomination.

To examine patterns of U.S. Attorney delay over time, Figure 3.1 plots the average number of days, by Congress, in which each nomination languished.

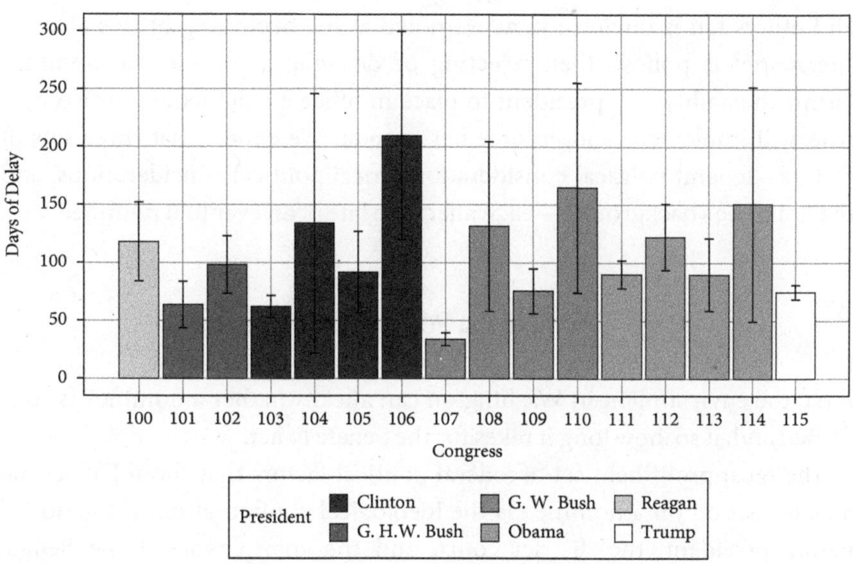

Figure 3.1 The average amount of delay (in days) for U.S. Attorney nominations, by Congress. Whiskers represent 95% confidence intervals.

The most striking feature of the plot is the fact that, on average, presidents' nominees are confirmed more quickly in their first two years in office than in their last two years in office. While nominees sent to the legislature in the first two years of a presidential term are confirmed, on average, in less than 100 days, those who are nominated in the latter half of a presidential term wait, on average, two more months before they are eventually confirmed by the Senate.

These lengthy delays are important. To the extent that appointing like-minded U.S. Attorneys can help presidents implement their policy priorities, stymying the confirmation of those individuals can help opposition-party senators halt the implementation of a presidential agenda. Thus, just as scholars have found that the delay facing bureaucratic (Bond et al. 2009; McCarty and Razaghian 1999; O'Connell 2009) and judicial nominations (Bell 2002; Binder and Maltzman 2002; Hendershot 2010; Shipan and Shannon 2003) responds to systematic factors, the delay experienced by U.S. Attorneys may also respond to observable features of the political environment.

3.6 What Affects a Nominee's Eventual Fate?

The importance of understanding why some nominees achieve confirmation and others fail is obvious: if, as we noted at the beginning of this chapter, "personnel is policy," then rejecting or delaying a presidential nominee harms the ability of a president to place in office a chief federal prosecutor who will implement and enforce her agenda. We expect that three sets of factors—federal political considerations, local political considerations, and the nominee's background—each affect the fate of an eventual nominee.

3.6.1 The Federal Political Environment

First, the environment in Washington can affect whether a nominee is confirmed and, if so, how long it takes for the Senate to act.

The most prominent set of federal political factors that should affect the Senate's action on a nominee is the ideological configuration of the nominating president, the district court, and the chairperson of the Senate Judiciary Committee. Recall that the district court's ideological location is important because it can unilaterally appoint a new U.S. Attorney to serve until confirmation if the Senate does not confirm a nominee within 120 days after an interim U.S. Attorney is appointed. Likewise, the Chair of the Senate Judiciary committee, more than anyone else, can advance or block a nomination's path through the chamber. Committee chairs have an extraordinarily large role to play in scheduling and managing nominations, and most nominations that eventually fail do so in committee (McCarty and Razaghian 1999, 1124–25).[9]

Most clearly, as the Senate and the president have more profound ideological disagreements, key senators may choose to slow down the nomination process, a phenomenon well-trodden in studies of executive (McCarty and Razaghian 1999) and judicial (Shipan and Shannon 2003) nominations. As a result, greater ideological distance between the Senate Judiciary Chair and the president should increase the delay time for U.S. Attorneys and be associated with a higher probability of failure.

Additionally, because it can only intervene when the president and the Senate do not reach a timely agreement, the local U.S. District Court steps in to appoint a nominee.[10] After 120 days of an interim U.S. Attorney's leadership, the district court has a unilateral power to determine who will fill the vacancy until the Senate successfully confirms a presidential nominee. If the president approves of the sort of nominee a court is likely to appoint, he may delay naming a new nominee or nominate a riskier nominee knowing that he is likely to suffer little policy loss from the actions of the interim appointee. Likewise, since presidents would prefer that an ideologically distant U.S. District Court does not remove their Attorney General's interim appointee, we expect that a president will be more likely to nominate easy-to-confirm nominees when the ideological distance between the president and the district court is high. We therefore expect that greater ideological distance between the president and the district court is associated with quicker confirmations and a lower probability that a nomination fails.

Similarly, we expect the speed and fate of a nomination will depend on the level of ideological disagreement between the U.S. District Court and

[9] In many applications, the Senate's median member is an appropriate pivotal actor in the Senate. However, Romer and Rosenthal (1978, 27) note that strong agenda control implies the median voter may not be the pivotal actor. This may be especially true in nominations where, without a favorable Chair, a nominee is unlikely to make it to the floor for consideration. Furthermore, the ideological position of the Chair is heavily influenced by which party controls the chamber and so chairs will be more distant during divided government when the Senate is controlled by a president's opposition. We therefore use the Senate Judiciary Committee Chair as the pivotal member of the Senate.

[10] The U.S. District Court therefore serves a role akin to a reversion point in a President-Senate bargaining model (Romer and Rosenthal 1978).

the Senate Judiciary Committee chairperson. Initially, the expectations seem straightforward: if the Senate Judiciary Committee Chair approves of a district court's likely nominee, he has little incentive to move quickly on the presidential nominee. Thus, increases in the level of ideological disagreement between the Senate Judiciary Committee Chair and the U.S. District Court should result in shorter delay and a higher probability that a nominee is eventually confirmed.

However, we do not believe the process will be this simple; the type of nominee a president will choose should also depend on this level of ideological congruence. When the distance between the Judiciary Committee Chair and the district court is high, the reversion point—the interim U.S. Attorney the district court could appoint—is relatively extreme. Because the Senate dislikes the reversion point so much under these circumstances, they are likely to confirm even a relatively unpalatable presidential nominee because the district court's nominee could be even worse. In this vein, Nokken and Sala (2000, 110) find that presidents are advantaged in nomination situations in which they face an extreme reversion point because they are likely to achieve confirmation of nominees that would otherwise fail. In these situations, we expect that presidents will nominate individuals closer to their own ideal point.

The result is a nominee and a reversion point that the Chair is apt to dislike. Under these circumstances, we expect the Chair to try to delay the nomination with the hopes of identifying scandal (Krutz, Fleisher, and Bond 1998) and eventually forcing the president to issue a "better" nominee. Thus, we expect that greater ideological distance between the relevant U.S. District Court and the Senate Judiciary Chair will be associated with an increase in the delay time for U.S. Attorneys and a decrease in the eventual likelihood that a nominee will be confirmed.

Aside from the ideological congruence between key actors in the Senate confirmation process, the institutional rules affecting the confirmation process could also affect its speed and disposition. As mentioned earlier, U.S. Attorneys pass through the blue slip procedure used to select appointees to the U.S. District and Circuit Courts. Though the formal blue slip process happens postnomination, presidents select a nominee knowing that they will have to satisfy home state senators before the nominee will eventually be confirmed. Therefore, we expect that much of the influence of these constraints takes place within the *prenomination process*, indirectly affecting the selection of a nominee (Binder and Maltzman 2009). Regardless of whether staff members perform informal consultations before naming a nominee or account for the home state senator's preferences on their own, knowing the home state senator will need to be satisfied before a nominee will be confirmed, the blue slip process should make presidents particularly attentive to the eventual confirmation process in their selection of a nominee.

Our expectations depend on the partisan alignment of a state's U.S. Senate delegation and the president. When the two senators and the president hail from the same party, there is no voice of home state dissent in the Senate, and we expect the process to move quickly through the legislature. Along those lines, nominations under this sort of weak constraint should be particularly likely to achieve confirmation and to do so fairly quickly.

Likewise, since the blue slip process induces presidents to bargain prenomination when both home state senators are of the opposition party (strong constraint), the nominee considered by the full Senate has already, in most cases, been vetted by two senators from the opposition party. We expect that the opposition's motivation to delay a nominee under such constraints would be commensurately lessened. As a result, nominations made under conditions of complete partisan division between the president and a state's Senate delegation also move along without much delay and are likely to be eventually confirmed.

In contrast, we expect the blue slip process to delay a confirmation when a state's Senate delegation is split. Under these circumstances, the president has a friendly voice in the Senate to help move the nominee along but also faces opposition from another home state Senator. This tricky situation makes it difficult for the president to please both home state senators while selecting a nominee, making it easier for one of the senators to object while the legislature is considering the nominee. We therefore expect the presence of a single opposition-party home state senator to be associated with an increase in legislative delay for a U.S. Attorney nominee and in the probability that a nomination eventually fails.

The political context may matter in other ways. First, prior research on the Senate confirmation process (Martinek, Kemper, and Van Winkle 2002; Scherer, Bartels, and Steigerwalt 2008) suggests that a president's popularity has an important role to play as nominations move through the Senate. More popular presidents are more likely to get their way, perhaps because senators expect that popular presidents will be able to rally the public to the president's position if necessary. As a result, we expect that the delay experienced by the nominees should decrease as a president's popularity increases. Similarly, the nominees of a popular president should be less likely to eventually fail.

Second, we expect that polarization should affect the outcome of a U.S. Attorney nomination. A wide body of scholarship on the legislative process (e.g., Binder and Maltzman 2009; McCarty and Razaghian 1999) has shown that increased polarization paralyzes the legislative process, making it hard for the president's agenda to pass. Thus as the chamber becomes more polarized, the amount of time a nominee must wait before confirmation should also increase; likewise, nominations sent to more polarized senates should be more likely to fail.

3.6.2 Local Considerations

While Washington politics might play an important role in determining a nominee's eventual fate, U.S. Attorneys are fundamentally local officials. We thus expect the local political context to also shape their confirmation process, as Eisenstein (1978) first suggested to be the case. For example, the size of the office managed by a U.S. Attorney affects the extent to which a nominee is a worthy target of delay for an opposition senator. Larger offices handle more cases, and increased confirmation delay provides more opportunities for an interim or acting U.S. Attorney to handle cases before a permanent U.S. Attorney can take office. As Eisenstein (1978) notes, office size also correlates positively with prestige: presidents are likely to spend additional time vetting nominees to lead prestigious offices in the prenomination process to ensure that they are confirmed as quickly as possible; the policy losses a president could face in these more prestigious offices are particularly important. As a result, we expect that nominees to lead U.S. Attorneys' offices in busier districts should be confirmed more quickly and be less likely to fail before the Senate.

Additionally, we look at the political leanings of the given judicial district. While most previous work on presidential popularity has prioritized a president's *national* popularity, U.S. Attorneys are confirmed to serve in a specific judicial district, and the president's popularity in that district might also affect a nominee's eventual confirmation. Indeed, a nominee to a district where a president is particularly popular might expect to sail through the Senate confirmation process, experiencing a quick confirmation.

3.6.3 The Nominee

Aside from the political factors that affect a nominee's eventual disposition before the Senate, studies of the Senate confirmation process also point to nominee-level characteristics that affect a nominee's fate in that body (Nixon 2001; Scherer, Bartels, and Steigerwalt 2008; Shipan and Shannon 2003). Most obviously, qualifications matter. Since the Senate is confirming a U.S. Attorney to perform legal work for the government, the qualifications of the nominee may affect the Senate's decision-making process. In the absence of recommendations by the American Bar Association (a measure commonly employed in studies of judicial delay), we examine work experience and education. First, individuals who have previously served as Assistant U.S. Attorneys are likely to be viewed by the Senate as particularly high-quality candidates because they are familiar with the work of a U.S. Attorney's office and have experience with federal law enforcement. Second, U.S. Attorneys who serve within a district come from the ranks of lawyers to practice there. Having strong local ties to the state in which they will work is an important consideration for prospective U.S. Attorneys. We therefore expect that nominees who previously served as an AUSA and who graduated from an in-state law school will experience quicker confirmations and be less likely to fail.

Beyond qualifications, prior research (e.g., Solowiej, Martinek, and Brunell 2005) suggests that a nominee's demographic background could affect the amount of time she languishes in the Senate and her eventual disposition. First, senators may view presidential nominees who are women or minorities as lower-quality nominees and subject them to more scrutiny, thereby lengthening the nomination process and making them less likely to be confirmed. Second, Asmussen (2011) suggests that presidents may use female or minority nominees strategically, believing that nominees from historically underrepresented backgrounds are more costly for senators to reject. By this logic, the president may select a nominee from a historically underrepresented background in the hopes of gaining enough votes for a nominee closer to the president's own ideal point than the Senate would normally tolerate. Because this nominee is one that would be otherwise unlikely to achieve confirmation, this strategy may have the effect of increasing the time taken to confirm a nomination. We are unable to differentiate between these mechanisms, though they lead us to the same hypothesis: nominees who are female and/or racial minorities will experience longer delay and be less likely to be eventually confirmed.

3.6.4 Methods and Data

We examine the outcomes of the Senate confirmation process for U.S. Attorneys using data from the Library of Congress about the U.S. Attorney nominations made by presidents from 1987–2016.[11] The unit of analysis is the nomination. These data are taken directly from the comprehensive list of nominations found on the Library of Congress's legislative information website. By starting in 1987, this discussion covers only nominations in the "post-Bork" era of heightened partisanship with respect to nominations (Carter 1994).

To examine how long a nomination takes to pass through the Senate, we employ a statistical method known as a duration model. Traditionally used in medical studies to measure the time until "death" for subjects given variation in treatment, political scientists have seized upon these models to study the time until a nomination "dies" (McCarty and Razaghian 1999; Nixon 2001; Shipan and Shannon 2003). Unlike in medical studies, where the research subject might actually pass away, "death" in this setting is a good thing since it represents a successful confirmation vote in the U.S. Senate. Following in the footsteps of many prior studies (Chiou and Rothenberg 2013; McCarty and Razaghian 1999; Nixon 2014; Ostrander 2016), we employ a Weibull survival model.[12]

Our dependent variable is the *Delay* experienced by the nominee. This is the number of days that pass from the date of nomination to the termination of nomination in confirmation, withdrawal, failure, or return to the president. Using the term "delay" is not intended to be pejorative. We use it merely to succinctly describe the time to decision within the Senate. Within our measure we do not account for congressional recesses, days out of session, or time between congressional sessions because U.S. Attorney nominations

[11] Because, as of June 2020, Donald Trump had not yet received a Common Space ideology score, his nominations could not be included in our model.

[12] Studies of executive nominations, such as Martinek, Kemper, and Van Winkle (2002, 353), often note that the nature of the nominations process, in which we expect nominations to be more likely to exit the system as time progresses, is a good theoretical fit for using a Weibull model. When the parametric assumptions of the Weibull model are justified by the data, the model achieves greater precision in estimates (Box-Steffensmeier and Jones 2004).

take place under a strict statutory time period until the district court can appoint a nominee; this happens regardless of the number of days the Senate is in session and conducting business.

To measure the federal political environment, we rely upon the level of ideological disagreement among the president, the Senate Judiciary Committee chairperson, and the median member of the U.S. District Court. To measure the ideology of the U.S. District Court, we expand upon federal district court judge ideology data collected by Boyd (2010) using data provided by the Federal Judicial Center (2012).[13] Our model includes three measures of ideological distance, calculated as the absolute value of the difference between the pairs of political actors: *Distance: Court—Judiciary Chair*, *Distance: President—Judiciary Chair*, and *Distance: President—Court*.

To account for the three varying levels of blue slip constraint, we use a set of dichotomous variables. When there are no senators from the president's party, the president faces *Strong Constraint*. When there is one senator from that state of the president's party, the president faces *Moderate Constraint*. when the president's party controls both Senate seats in the state, the president faces *Weak Constraint*. The data fall fairly equally across regimes: 30% of cases are those in which the president faces *Strong Constraint*, 35% are *Moderate Constraint* cases, and the remaining 35% cases are instances of *Weak Constraint*. Because all cases fall into one of these three regimes, we exclude one of these categories, *Strong Constraint*, as a baseline category.

We include two other measures of the federal political environment. To measure *Presidential Approval*, we use data compiled by the American Presidency Project on the average approval ratings for each president. For each nominee, we use the average monthly approval rating for the president in the month in which he submitted the nomination to the Senate. Finally, to measure *Polarization*, we follow McCarty, Poole, and Rosenthal (2006) by taking the absolute difference in mean scores of the Democratic

[13] Using methodology established by Giles, Hettinger, and Pepper (2001); and Epstein et al. (2007), these scores rely upon Poole's (1998; 2009) common space scores of the ideology of home state senators and the president to create an estimate of the policy preferences of U.S. District Judges. The Common Space score of the District Court judge is the president's score if there are no same-party home state senators, the same-party home state senator's Common Space score if there is one same-party home state senator, and the average of the two Senators' Common Space scores if both senators are from the president's party. Since the Boyd District Court scores are calculated using Poole's common-space estimates, both the District Court and the Senate scores are on the same ideological space, making the calculation of the distance both possible and valid (Poole 1998, 2009). We use the ideal point for the median judge on the U.S. District Court since they often choose their nominee by majority vote, making the median judge the most accurate predictor of the district court's eventual choice.

and Republican Parties in the chamber along the first dimension of the NOMINATE scores.

By contrast, we hypothesized that the local political environment could also speed up confirmation. Based on data we received following a FOIA request to the Executive Office for U.S. Attorneys, we measure the relative U.S. Attorney *Office Size* based on the number of Assistant U.S. Attorneys in each district in every year.[14] Our other measure of local-level political context is district-level *Incumbent President Support*. This variable is the percentage of the vote that the incumbent president received in the judicial district where the vacancy arose.

Finally, we also expect the nominee's background to affect her confirmation. We rely on the data presented in Table 3.1 to measure these characteristics: whether the nominee was a *Female Nominee*, whether the nominee was a historically underrepresented *Minority Nominee*, whether the nominee went to a *Home State Law School*, and whether the nominee had previously served as an Assistant United States Attorney (*Former AUSA*). These variables are all dichotomous and take a value of 1 if the nominee has that background characteristic. Summary statistics for all of the variables we use in our analyses are available in Table 3.4 in the chapter's Data Appendix.

3.6.5 Results and Analysis

Table 3.2 shows the results of the survival model. The outcome variable in this analysis is the number of days that elapsed between a candidate's nomination and the Senate's last action on the nomination. The coefficients in the table are hazard ratios. Coefficients above the baseline of 1 correspond to faster confirmations as an independent variable increases, all else equal. Estimates below 1 suggest that a nominee will experience more delay as the associated independent variable increases.

The overwhelming conclusion from Table 3.2 is the dominance of federal political factors on the amount of time in which a nominee languishes before the U.S. Senate. First, the delay experienced by a nominee is dependent on

[14] The Executive Office for U.S. Attorneys provided us with data on the number of Full Time Equivalent U.S. Attorneys for the years prior to 1992; after that date, the measure is simply the number of Assistant U.S. Attorneys. While, in practice, the measures are very similar, we normalized by year to avoid the possibility that the measurement change affects our empirical results. We standardized the size of all U.S. Attorney's Offices by year to form our measure.

Table 3.2 Duration of Nomination Final Outcomes, 100th to 114th Congresses (1987–2016).

	Coefficient	Standard Error
Federal Political Environment		
Distance: President—Judiciary Chair	0.71*	(0.11)
Distance: Court—Judiciary Chair	0.92	(0.16)
Distance: President—Court	1.04	(0.17)
Weak Constraint	1.18	(0.16)
Moderate Constraint	1.41*	(0.19)
Presidential Approval	1.02*	(0.00)
Polarization	0.44	(0.57)
Local Considerations		
Office Size	0.97	(0.05)
Incumbent President Support	0.89	(0.58)
The Nominee		
Former AUSA	0.98	(0.10)
Female Nominee	0.87	(0.11)
Minority Nominee	1.01	(0.15)
Home State Law School	1.07	(0.12)
Top Law School	0.85	(0.14)
Constant	0.00*	(0.00)
N	491	

The model is a Weibull survival model. The listed entries are hazard ratios with standard errors in parentheses. * Significant at $p < 0.05$. The outcome variable is the amount of time, in days, between the date of the nomination and the Senate's final action on the nominee.

the level of ideological disagreement between the president and the Senate Judiciary Committee Chair. As shown in Figure 3.2, a nominee languishes longer when *Distance: President—Judiciary Chair* increases. Across the interquartile range, this effect is substantively large, corresponding to about 19 days. In practice, this result suggests that presidents may be forced to compromise heavily in their selection of a nominee in times of divided government—when the distance between the president and the Senate

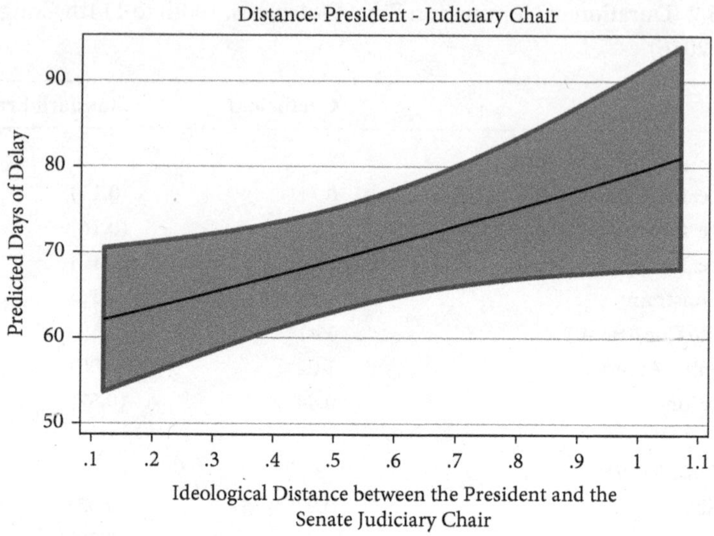

Figure 3.2 Estimated number of days of delay experienced by the nominee given the changing values of the ideological distance between the president and the Senate Judiciary Committee chair.

Judiciary Chair is likely to be large—in order to achieve confirmation for his nominees.

We find evidence that the level of blue slip constraint experienced by the president has an influence on the amount of delay experienced by a nominee, as shown in Figure 3.3. Contrary to expectations, however, we find that, when the president faces *Moderate Constraint*—in which there is only one home state senator from the president's party—the process moves about 20 days more quickly than if there were no home state senators from the president's party. Moreover, and as hypothesized, there is no significant difference in confirmation times between those nominees who come from states in which there are no home state senators from the president's party (*Weak Constraint*) and those with two home state senators from the president's party (*Strong Constraint*), suggesting, somewhat surprisingly, that there is more prenomination bargaining when delegations are divided than when they are united.[15]

[15] Similarly, there is no difference between the amount of delay experienced under *Moderate Constraint* and *Weak Constraint*.

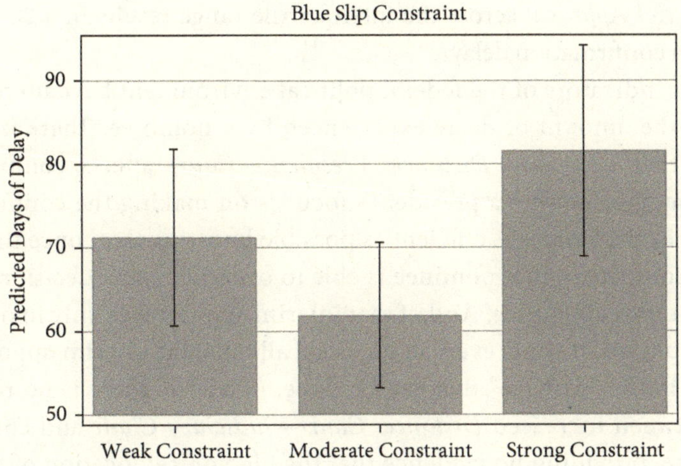

Figure 3.3 Estimated number of days of delay experienced by the nominee given the changing values of blue slip constraint.

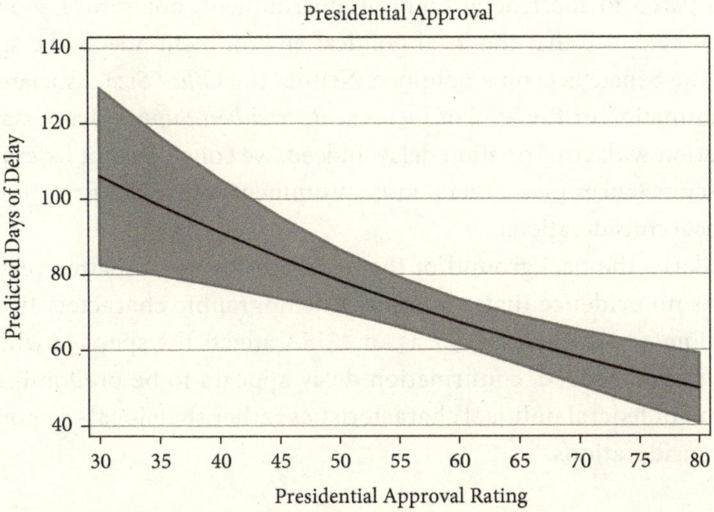

Figure 3.4 Estimated number of days of delay experienced by the nominee given changing values of presidential approval.

More in line with our expectations, the speed at which a president's U.S. Attorney is confirmed depends solidly on the president's popularity (Figure 3.4). More popular presidents are able to achieve a final disposition for their nominees more quickly than less popular presidents. An increase in

Presidential Approval across the interquartile range results in a 20-day decrease in confirmation delay.

Other indicators of the federal political environment have no relationship to the amount of delay experienced by a nominee. There is no evidence that increased *Distance: President—Court* affects confirmation times, suggesting that a president's focus is on making the confirmation process in the Senate as efficient as possible knowing that, once the nominee is confirmed, that nominee is able to override many decisions made by an interim appointee. And, if that interim appointee is only in office for a short period of time, even an ideologically distant interim appointee is limited in the "damage" that can be done. Likewise, there is no relationship between increased *Distance: Court—Judiciary Chair* and confirmation time, providing no evidence that the ideological location of the U.S. District Court seems to affect the nominee's speed through the Senate. Similarly, there is no evidence that increased *Polarization* is associated with more drawn-out confirmations.

Compared to the federal political environment, our results provide us with no evidence that the local political environment affects the speed at which the Senate acts on a nominee. Neither the *Office Size* associated with the nomination or the level of *Incumbent President Support* has a statistical association with confirmation delay. Indeed, we conclude that federal political circumstances play a much more prominent role in confirmation delay than local considerations.

Similarly, the background of the nominee seems to matter very little. There is no evidence that a nominee's demographic characteristics, legal education, or previous service as an AUSA affects the speed at which she is confirmed. Indeed, confirmation delay appears to be predominantly a function of federal political characteristics rather than local- or nominee-level considerations.

3.7 What about Failure?

We are also interested in the outcome of each confirmation. While less than 10 of the nominees in our data were rejected on the Senate floor, a sizable proportion of the observations in our data are censored—individuals who were never explicitly rejected by the Senate but were never given an up-or-down vote on the floor of the Senate. In other words, they were "delayed to death." The dependent variable in our second analysis, *Failure*, is dichotomous and indicates whether or not a nomination failed to be confirmed by the U.S. Senate, either because it never received a vote or because the Senate voted to reject the nomination. Values of 1 indicate that the nomination failed to be confirmed. About 15% of our sample consists of cases that were never confirmed by the Senate. Given the dichotomous nature of the dependent variable, we use logistic regression to estimate the likelihood that a nomination will not be confirmed by the Senate.[16]

Our estimates of the likelihood of a nomination's failure before the Senate, shown in Table 3.3, tell the same, unambiguous story: when it comes to the success or failure of an individual nominee, national-level concerns matter far more than individual or district-level considerations. Indeed, the model estimates provide no evidence that either local-level considerations or a nominee's background have any effect on the probability that an individual's nomination will fail before the Senate.

The model results indicate that ideological considerations and presidential popularity exert a powerful influence on the success of a nomination. Figure 3.5 displays the predicted probability that a nominee fails as the ideological distance between the president and the Senate Judiciary Committee Chair changes. An increase in *Distance: President—Judiciary Chair* across the interquartile range corresponds to a 0.28 increase in the probability that the Senate will not confirm a nominee.

Figure 3.6 demonstrates that higher levels of *Presidential Approval* tend to decrease the probability that an individual nomination will fail. An increase in *Presidential Approval* across the interquartile range corresponds to a 0.07 decrease in the probability that a nominee will fail to be confirmed by the Senate. These findings comport well with expectations derived from prior studies of the nominations process and are broadly similar to the results of the previous analysis.

A notable difference between our results for delay and those for failure concerns the role of the blue slip. While we uncovered evidence in the

[16] There is a slight difference in the number of observations between the Weibull model and the logistic regression. This happens because a handful of nominees were confirmed on the day they were nominated. Because they experienced no delay, they are excluded from the Weibull model but included in the logistic regression.

Table 3.3 Nomination Final Outcomes, 100th to 114th Congresses (1987–2016)

	Coefficient	Standard Error
Federal Political Environment		
Distance: President—Judiciary Chair	3.02*	(0.51)
Distance: Court—Judiciary Chair	0.78	(0.64)
Distance: President—Court	0.66	(0.58)
Weak Constraint	0.40	(0.40)
Moderate Constraint	0.25	(0.38)
Presidential Approval	−0.04*	(0.01)
Polarization	5.73	(3.62)
Local Considerations		
Office Size	−0.02	(0.17)
Incumbent President Support	−0.76	(1.95)
The Nominee		
Former AUSA	−0.21	(0.30)
Female Nominee	−0.10	(0.42)
Minority Nominee	0.02	(0.47)
Home State Law School	−0.15	(0.31)
Elite Law School	−0.08	(0.51)
Constant	−5.87*	(2.99)
N	499	

The listed entries are logistic regression coefficients with standard errors in parentheses. * Significant at $p < 0.05$. The outcome variable takes a value of 1 if a nomination fails and 0 if a nominee is confirmed.

previous section that the presence of a home state senator can affect the speed at which a nominee is confirmed, the results in Table 3.3 provide no evidence that the partisan configuration of home state senators affects the probability that a nominee fails. This finding is likely because while such senators may be able to delay a nominee through hearings and raising issues, without finding disqualifying information or expanding the scope of conflict during this delay it is difficult to overcome the

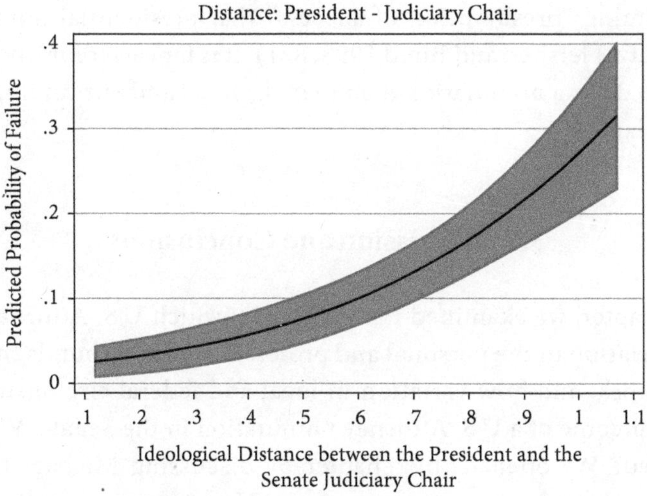

Figure 3.5 Marginal effects of the ideological distance between the president and the Senate Judiciary Committee chair on the probability that a nominee fails to be confirmed by the Senate.

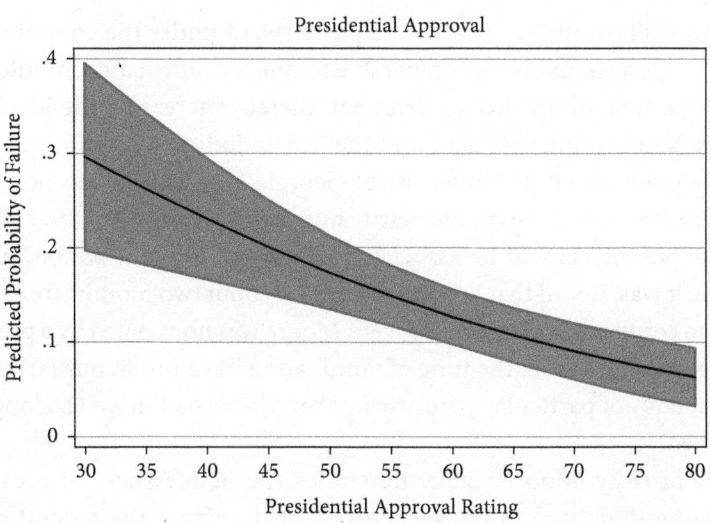

Figure 3.6 Marginal effects of presidential approval on the probability that a nominee fails to be confirmed by the Senate.

overwhelming "presumption of success" that presidential nominations have (Krutz, Fleisher, and Bond 1998, 871). It is far easier for a home state senator to delay a nomination than to make it fail and our findings reflect this imbalance.

3.8 Discussion and Conclusions

In this chapter, we examined the process by which U.S. Attorneys reach office, variation in the personal and professional backgrounds they bring to their work, and how variation in local and federal circumstances affect the outcome of a U.S. Attorney nomination in the Senate. What have we learned? We opened this chapter by discussing Michael J. Moore, President Obama's nominee to serve as U.S. Attorney for the Middle District of Georgia. What might our results suggest about why Moore, compared to the other nominations we mentioned, waited so long to be confirmed? To answer that question, let's compare the circumstances of Moore's nomination to those surrounding Maxwell Wood, his predecessor in office.

Wood is illustrative of a nominee put forward under the conditions our results suggest should be very favorable to quick confirmation. While nominated in a time of divided government, thereby increasing the ideological distance between the president and the Senate Judiciary Committee Chair, Wood, a graduate of the University of Georgia Law School, was nominated by a president with the extraordinarily high approval rating of 85%. This extreme popularity should be associated with a quick confirmation. And, in practice, it was. Recall that Wood only waited about two months from nomination to confirmation. Comparatively, Moore was nominated by a president who was less popular at the time of nomination. As a result, our results suggest that it is not particularly surprising that Moore had to wait so long to be confirmed.

More broadly, Moore's story illustrates the helplessness of presidents against the structural political factors that dominate the federal confirmation process for U.S. Attorneys. Aside from presidential popularity, the factors related to the outcome of Senate confirmation—ideological distance and blue slip configuration—are difficult (if not impossible) for a president to manipulate. In this way, our results suggest that presidents may want to put their allies in office quickly, but the structural realities of modern American politics stand as real impediments along the way.

Still, even though presidents are wildly successful at eventually getting their nominees confirmed, U.S. Attorneys often experience significant delay in the Senate. These nominees are rich targets because they serve as the gatekeepers of federal law within their districts and have wide discretion in how they perform and prioritize their tasks. For opposition-party senators, delaying these nominees can be an effective way to stymie a president's agenda. Still, though nominees may languish for a long time in the Senate, they are rarely rejected outright. Instead, when nominees fail, they generally do so out of malign neglect, waiting so long for an up-or-down vote that the congressional session ends without the nomination receiving a resolution (Bond, Fleisher, and Krutz 2009).

Additionally, we found that presidents vary widely in the extent to which they attempt to advance demographic or professional diversity in the U.S. Attorney ranks. Importantly, we found that Democratic presidents have, on average, been much more likely than their Republican counterparts to nominate women or members of historically underrepresented populations to serve as U.S. Attorneys in recent years. The results for professional diversity are less pronounced, with presidents of both parties generally preferring graduates of home state law schools and nominees who have previously served as Assistant U.S. Attorneys.

The biggest lesson we take from this chapter is the structural dominance of federal-level political factors on U.S. Attorney nominations. Local-level factors appear to play no statistically distinguishable role in predicting the amount of delay a nominee will face or whether or not her nomination will eventually fail. Rather, fundamental features of American national government—ideological disagreement, partisanship, and presidential popularity—play statistically meaningful and substantively large roles in affecting a nominee's fate before the Senate.

Still, our results in this chapter address only how U.S. Attorneys reach confirmation. Do similar federal-level political concerns affect how they perform their work and their future career paths? These are the questions we seek to answer in the remainder of this book. We begin this inquiry in Chapter 4 by jumping ahead to the end of a U.S. Attorney's term, exploring why U.S. Attorneys leave office and where they work after they leave their post as a chief federal prosecutor.

Chapter 3 Data Appendix

Table 3.4 Summary statistics for dependent and independent variables used in the models estimated in Table 3.2 and Table 3.3.

	Mean	Standard Deviation	Range
Delay	78.86	80.01	0–646
Confirmation Failure	0.13	0.34	0–1
Distance: Court—Judiciary Chair	0.46	0.29	0.00–1.01
Distance: President—Judiciary Chair	0.59	0.44	0.02–1.06
Distance: President—Court	0.57	0.31	0.01–1.13
Weak Constraint	0.35	0.48	0–1
Moderate Constraint	0.35	0.48	0–1
Presidential Approval	55.87	13.44	30.33–88.00
Polarization	0.67	0.04	.61–.82
Office Size	0.00	0.92	−0.85–4.64
Incumbent President Support	0.50	0.90	0.25–0.74
Former AUSA	0.52	0.50	0–1
Female Nominee	0.18	0.38	0–1
Minority Nominee	0.14	0.34	0–1
Home State Law School	0.59	0.49	0–1

4
Departures and Removals

At 2:20 p.m. on March 11, 2017, the U.S. Attorney for the Southern District of New York, Preet Bharara, tweeted: "I did not resign. Moments ago I was fired. Being the US Attorney in SDNY [Southern District of New York] will forever be the greatest honor of my professional life." Bharara's tweet marked the end of a day-long standoff between the Obama-appointed U.S. Attorney and the Trump Administration. The previous day, the Department of Justice announced that it had asked the 46 remaining Obama-appointed U.S. Attorneys to resign (Stefansky and Makarechi 2017).

The Trump Administration's decision to demand these resignations was made all the more remarkable because of its timing. The Administration's decision followed a growing chorus of calls from conservative media outlets to purge Obama appointees throughout the executive branch and to replace them with allies of the new administration (Haberman and Savage 2017). Indeed, just the evening before the Administration sought these resignations, Fox News host Sean Hannity called on the Administration to fire the Obama-era U.S. Attorneys. Hannity implored:

> President Trump would do well to follow Lincoln's example and fire anyone and everyone who is actively working against him in government.
>
> After all, even former president Bill Clinton utilized this tactic back in 1993. He fired all 93 U.S. attorneys. According to Conservative Review's Daniel Horowitz, sacking subversive government employees is best done at the start of an administration.
>
> "Clinton easily fired all 93 U.S. attorneys on Day 1," Horowitz noted. "Nobody blinked an eye. Yet when Bush's attorney general fired eight U.S. attorneys well into his second term, well, that became a national scandal."
>
> It's . . . very important for President Trump to act now. (Hannity 2017)[1]

[1] As we will see, Hannity's account of the Clinton Administration's actions was incorrect. While Clinton's Attorney General did seek the resignation of the remaining Bush-era U.S. Attorneys, there were not 93 Senate-confirmed U.S. Attorneys in office when she made the request. And, the move

The Politics of Federal Prosecution. Christina L. Boyd, Michael J. Nelson, Ian Ostrander, and Ethan D. Boldt,
Oxford University Press (2021).
DOI: 10.1093/oso/9780197554685.003.0004

And, while the Department of Justice was seeking these resignations, President Trump's Press Secretary Sean Spicer justified the Administration's decision to seek the replacement of Obama appointees, saying:

> I think that there's no question when you have eight years of one party in office, there are people who stay in government—and continue to espouse the agenda of the previous administration. So I don't think it should come as any surprise there are people that burrowed into government during eight years of the last administration and may have believed in that agenda and may continue to seek it. (Brown et al. 2017)

While the Obama appointees gradually submitted letters of resignation to Trump's Department of Justice that afternoon, Bharara was defiant, refusing to submit a letter of resignation and publicly demanding to be fired. Bharara's firing came the following day, in a phone call from Dana Boente, himself a U.S. Attorney serving as the acting deputy attorney general (Henning 2017). This firing led to widespread media furor, in part because Bharara had built a reputation as a crusader against corruption and because the SDNY office he led was in the midst of investigating allies of Donald Trump for possible corruption.[2]

Were the Trump Administration's actions unusual? This chapter answers that question by exploring the end of a U.S. Attorney's tenure. Importantly, the end of a U.S. Attorney's time in office can be just as (or even more) political than the initial appointment. We examine when and how U.S. Attorneys leave their jobs and where their careers take them after they leave office. Reviewing the past five presidential transitions, we will see that, while the timing and execution of the Trump Administration's decision was somewhat unusual, its desire to replace Barack Obama's appointees with its own selections was business as usual for a new administration.

Indeed, after they are confirmed by the Senate, most U.S. Attorneys are able to continue serving until a new administration takes office, even if it means that they serve beyond their official four-year term in office. In fact, though U.S. Attorneys formally serve at the pleasure of the president, they

sparked such an uproar that neither the George W. Bush nor Barack Obama Administrations took the same path.

[2] Bharara had met with Trump after the 2016 presidential election and issued a statement saying that Trump had agreed to keep him as U.S. Attorney for SDNY (Henning 2017).

are rarely removed from office in the middle of a president's term. By examining a controversial decision by the George W. Bush Administration to fire a handful of U.S. Attorneys in the middle of his term, we will see that firing U.S. Attorneys is an action that comes with political costs for an administration.

Beyond their service in office, we also examine U.S. Attorneys' career paths in the years following their tenure. Consistent with intuitions from prior literature, we find that for most U.S. Attorneys their time in office is likely an ambition for future employment rather than an endpoint in itself. Because they serve short terms at the pleasure of the president, U.S. Attorneys must think about their next steps while serving in government office, which may influence how they perform their tasks. For many U.S. Attorneys, the next step is a future political career, perhaps even a coveted position as a federal judge. Other former U.S. Attorneys use their skills to run for elected office. Thus, the power to nominate U.S. Attorneys has both powerful short- and long-term consequences for a presidential legacy. In the short term, the selection of U.S. Attorneys allows presidents to wield ongoing power over the application of federal law. Over the longer term, presidents are choosing the next generation of political elites, as many of these individuals continue to other important political offices.

4.1 Departures and Independence

Federal law provides some basic information about the terms of U.S. Attorneys:

(a) The President shall appoint, by and with the advice and consent of the Senate, a United States attorney for each judicial district.
(b) Each United States attorney shall be appointed for a term of four years. On the expiration of his term, a United States attorney shall continue to perform the duties of his office until his successor is appointed and qualifies.
(c) Each United States attorney is subject to removal by the President (28 U.S. Code §541).

The statute indicates that each Senate-confirmed U.S. Attorney serves for a four-year term. Because most presidents try to fill U.S. Attorney positions in the first year of their term and presidential terms are also four years long, the terms of presidents and U.S. Attorneys are roughly coterminous. However, presidents rarely nominate U.S. Attorneys as their first act in power, and even if they did, it may take the Senate several months to process these nominations. In practice, the terms of U.S. Attorneys often expire during or well after the first year of a new presidential administration.

But there is a tension in the statutory language. U.S. Attorneys are *also* "subject to removal by the President." The statute provides no information about the conditions under which the president may remove U.S. Attorneys. Congress could have insulated U.S. Attorneys from presidential control by specifying that these officials could only be removed by the president for incompetence, malfeasance, or other inappropriate behavior. But it did not. As a result, the president can remove U.S. Attorneys from office for any reason at all, including for partisan or ideological reasons.

Though presidents have the formal power to remove U.S. Attorneys from their position for any reason, presidents have rarely exercised this authority. The Congressional Research Service conducted an exhaustive investigation of every Senate-confirmed U.S. Attorney who served from 1981–2006, the year when President George W. Bush fired seven U.S. Attorneys in the middle of his term (a decision we will explore at length later in this chapter). The report found that, not counting those officials whose term was interrupted by a change in presidents, only two were dismissed by their appointing president (Scott 2007). William Kennedy, who led the U.S. Attorney's Office for the Southern District of California, was dismissed by President Reagan in 1982 for publicly releasing the name of a confidential CIA informant to the media after the CIA blocked his attempt to prosecute the informant (Pound 1982). J. William Petro, an Ohio U.S. Attorney, was fired by President Reagan in 1984 for revealing to a friend information about an impending indictment, which compromised an undercover investigation. Ultimately, Petro was convicted on charges of criminal contempt (Werner 1984; *New York Times* 1985).[3]

According to the Congressional Research Service, three other U.S. Attorneys resigned in the middle of their terms due to scandal. One of them,

[3] Even before 1981, presidents have been reluctant to remove U.S. Attorneys in the middle of their term. Johnston (1993) cites two additional cases: Robert Morganthau resisted efforts by the Nixon Administration to replace him as a New York U.S. Attorney in 1969 until he received a personal "ultimatum" by President Nixon. And "In 1978, Attorney General Griffin B. Bell removed David W. Marston as United States Attorney in Philadelphia, provoking charges, never proved, that a lawmaker under scrutiny by Mr. Marston's office had urged President Jimmy Carter to remove the prosecutor."

Larry Colleton, served as U.S. Attorney for the Middle District of Florida and resigned in 1994 after he was videotaped grabbing a Jacksonville television reporter by the throat when the reporter confronted Colleton about decisions made by his office (Groer 1994). The second, Frank L. McNamara Jr., who served as U.S. Attorney in Massachusetts, resigned in 1989 following the launch of a Justice Department probe into whether McNamara had falsely accused his predecessor of smoking marijuana (Neuffer and Kurkjian 1989). Lastly, Kendall Coffey, U.S. Attorney for the Southern District of Florida, resigned in 1996 "amid accusations that he bit a topless dancer on the arm during a visit to an adult club after losing a big drug case" (Associated Press 1996). These sorts of incidents are uncommon.

Thus, across a 25-year time period, only five U.S. Attorneys left office involuntarily in the middle of their terms. It is rather typical then, that barring a change in presidential administration, nearly all U.S. Attorneys are able to serve their full four-year term. To be sure, some individuals choose to resign for personal or career-based reasons (such as to run for office or to accept a judicial appointment). But, while presidents technically have the power to remove U.S. Attorneys from office, they rarely exercise that power after the start of an administration.

4.2 Presidential Transitions

Presidential transitions, especially where the party in control of the executive changes, are often difficult and chaotic times for a new administration (Joynt Kumar et al. 2000). In their early months, presidents face public pressure to live up to Franklin Roosevelt's first 100 days of legislative successes (Neustadt 2001) while also trying to fill hundreds of key bureaucratic posts in order to ensure that the machinery of government continues to function (Joynt Kumar 2008). After a presidential transition, time and attention are in short supply while any missteps at this early stage can be costly for the future of the administration (Pfiffner 1996). This forces an administration to carefully prioritize their early actions.

New administrations face several constraints when considering how to start staffing U.S. Attorney offices. Immediately upon taking office a new president will inherit their predecessor's confirmed U.S. Attorneys who have not already resigned. Many U.S. Attorneys do resign upon a presidential transition. As James S. Brady, a U.S. Attorney under Jimmy Carter explained,

"When Carter lost in November of 1980, I resigned . . . Nobody asked me, but that's the tradition of the office. U.S. Attorneys serve at the pleasure of the president, and when a new administration comes in, everybody knows you will have a new U.S. Attorney" (quoted in Savage 2007).[4] Retaining a prior administration's officials, even for a few months, risks an application of federal law that is out of step with a president's priorities. As such, new administrations often ask for the resignations of sitting U.S. Attorneys. However, sweeping all U.S. Attorneys aside at once risks the interruption of ongoing investigations.

Every new administration faces this choice between retention for stability and asking for resignations in order to promote one's own U.S. Attorneys. Historically, the manner in which new administrations handle their transition has varied widely. To illustrate these differing strategies, we briefly review how the past five administrations sought to handle their nomination of U.S. Attorneys. These cases provide insight into how presidents prioritize U.S. Attorneys as well as demonstrate the politics of staffing these positions.

4.2.1 Ronald Reagan

The Reagan Administration demonstrates the recurrent difficulties that presidents face in replacing U.S. Attorneys after a transition. When President Reagan took office in 1981, he arguably "hit the ground running" with both his policy proposals and efforts to build an administration composed of personnel loyal to the president's agenda (Pfiffner 1983, 623). But even in a well-ordered transition, President Reagan's nominations to U.S. Attorney positions still took months to unfold.

President Reagan inherited a team of U.S. Attorneys that were either acting/interim officials or holdover appointees from the Carter Administration (Savage 2007). But while Reagan took office on January 20, the first appointment to a U.S. Attorney position did not take place until Henry Dargan McMaster was nominated to be the U.S. Attorney for the District of South Carolina on May 11. By the time McMaster was nominated, roughly 30 U.S. Attorney positions were vacant due to resignations, two were vacant due to deaths (including the position McMaster was nominated to

[4] There are exceptions to this rule. Some U.S. Attorneys, as we will see, are asked to remain in their positions. Others (rarely) will go to extreme lengths—even changing their own party affiliation—to keep their jobs (Graybiel 2001; Rosica 2001).

fill), and a further 15 positions were occupied by officials who had already turned in their resignations (O'Toole 1981). This lag in filling vacancies, let alone replacing remaining Carter appointees, demonstrates the difficulties that new administrations face in filling positions while presidents are simultaneously trying to meet other demands.

The Reagan Administration, who coined the phrase "personnel is policy," also serves as a good example of how political and ideological considerations influence U.S. Attorney staffing. In order to fill U.S. Attorney vacancies, President Reagan relied on copartisans in the Senate to help produce recommendations and weigh in on candidates. In a sign that the Reagan Administration was attuned to the quality of his U.S. Attorney nominees, the Reagan Department of Justice encouraged senators to have candidates screened by a commission or committee and to give the Department of Justice a short list of possible appointees rather than selecting a single prospective nominee (Pear 1981). The Reagan Administration went so far as to provide particular qualifications for senators to look for in quality candidates:

> [We look for a] good undergraduate and legal education, at least five years trial experience, demonstrated administrative ability, a willingness to carry out the policies of President Reagan, a reputation of fitness and integrity among local lawyers and demonstrated experience in criminal matters. (Sniffen 1981)

In this way, while U.S. Attorneys were not patronage positions, the administration was explicitly valuing fidelity to Reagan's policy goals as a criterion for selecting U.S. Attorneys.

4.2.2 George H.W. Bush

When George H.W. Bush was inaugurated on January 20, 1989, he was taking the reins of the presidency from a copartisan predecessor, Ronald Reagan, after having served within the prior administration as vice president for eight years. He was the only president among recent administrations to immediately succeed a copartisan through election. As such, the politics of his transition were unique in that U.S. Attorneys already confirmed and serving in office were of the same party as the incoming president.

The symbiosis of a friendly transition enabled the Bush Administration to move forward on filling U.S. Attorney vacancies without formally asking those attorneys currently in office to tender their resignation. Where local officials and Department of Justice officials had no problem with an incumbent U.S. Attorney, the Bush Administration was often willing to let that person remain in office.[5] As an administration spokesperson described Bush's approach, there was no "blanket rule"; instead, holdover U.S. Attorneys were evaluated on "a case by case basis" (Koenig 1990).

Overall, the administration avoided public controversy in transitioning from the Reagan Administration's personnel to its own nominees (Nelson and Gerstenzang 1989). However, the administration struggled organizationally. In fact, by mid-March 1989, two months after Bush's inauguration, the administration still lacked an established procedure for selecting federal judges and U.S. Attorneys. This lack of a general rule for making decisions coupled with keeping Reagan-era U.S. Attorneys greatly slowed the pace of appointments after the transition: President G.H.W. Bush only reached his 10th U.S. Attorney nomination, Robert Genzman on September 15,1989, about 8 months into his term. In contrast, 8 months into the Reagan Administration, Reagan had nominated about 30 U.S. Attorneys. So while G.H.W. Bush avoided controversy, he was less influential as a result of his decision to retain existing personnel.

4.2.3 Bill Clinton

The placid transition between Ronald Reagan and George H.W. Bush stands in stark contrast to the enormous controversy that swirled around Bill Clinton's handling of U.S. Attorney nominations. On March 24th, 1993, about two months into Clinton's first term in office, Attorney General Janet Reno demanded the immediate resignation of all 77 incumbent U.S. Attorneys (Bernac 1993).[6] Reno justified the request on the grounds of both transparency and partisanship, stating in a press conference that her purpose was "that the U.S. Attorneys presently in position will know where they stand and that we can begin to build a team" (Johnston 1993).

[5] Evidence for this willingness to rely on Reagan holdovers can be found in the longer average service times for Reagan-appointed U.S. Attorneys as demonstrated in Figure 4.2.

[6] At this point in Clinton's presidency, 16 incumbent U.S. Attorneys had already submitted their resignations (Johnston 1993).

President Clinton, in an exchange with reporters, defended Reno's decision against claims that it was politicized, saying "all those people are routinely replaced, and I have not done anything differently . . . And I think the blanket decision is less political than picking people out one by one" (Clinton 1993). In other words, Clinton argued that asking all of the Bush appointees to simultaneously tender their resignations treated them all equally rather than an alternative process in which the Clinton Justice Department reviewed their performance on a case-by-case basis and allowed that review to determine when each U.S. Attorney would be asked to resign.

Republicans in Congress expressed deep displeasure with Reno's actions. At the time, Senate Majority Leader Bob Dole (R-KS) labeled it the "March Massacre," drawing on the corruption of the Nixon era. Dole took issue with both the timing of the decision and its politicized veneer, saying "[t]he president's political—and, yes, impatient—desire to select his own U.S. attorneys will force much of the department's important work to come to a screeching halt. . . . Justice will suffer" (Bernac 1993).

The reactions of sitting U.S. Attorneys were mixed. On the one hand, Jean Paul Bradshaw II, U.S. Attorney for the Western District of Missouri, said Reno "compromised the integrity" of the Justice Department (Associated Press 1993). Other U.S. Attorneys, by contrast, told their local media outlets that the notice was expected even if the timing was sudden. Tom Corbett, a former Pennsylvania U.S. Attorney, pinpointed the controversy as one of timing more than substance: "We knew this was coming, but it broke with tradition to do it this way . . . It didn't make for a smooth transition. It was how the message was delivered more than what actually occurred" (Savage 2007).

While many U.S. Attorneys spoke out about the "timing" issues and break in tradition associated with Reno's actions, much of the ire of congressional Republicans concerned an ongoing investigation by Jay Stephens, the U.S. Attorney for the District of Columbia, of Rep. Daniel Rostenkowski (D-IL). Stephens had informed Reno and other Justice Department officials that he would make a decision about whether or not to charge Rostenkowski within the next 30 days. Shortly thereafter, Reno made her announcement that U.S. Attorneys should immediately submit their resignations and to make them effective just a few days later, effectively denying Stephens the ability to make a charging decision in the Rostenkowski case. Because Rostenkowski was a Clinton ally, Republicans argued that Reno's timing was politically motivated.[7] Republicans pounced on the Rostenkowski case as evidence that the Clinton Administration was behaving inappropriately, with House Republican Whip Newt Gingrich (R-Ga.) claiming, "The whole thing has a very unsavory look to it. Clearly the administration has the right to get Democratic U.S. attorneys, but to have somebody report that they need 30 more days in a very complex major case that may have national implications and then have them summarily dumped with 10 days' notice frankly just smells. It strikes me as clearly, blatantly political" (quoted in Briggs and Talbott 1993).

Perhaps because of this controversy, Reno backed off from making many of the U.S. Attorneys' resignations immediately effective, allowing them to remain in office until their successors were confirmed (Savage 2007). President Clinton's first nominations for replacements started in mid-June 1993, or about three months after the initial announcement that all U.S. Attorneys would be replaced. Overall, the Clinton transition demonstrates both that the political optics of blanket firings as well as their practical logistics may not be worth the benefits of entirely sweeping out a prior administration's appointees at the start of an administration.

4.2.4 George W. Bush

The George W. Bush administration had Clinton's controversy on its mind as it decided how to handle transitioning U.S. Attorneys in 2001. Rather than asking all U.S. Attorneys to immediately submit their resignations, the Bush Department of Justice worked on a case-by-case basis with incumbent U.S. Attorneys to schedule transitions that took into account the office's workload and U.S. Attorneys' personal circumstances (Gullo 2001). In the words of Attorney General John Ashcroft, the Department of Justice was "committed to making this an orderly transition to ensure effective, professional law enforcement that reflects the President's priorities" (U.S. Department of Justice 2001).

[7] The D.C. U.S. Attorney's office, led by U.S. Attorney Eric Holder, did bring charges against Rostenkowski. Rostenkowski would eventually plead guilty for charges stemming from "sending official payroll checks from his office in Washington to his office in Chicago to pay employees who did no official work but did personal services for him" and "an official check he mailed to buy, through the House Stationery Store, a piece of china that he intended as a personal gift" (Rosenbaum 1996; Thomas 1994).

The Administration formally started to transition U.S. Attorneys offices in mid-March 2001. By this point, about one-third of Clinton's appointees had already resigned, and nearly all had offered to resign (Ziner 2001). The Bush Department of Justice worked to schedule transitions that enabled Clinton U.S. Attorneys to have generally left office by July 1, 2001 (U.S. Department of Justice 2001). The only Clinton appointee to be allowed to remain in office indefinitely was Mary Jo White, who led the U.S. Attorney's Office for the Southern District of New York. White's office was investigating several high-profile matters, including the legality of pardons that Clinton issued while leaving office and the prosecution of terrorists with alleged ties to Osama bin Laden who were accused of bombing African U.S. Embassies. Due to the high-profile nature of these cases, the Bush Administration allowed White to remain in office. To do otherwise risked lending a perception of politicization to the investigation into the pardons (Martineau 2001a).

The Bush Administration's U.S. Attorney transition was not without controversy, however. That Mary Jo White, a Clinton appointee, was allowed to remain in her office during the Bush Administration while her Clinton-appointed colleagues in other New York U.S. Attorneys' Offices were forced to resign violated a long-standing practice between Democrats and Republicans in the state. The practice, which began in 1977 with a bipartisan agreement between Senators Daniel Patrick Moynihan and Jacob Javitz, had allowed U.S. Attorneys in New York to serve out their terms even when the presidency changed parties (Mansnerus 2001). When George W. Bush came to office, both New York State senators were Democrats, and Senator Chuck Schumer asked the Bush Administration to honor this practice, writing in a letter that "Allowing U.S. Attorneys to serve out their terms has the great benefit of reducing the role politics plays in the administration of justice in our federal courts" (McCaffrey 2001). Schumer further called for the Bush Administration to allow the other New York U.S. Attorneys to remain in office, saying that serving full four-year terms "promotes the good government that flows from having leaders with experience and institutional memory" (Martineau 2001a).

However, the Bush Administration did not relent, and the U.S. Attorneys—including eventual Attorney General Loretta Lynch—tendered their resignations. The U.S. Attorney for New York's Northern District, Daniel French, publicly expressed his displeasure, saying Bush's decision ruined "the tradition of depoliticizing prosecution in New York" (Martineau 2001b). Still, he tendered his resignation voluntarily.

4.2.5 Barack Obama

Upon taking office the Obama Administration moved carefully, and slowly, to replace U.S. Attorneys. The administration continued the practice of working individually with U.S. Attorneys to transition their offices to new leadership. Attorney General Holder expressly stated the administration's desire to avoid the turmoil experienced by the Clinton Administration, saying "We have made the determination that we are not going to replace wholesale all of the U.S. attorneys in the way that was done, I guess, in the Clinton administration" and promising that some Bush-era U.S. Attorneys would remain under the Obama Administration (Bishop 2009). Holder's knowledge of the controversy was personal; he served as the U.S. Attorney who indicted Daniel Rostenkwoski in the Clinton Administration, the prosecution that was at the root of the controversy of the Clinton-era U.S. Attorney dismissals (Thomas 1994). The result of this caution, however, was that the administration was perceived by allies as moving slowly in making these key nominations.

In early January 2009, the Department of Justice emailed all incumbent U.S. Attorneys, asking them to remain in office (Shapiro 2009). While some incumbents did tender their resignations, at the end of Obama's first month in office, 54 of the 93 U.S. Attorneys were Senate-confirmed U.S. Attorneys held over from the Bush Administration. Three U.S. Attorneys' offices were led by interim appointments made by the prior Bush Administration that had not yet been Senate confirmed, 18 U.S. Attorneys had been appointed by the local district court, and the remaining offices had career prosecutors serving as Acting U.S. Attorney (Shapiro 2009). President Obama did not submit his first batch of replacement U.S. Attorney nominations until June 4, 2009.

While this gradual approach avoided any major controversy, the relatively slow pace by which the Obama Administration worked to fill U.S. Attorney positions with Democratic appointees caused some members of Congress to raise public concerns. Consider, for example, this July 31, 2009 exchange before the House Judiciary Committee between Maxine Waters (D-CA) and Attorney General Eric Holder:

WATERS: Finally, U.S. attorneys, many jurisdictions are waiting desperately to see what's going to be done. As we understand it, the protocol has been that U.S. attorneys would hand in their resignations and would give the new administration an opportunity to make new appointments. We don't see that happening quite fast enough, and there are many of these jurisdictions where there are real complaints against U.S. attorneys such as in Louisiana, Mississippi, Alabama. What are you doing about that? And how fast are you going to move on that? Or have you changed how it is normally done?

HOLDER: We are working as quickly as we can to put new U.S. attorneys in place. I expect that we'll have an announcement in the next couple of weeks with regard to our first batch of U.S. attorneys. I have met with some of the candidates whose names I expect we will be announcing pretty soon. They come [to] Washington as part of the process. And so we will have our people in place, I think, relatively soon. One of the things that we don't want to do was to disrupt the continuity of the offices and pull people out of positions where we thought there might be a danger that that might have on the continuity—the effectiveness of the office. But it is our intention—elections matter. It is our intention to have U.S. attorneys that are selected by President Obama in place as quickly as we can. And as I said, our first batch will be announced very soon.

WATERS: Thank you very much. I'd just like to say there is a danger with some of them being left there. So whatever you can do to move them, we appreciate it. Thank you. (House Judiciary Committee 2009)

This exchange highlights a different type of problem administrations can face when transitioning into office. While the Clinton Administration took heavy criticism for dismissing incumbent U.S. Attorneys too hastily, the Obama Administration took heat for moving too *slowly*. Further, Waters's statement that there was a "danger" in leaving Bush-era U.S. Attorneys in office during the Obama Administration further highlights the political stakes of these appointments. Waters's stated reason for wanting the Obama Administration to push forward to name new nominees is distinctly partisan in nature.

4.2.6 Donald Trump

Unlike the relatively smooth transition between Presidents G.W. Bush and Obama, President Trump's transition has been likened to a train wreck (Burke 2018). Additionally, President Trump's management of the White House has been characterized generally as lacking "a regular policy process" (Pfiffner 2018, 153). Perhaps as a result of a rough transition and a unique style, the Trump Administration's handling of the U.S. Attorney transition was most similar to the Clinton Administration's abrupt move to fire remaining U.S. Attorneys at the start of the administration. As the anecdote that began this chapter suggests, the Trump Administration's handling of the U.S. Attorney transition was similarly controversial.

On March 10, 2017, only shortly after Acting Deputy Attorney General Dana Boente had begun contacting USAs individually, the Department of Justice publicly announced that all Obama-era U.S. Attorneys were to resign immediately. This public announcement blindsided many U.S. Attorneys and unleashed a media firestorm (Brown et al. 2017). The Trump Department of Justice, like the Clinton Administration before it, justified the actions on the basis of uniformity, as this statement by spokesperson Sarah Isgur Flores illustrates:

> As was the case in prior transitions, many of the United States attorneys nominated by the previous administration already have left the Department of Justice. The attorney general has now asked the remaining 46 presidentially appointed US attorneys to tender their resignations in order to ensure a uniform transition. (quoted in Brown et al. 2017)

The major difference between the Trump Administration's actions and those taken by the Clinton Administration concern the effective date of the resignation letters.[8] Whereas the Clinton Administration accepted the resignation of U.S. Attorneys effective when their successor was confirmed, the Trump Administration sought the immediate resignation of all Obama-era U.S. Attorneys. Indeed, at least one U.S. Attorney said that he was told to clear out his office by the end of the day (Gerstein and Dawsey 2017). A law enforcement source quoted by CNN illustrated how sudden the firings were

[8] Interestingly, Trump's first Attorney General, Jeff Sessions, was one of the U.S. Attorneys told to submit his resignation by Janet Reno at the beginning of the Clinton Administration (Horwitz and Barrett 2017).

for many: "you don't tell them to clean out their desks the same day effective midnight tonight. There are people traveling on official business—are they supposed to turn [in] their cell phones today? Can they come into their office tomorrow to check email?" (Brown et al. 2017).

While the administration said that the actions had been long planned, they violated an agreement between the administration and the ranking Democrat on the U.S. Senate's Judiciary Committee, Dianne Feinstein, who expressed dismay and surprise at the administration's actions:

> Under previous administrations, orderly transitions allowed U.S. attorneys to leave gradually as their replacements were chosen. This was done to protect the independence of our prosecutors and avoid disrupting ongoing federal cases.
>
> In January, I met with Vice President Pence and White House Counsel Donald McGahn and asked specifically whether all U.S. attorneys would be fired at once. Mr. McGahn told me that the transition would be done in an orderly fashion to preserve continuity. Clearly this is not the case. I'm very concerned about the effect of this sudden and unexpected decision on federal law enforcement. (Feinstein 2017)

The result of the Trump Administration's action was that each office would be led by an Acting career prosecutor rather than an Obama appointee until Trump's nominee was confirmed.[9] At this point in the presidential transition, the Trump Administration had not yet nominated a single U.S. Attorney, and the administration did not nominate any replacements for months after demanding the resignations of the Obama-era U.S. Attorneys (Horwitz 2017a; Shear 2017).

4.2.7 Summary

We draw several conclusions from this review of the past several presidential transitions. Perhaps most importantly, there is a strong presumption that a new presidential administration will be able to fill all 93 U.S.

[9] The Trump Administration did not accept the resignation of two Obama-era prosecutors: Dana Boente, who was serving as acting deputy attorney general; and Rod Rosenstein, who was the Trump Administration's nominee to hold the deputy attorney general position on a permanent basis (Horwitz and Barrett 2017).

Attorney positions even if there are Senate-confirmed U.S. Attorneys in those positions who have not yet completed their four-year terms (Scott 2007). In fact, this understanding is so strong that many U.S. Attorneys preemptively tender their resignations when a new president comes into office. Practically speaking, this means that a U.S. Attorney's tenure is determined less by their four-year term and more by the partisan implications of presidential turnover. Each new administration is able to nominate its own team of U.S. Attorneys who, subject to delay (or even failure) in Senate confirmation, are able to ensure that local prosecutions are conducted according to the incoming administration's policy priorities.

As the analysis in this section suggests, administrations handle these transitions very differently. The George H.W. Bush, George W. Bush, and Obama Administrations worked on an individual basis with incumbent U.S. Attorneys, keeping incumbents in office to enable continuity and to keep confirmed U.S. Attorneys in control of their offices until a replacement was at hand. The Clinton and Trump Administrations used a more rigid approach, simultaneously demanding resignations from all incumbent U.S. Attorneys. This approach was roundly criticized, even as the administrations tried to justify the actions on the grounds of uniformity. But caution can also create problems, as the exchange between Eric Holder and Maxine Waters illustrated; delay in filling U.S. Attorneys' offices with an administration's own nominees opens the administration up to criticism from copartisans and can frustrate the administration's ability to implement its justice priorities.

4.3 Midterm Departures

As we saw earlier, presidents rarely fire U.S. Attorneys. Instead, U.S. Attorneys typically serve until they choose to pursue other career opportunities or there is a change in presidential administration. What happens when an administration chooses to dismiss U.S. Attorneys in the middle of their terms for reasons not related to unsavory conduct by that federal prosecutor? To answer this question, we examine two high-profile decisions to fire U.S. Attorneys in the middle of a presidential administration, one by the George W. Bush Administration in 2006 and one by the Donald Trump Administration in 2020.

4.3.1 The 2006 U.S. Attorney Firings

On December 7, 2006, the George W. Bush administration asked for the resignation of seven U.S. Attorneys.[10] All seven of these U.S. Attorneys were originally appointed by George W. Bush and confirmed by the Senate during Bush's first term in office. Indeed, "the Department of Justice had never removed a group of U.S. Attorneys at one time because of alleged performance issues" until the Bush Administration sought these resignations (U.S. Department of Justice 2008, 325).

These firings coincided with a change in the procedures used to fill vacancies in U.S. Attorney positions. When Congress reauthorized the PATRIOT Act in 2006, it amended the procedures surrounding interim U.S. Attorneys. As Chapter 3 explained, interim U.S. Attorneys have historically been appointed by the Attorney General and serve for 120 days, at which point the local U.S. District Court appoints a replacement. The PATRIOT Act revisions removed the local U.S. District Court from the equation, allowing the Attorney General's nominee to serve *indefinitely*. Thus, these new rules enabled the Bush Administration to fill vacant U.S. Attorney positions with their chosen appointees *without congressional approval* (Nelson and Ostrander 2016).

The administration's rationale for the firings shifted in the following months, especially after a Democratic Congress began an investigation into the firings. Initially, administration officials denied that politics played a role in the firings, saying instead that poor performance was behind the request for resignations (Johnston 2007a; Stolberg 2007). Attorney General Alberto Gonzales went so far as to testify that he would "never, ever make a change in a United States attorney for political reasons or if it would in any way jeopardize an ongoing serious investigation. I just would not do it" (Eggen 2007). However, conflicting evidence eventually came to light; six of the attorneys had been rated "well regarded," "capable," or "very competent" in their Justice Department evaluations (Johnston 2007b). The administration then shifted their rationale to the department's national priorities, suggesting that the fired U.S. Attorneys were insufficiently using their office to enforce

[10] The seven U.S. Attorneys were David Iglesias (DNM), Carol Lam (SDCA), John McKay (WDWA), Daniel Bogden (DNV), Paul Charlton (DAZ), Kevin Ryan (NDCA), and Margaret Chiara (WDMI). Two other U.S. Attorneys, Thomas DiBiagio (DMD) and Kasey Warner (SDWV), were dismissed in early 2005 and two others, Todd Graves (WDMO) and Bud Cummins (EDAK), were dismissed in 2006.

national priorities on issues like voter fraud and immigration (Johnston 2007b; Johnston and Lipton 2007; Serrano 2007b). Documents released by Congress, coupled with an internal investigation by the Department of Justice, painted a starkly different picture.

The congressional investigation revealed that the dismissals had been premeditated, with planning among top-level DOJ officials originating in January 2005, just as Bush's second term began. On that day, Bush's political advisor Karl Rove asked another official in the White House Counsel's office "how we planned to proceed regarding U.S. attorneys, whether we were going to allow all to stay, request resignations from all and accept only some of them or selectively replace them, etc" (*ABC News* 2007). At one point, the White House Counsel's office considered asking all U.S. Attorneys to resign. This decision evokes the decision by the Clinton Administration to dismiss all Bush-holdover USAs, however, there is one important distinction. While the Clinton Administration had asked for the resignations at the beginning of the presidential transition, the Bush Administration was considering dismissing U.S. Attorneys *in the middle of an administration* (Weiss 2008). This stands in stark contrast to the precedent set by Reagan and Clinton, neither of whom dismissed a U.S. Attorney between his first and second terms in office.

The Department of Justice, led by the Attorney General's Chief of Staff, Kyle Sampson, responded to Rove's question in an email with a suggestion that the administration replace a smaller number of U.S. Attorneys, though he recognized that the decision was likely to be controversial:

> As an operational matter, we would like to replace 15–20 percent of the current U.S. Attorneys—the underperforming ones . . . The vast majority of U.S. Attorneys, 80–85 percent, I would guess, are doing a great job, are loyal Bushies, etc., etc. Due to the history, it would certainly send ripples through the U.S. Attorney community if we told folks they got one term only. (Sampson 2005a)

There was no immediate response to Sampson's email, though Gonzales authorized Sampson to begin to review the U.S. Attorneys' performance to identify some for possible removal, and White House Counsel Harriet Miers asked Sampson in February 2005 for recommendations for U.S. Attorneys for the administration to consider dismissing (U.S. Department of Justice

2008). Sampson responded on March 2, 2005, sending Harriet Miers a list of U.S. Attorneys ranked into three categories:

bold = Recommend retaining; strong U.S. Attorneys who have produced, managed well, and exhibited loyalty to the President and Attorney General.
strikeout = Recommend removing; weak U.S. Attorneys who have been ineffectual managers and prosecutors, chafed against Administration initiatives, etc.
nothing = No recommendation; have not distinguished themselves either positively or negatively (Sampson 2005b).

Sampson's first list targeted 14 U.S. Attorneys for possible removal, though only 4 of the attorneys on that list were eventually asked to resign in 2006 (U.S. Department of Justice 2008).[11] Note that Sampson rated U.S. Attorneys based both on their "loyalty" to the administration but also the attorneys' support of the administration's prosecutorial initiatives.

The administration took no immediate action on Sampson's list. It was not until January 2006—nine months later—that Sampson provided Miers with an updated list of attorneys to consider dismissing. This list contained nine candidates for dismissal. This process continued through December 2006. All told, Sampson assembled seven lists of possible dismissal candidates (U.S. Department of Justice 2008). Sampson met with Attorney General Gonzales on November 27, 2006, to discuss the dismissals,[12] and the White House approved the plan on December 4, 2006, with an email acknowledging the coming controversy: "We're a go for the US Atty plan. WH leg, political, and communications have signed off and acknowledged that we have to be committed to following through once the pressure comes" (U.S. Department of Justice 2008). Sampson replied that all U.S. Attorneys were currently in D.C. for a conference, and they planned "to wait until they are back home and dispersed, to reduce chatter" (U.S. Department of Justice 2008).

When the U.S. Attorneys were personally called by Michael Battle, the Director of the Executive Office for U.S. Attorneys on December 7, 2006,

[11] Two of Sampson's bolded ("Recommend retaining") attorneys—Iglesias and Ryan—were among those asked to resign in December 2006.

[12] Though Gonzales claimed in a March 13, 2007, press conference that he was not involved in any talks about dismissals, he later affirmed that he "signed off on the recommendations and signed off on the implementation plan" enforced in December 2006.

they were not provided with any formal rationale for their dismissal. Because the dismissals were conducted privately, they initially escaped media attention. It wasn't until January 2007 that the firings came to light and the controversy unfolded (Weiss 2008).

Congressional and executive branch investigations into these firings provided hard evidence that at least some of the dismissals were based on politics rather than performance. For example, David Iglesias communicated with Republican Senator Pete Domenici and Representative Heather Wilson in October 2006 (two months before the firings) about investigations into Democrats, especially as they pertained to Wilson's upcoming election.[13] The investigation eventually revealed that Domenici explicitly asked Karl Rove and President Bush to fire Iglesias. Indeed, the Department of Justice's investigation into the firings concluded that Iglesias's removal was ultimately motivated by New Mexico Republicans' complaints over his handling of voter fraud and corruption cases against Democrats. Iglesias didn't appear on any of Sampson's list of low-performing U.S. Attorneys until after the October conversation with Domenici and Wilson. In fact, Iglesias was listed as one of the "strong" U.S. Attorneys on Sampson's first list (U.S. Department of Justice 2008, 151).

Or consider the case of Carol Lam, former U.S. Attorney for the Southern District of California. Lam was investigating Republican Representative Randy Cunningham for possible corruption. Soon after search warrants for two of Cunningham's associates were issued, Sampson sent an email seeking to discuss "the real problem we have right now with Carol Lam" (Serrano 2007a). Overall, the Department of Justice's Inspector General concluded there was "significant evidence that political partisan considerations were an important factor in the removal of several of the U.S. Attorneys" (U.S. Department of Justice 2008, 325–26).

The fallout from the Bush Administration's decision to purge these U.S. Attorneys was widespread. Harriet Miers resigned her position in January. Battle resigned in early March, testifying to the Senate Judiciary Committee that he was not aware of performance issues until he was instructed to make the calls to the seven attorneys. Other senior administration and DOJ officials (including Kyle Sampson) also resigned in the following months. Ultimately,

[13] Interestingly, David Iglesias may have been the inspiration for Tom Cruise's character in *A Few Good Men* (Glaberson 2011).

on August 27, 2007, Gonzales resigned as well, after testimony from officials contradicted his sworn testimony that he was not involved in the firings.

The reaction involved more than personnel. Congress passed a law restoring the pre-PATRIOT Act rules for the appointment of U.S. Attorneys in March 2007.

4.3.2 The 2020 Berman Firing

Late on Friday night June 19, 2020, U.S. Attorney General William Barr issued an unusual press release. In it, he thanked Geoffrey Berman, the interim U.S. Attorney for the Southern District of New York (SDNY), for his years of service, announced Berman's resignation, and named Jay Clayton—then chair of the Securities and Exchange Commission and frequent Trump golfing partner—as the presidential nominee to be sent to the Senate for confirmation (Feuer et al. 2020; U.S. Department of Justice 2020c).[14] Contrary to the tradition of having intra-office assistants perform the duties of the U.S. Attorney in the absence of a confirmed nominee, the announcement named Craig Carpenito—then U.S. Attorney for New Jersey—to serve as the acting U.S. Attorney for the SDNY. Just hours after Barr's press release, however, Geoffrey Berman issued his own stunning public statement:

> I learned in a press release from the Attorney General tonight that I was 'stepping down' as United States Attorney. I have not resigned, and have no intention of resigning, my position to which I was appointed by the Judges of the United States District Court for the Southern District of New York. I will step down when a presidentially appointed nominee is confirmed by the Senate. Until then, our investigations will move forward without delay or interruption. I cherish every day that I work with the men and women of this Office to pursue justice without fear or favor—and intend to ensure that this Office's important cases continue unimpeded. (Berman 2020)

After Berman's public rebuke of Barr's statement, confusion, outcry, and speculation quickly ensued. At the time of these events, the SDNY office was

[14] This announcement came after Barr offered Berman (and Berman declined) ostensible "promotions" within the Department of Justice in exchange for stepping down as Manhattan's U.S. Attorney (Weiser et al. 2020).

investigating several politically salient cases involving figures like President Trump's personal attorney (and former New York City mayor) Rudy Giuliani (Feuer et al. 2020). As such, critics suggested that the move to remove Berman was orchestrated by the Trump Administration to gain political control over the high-profile caseload of the SDNY office (Rosenzweig 2020) while tenuous comparisons were even made to Richard Nixon's infamous "Saturday Night Massacre" during the Watergate scandal (Collinson 2020). Chuck Schumer, the Senate Minority Leader (representing New York) put out a press release calling Barr's actions "blatantly corrupt" and urged the DOJ Inspector General to investigate Barr's decision to remove Berman from office (Schumer 2020). In addition to the more sinister speculation, the botched attempt by Attorney General Barr to immediately oust Berman from office conveyed a sense that the Trump Administration's DOJ management was chaotic and unprofessional (Benner and LaFraniere 2020).[15]

Ultimately, Berman would quickly depart his office. Just one day after the dueling Barr and Berman press releases of June 19, Barr wrote to Berman to report that President Trump was firing him. Berman capitulated at once in the face of this more formal action (Orden et al. 2020).[16] Perhaps in recognition of the new optics, immediate control of the SDNY office was given to Berman's chief deputy rather than Carpenito as originally suggested by Barr's Friday night press release (Rosenzweig 2020).[17] While Berman's defiant act did not save his job, it forced the administration to fire him publicly, with all of the attention and criticism entailed in that decision, rather than bury the "resignation" quietly on a Friday night (Benner and LaFraniere 2020). The increased public scrutiny also helped to ensure that Berman's second-in-command, rather than Barr's handpicked selection, would oversee the office in the immediate aftermath of Berman's departure.

Also on Saturday the 20th, Republican Senate Judiciary Committee Chair Lindsey Graham announced that he would enforce the traditional blue

[15] In this vein, Attorney General Barr was also criticized for attempting to replace Geoffrey Berman with Jay Clayton, an individual who did not have prior experience as a prosecutor (Weiser et al. 2020).

[16] Because Berman was appointed by the district court, rather than confirmed by the Senate, there was uncertainty about whether President Trump had the legal authority to fire him (Savage 2020). Some would suggest that despite Berman's method of appointment, he still served at the pleasure of the president and that the presidential removal order was essentially self-executing (Neustadt 1990). Ultimately, because of how quickly events played out, there was no opportunity for courts to weigh in on the question.

[17] This decision was particularly important because the deputy, Audrey Strauss, had led the office's investigations on many of the most politically sensitive cases because Berman was forced to recuse himself due to his connections to Trump (Feuer et al. 2020).

slip protocol on Jay Clayton, the administration's pick to replace Berman. Graham's decision meant that he would not allow a nominee to be confirmed by the Senate unless that person satisfied New York's two Democratic senators (Feuer et al. 2020). The New York senators quickly signaled that they would not support Clayton's nomination (Carney 2020). As a result, Graham's decision instantly diminished the probability that the Senate would be able to confirm a Trump nominee, the ostensible purpose behind Barr's actions.

As a former federal prosecutor told CNN: "After all this what did they gain by getting rid of Berman? Nothing" (Orden et al. 2020).

4.3.3 Implications

It is always difficult to extrapolate from just a few historical circumstances to a broader lesson. But, still, we can try. The most obvious conclusion that we are able to draw from the dismissal of these U.S. Attorneys is their high cost. These actions are highly visible, were covered widely by the media, and required significant concessions from the administration that contradicted their goals for the firings in the first place. U.S. Attorneys can and, as we have shown, often do protest their ousting. Furthermore, dismissals that are resisted are immediately decried as attempts to subvert the normal course of justice through politicization of the U.S. Attorneys' offices. However, removals outside of transitions are rare. Indeed, that we have so few instances of presidents dismissing U.S. Attorneys may well be due to the fact that presidents act strategically in this regard. Because they know they will face severe repercussions from firing U.S. Attorneys midterm, they choose to let U.S. Attorneys—even those they may otherwise like to replace—remain in office.

Though quite rare, these cases do exist as a warning to serving U.S. Attorneys. If an administration deems that it is worth the political costs to remove a U.S. Attorney, they will. While a U.S. Attorney can raise the cost of removal by going public, they can do nothing to fight the dismissal itself. U.S. Attorneys ultimately serve at the pleasure of the president.

4.4 Leaving (or Not) the U.S. Attorney's Office

Though U.S Attorneys are appointed for a four-year term, they are able to remain in office after their term has expired. Individuals who serve beyond their statutory term length are said to be serving as a "holdover" during this time. Holdover capacity is designed to allow bureaucratic institutions to function in the absence of Senate-confirmed replacements. But the existence of holdover capacity can also change the dynamics of confirming replacements as compared to a true vacancy where no one is serving in the position (Madonna and Ostrander 2017).

There are several reasons that presidents may choose to allow U.S. Attorneys to continue to serve in a holdover capacity. First, presidents often are not able to address new U.S. Attorney nominations within their critical first months of office. One reason for this is that presidents often have to prioritize their judicial (King and Ostrander 2020) and bureaucratic nominations while forming their governing team in early days. Nominations to high-level agency posts and judicial vacancies frequently take priority over other issues, such as replacing holdover US Attorneys. As such, we often do not see any U.S. Attorney nominations within the first 100 days of a new administration.

Second, as noted in the discussion of recent presidential transitions, a blanket firing of all U.S. Attorneys would be disruptive to their respective offices while also attracting bad press and the condemnation of the president's opposition party in Congress. As a result, presidents often—but not always—wait to replace a U.S. Attorney from a prior administration until one has a permanent replacement ready. In the interim, even officials serving in a holdover capacity from the prior administration are kept in office for several months while waiting for a replacement.

Third, U.S. Attorneys often handle cases that can be perceived as political, and replacing such an official may be seen as an act designed to tip the scales of justice. For example, Shapiro (2009) noted that President Obama held off on replacing Patrick Fitzgerald, a George W. Bush appointee, as Fitzgerald was investigating Rod Blagojevich, the former Democratic Governor of Illinois.

Fourth and finally, presidents often allow their U.S. Attorney appointments to continue to serve in office as a holdover because of convenience. If a president is satisfied with the job a holdover is doing, there is no urgent need to nominate a replacement. And, as a president transitions from his first term in office to a second, he may not want to expend energy on a new slate of U.S. Attorneys and will allow the prosecutors in office to remain until the end of his term. Additionally, as discussed before, when administrations transition from a predecessor president of the same party, presidents may not feel the urgency to replace a U.S. Attorney once their official term of office is complete. They likely have similar policy goals as their predecessor and choose to spend their political capital on other, more pressing, concerns.

To examine the prevalence of holdovers among the U.S. Attorney ranks, we turn to data on the average length of service for U.S. Attorneys. Based on records kept by the Library of Congress, we compiled a dataset containing all U.S. Attorney nominations confirmed by the Senate.[18] We then used official reports, future nominations, resumes, and media sources to note the length of service and subsequent career history for each U.S. Attorney within our data. Our data include all U.S. Attorneys nominated by Ronald Reagan, George H.W. Bush, Bill Clinton, George W. Bush, and Barack Obama. The data therefore span from early 1981 until Donald Trump requested the resignation of Barack Obama's U.S. Attorneys in early 2017. The unit of analysis in the dataset is the individual U.S. Attorney, and there are approximately 500 cases for which we have full data.[19]

Figure 4.1 presents a histogram of the amount of time spent in office by each confirmed U.S. Attorney. The black dashed vertical line in the figure marks four years, the statutory term of office for U.S. Attorneys. The major conclusion we can draw from this graph is that *most* U.S. attorneys serve beyond just one four-year term. The figure also shows a spike in departures just before the eight-year mark, suggesting that some U.S. Attorneys appointed early within a two-term administration stay for the full presidency and perhaps even a bit beyond. The cases stretching beyond eight years in our data are most often President Reagan's appointees serving in a holdover capacity after the friendly transition to the G.H.W. Bush Administration, the only copartisan transition in our data.[20] For one notable example, Jeff Sessions served as the U.S. Attorney for the Southern District of Alabama for 12 years

[18] There exist a great number of acting and interim U.S. Attorneys who serve in the absence of a confirmed nominee. However, as noted in Chapter 3, the circumstances of such temporary appointments—including how they received their position and how long they may serve—varies greatly and as such they are not always comparable cases to Senate-confirmed appointees.

[19] While we have complete data for U.S. Attorney nominations due to Senate records, no similar source exists to accurately track departures. As such, there are a handful of cases for which we do not have departure dates. These cases have been excluded from our analysis. Trump Administration nominations, for which there is not yet full departure data, are excluded.

[20] There are a handful of long-serving cases occurring after the Reagan Administration. Such cases are appointees from the G.W. Bush Administration who were allowed to continue serving under President Obama for an extended period of time. For example, in May 2005 Rod Rosenstein was appointed by G.W. Bush to be the U.S. Attorney for the District of Maryland. President Obama kept Rosenstein serving as a U.S. Attorney throughout his entire administration. Rosenstein only left in 2017 upon his appointment as the Deputy Attorney General by the Trump Administration (U.S. Department of Justice 2019b).

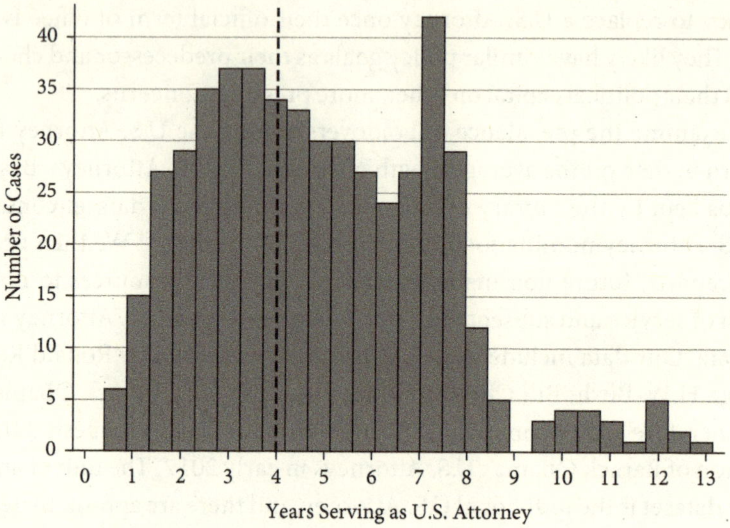

Figure 4.1 Histogram showing the distribution of U.S. Attorneys' time in office. Data include Senate confirmed appointees from the Reagan through Obama Administrations.

through the entire Reagan and George H.W. Bush administrations before resigning in 1993 after Bill Clinton's election (Gray 2018).[21]

How has length of service varied across recent presidential administrations? Figure 4.2 provides the average length of service for U.S. Attorneys nominated by each president for which we have complete data. The dashed gray line shows the four-year statutory term of service for U.S. Attorneys. Again, these data show that most U.S. Attorneys serve far more than the four-year term. In fact, the average service length for our data is 4.9 years, and the *only* president to have their appointees serve on average less than their full term is George H.W. Bush, who—not coincidentally—is also the only president in the data to serve a single term in office. Likewise, that George H.W. Bush succeeded a copartisan president is seen in the comparatively long average term of office served by President Reagan's appointees; as noted before, many of these Reagan-era prosecutors continued to serve as U.S. Attorneys well into the George H.W. Bush Administration.

[21] Sessions did attempt to leave his position during the Reagan Administration to receive a federal judgeship; however, he was not confirmed (Gray 2018).

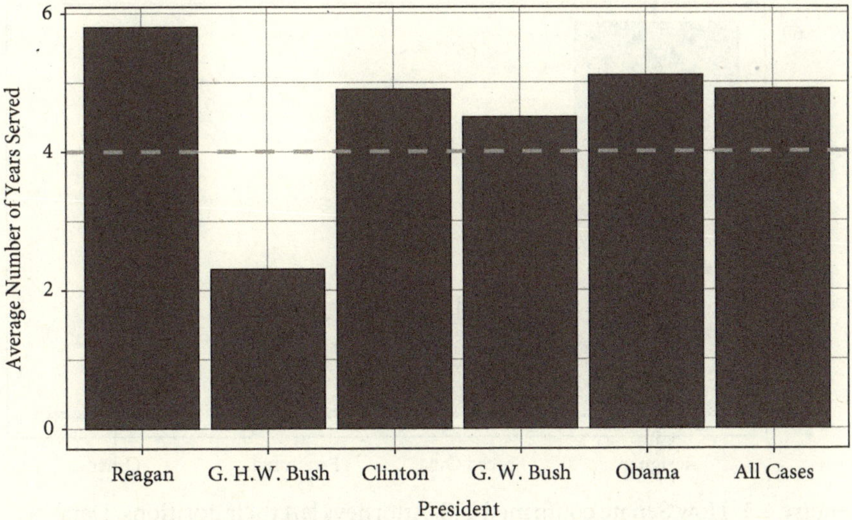

Figure 4.2 Average length of appointee service in years by appointing president. The number of U.S. Attorneys in the data for each president are Reagan (114), G.H.W. Bush (31), Clinton (117), G.W. Bush, (131), Obama (109). The dashed gray line shows the 4-year statutory term of service for U.S. Attorneys.

What finally prompts people to leave their position as a U.S. Attorney? Figure 4.3 shows the proportion of all U.S. Attorneys confirmed between 1981 and 2016 that exited their position through a voluntary resignation, being forced out either through firing or far more often by having their resignation requested by the administration, leaving through a promotion to a higher office such as becoming a federal judge, or through some other pathway. By an overwhelming margin (62% of cases), most U.S. Attorneys resign their posts voluntarily. Interestingly, the next highest category (19%) are those who are forced out of their positions. While this category may seem high, recall that the Clinton and Trump Administrations formally sought the resignations of U.S. Attorneys appointed by their predecessors. Almost the same proportion of chief federal prosecutors (18%) leave their office for a promotion to a new federal position. Very few U.S. Attorneys leave in any other manner. Only about 1% of cases depart through some other mechanism (usually dying while in office).

Given that U.S. Attorneys serve at the pleasure of the current president, their exits may be timed according to the electoral calendar. Figure 4.4 shows when U.S. Attorneys exit (voluntarily or otherwise) based on presidential

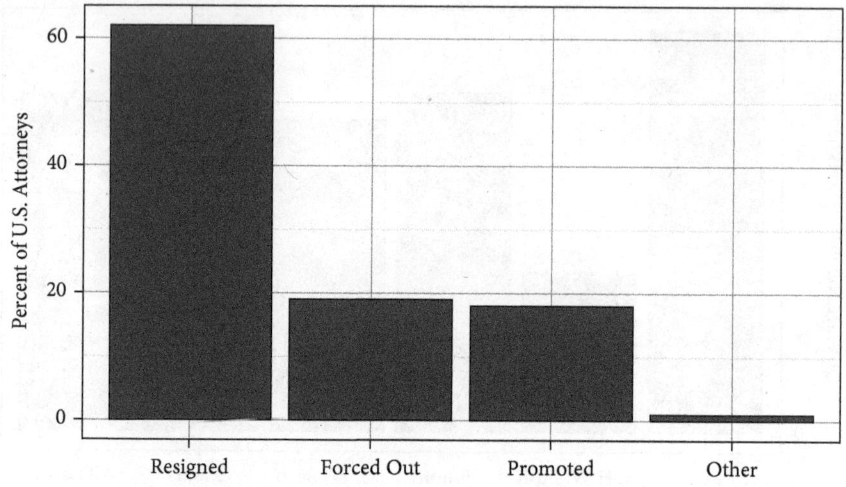

Figure 4.3 How Senate confirmed U.S. Attorneys left their positions. Data range from President Reagan's first appointments in 1981 through the dismissal of Obama Administration appointments by President Trump in 2017.

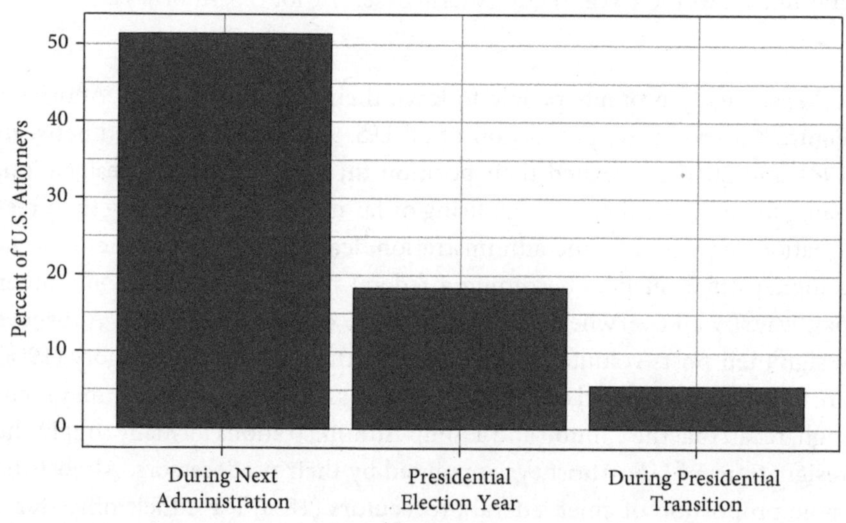

Figure 4.4 Timing of U.S. Attorney departures from office relative to presidential calendar. Categories are independent and not exclusive.

timing. First, we see that more than 50% of U.S. Attorneys end up serving some time in a new administration. Many of these cases represent brief periods of service after a presidential transition before a blanket request for resignations. Perhaps because holdover service is so common, there does not appear to be a large exodus of U.S. Attorneys leaving either during presidential election years (every four years) or while a presidential transition (defined as the period of time between a presidential election and a new president taking office) unfolds. Overall, these data suggest presidential elections influence U.S. Attorney turnover but they do not provide the absolute barriers that some anecdotes would suggest.

4.5 The Springboard to Higher Office

While U.S. Attorneys have extraordinary amounts of power while in office, service as a U.S. Attorney also provides a valuable credential for the politically ambitious. Political scientists have long argued that judicial appointments are an important component of a president's legacy because judges will continue to serve on the bench long after a president leaves office (Goldman 1997; Steigerwalt 2010). U.S. Attorney nominations have a similar legacy-burnishing feature for presidents. Because so many U.S. Attorneys will become power players in the American political system, presidential decisions about who to nominate as a U.S. Attorney are also choices about what the future of the political party will look like.

Like other types of prosecutorial offices, the position of U.S. Attorney is often a steppingstone within an official's career rather than a destination itself (Boylan 2005; Engstrom 1971). This fact dates back to the nation's founding. Among the nation's first U.S. Attorneys were John Marshall who later became the chief justice of the United States and Christopher Gore who later served as the governor of Massachusetts (Executive Office for U.S. Attorneys 1989). The trend has continued. Eisenstein (1978) examined the careers of U.S. Attorneys serving between 1896 and 1960.[22] He found that approximately 26% of his cases were "successful" U.S. Attorney alumni, going on to serve as governor, judge, state attorney general, member of Congress, or in a high-level DOJ position. Similarly, Eisenstein (1978) was able to compile data on

[22] Eisenstein (1978) randomly sampled a set of 30 districts, successfully locating data on 272 of the 352 U.S. Attorneys.

101 of the 186 U.S. Attorneys who served between 1961 and 1973 and concluded their service by 1975; 32 of those men were "successful" alumni, and 27% were holding a governmental position in 1975. Thus, across U.S. history, many chief federal prosecutors have left office and moved to other important political positions.

Indeed, based on anecdotes and evidence from the career choices of former U.S. Attorneys (Miller and Curry 2019), it is likely that many U.S. Attorneys begin their service with an eye toward these related career ambitions. Surveying 49 U.S. Attorneys in 1965, Eisenstein (1978) found that 28 (57%) had their eye on a federal judgeship. Eisenstein also reports the results of a survey of U.S. Attorneys who served from 1961 and 1973; more U.S. Attorneys (31% of respondents) said they wanted to be a federal judge than any other career path, including achieving partner at a private law firm. This ambition was based on prior precedent. Eisenstein (1978) found that of 187 district judges who served in 1916, 1936, and 1959, 15% had served as a U.S. Attorney, and another 7% had served as an Assistant U.S. Attorney.

The trend continues even today. In Figure 4.5, we outline the immediate future career paths of former U.S. Attorneys once they leave their office. While many U.S. attorneys move on to work in a private legal practice (42%), nearly one-third of U.S. Attorneys move immediately to another political position.

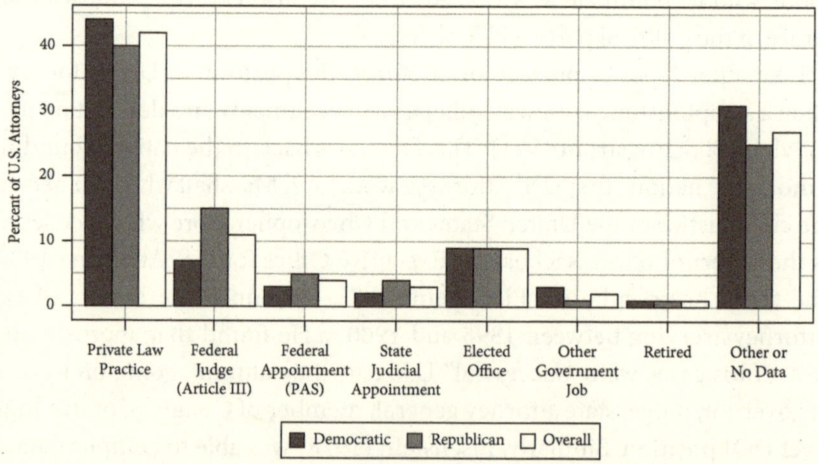

Figure 4.5 Appointee occupations immediately after leaving the U.S. Attorney position. Data range from President Reagan's first appointments in 1981 through the dismissal of Obama Administration appointments in 2017.

One-in-ten U.S. Attorneys become a federal judge immediately after they leave office. Other former U.S. Attorneys decide to run for elected office (9%), while still more (4%) are appointed to another presidentially nominated federal post requiring Senate confirmation (a "PAS" appointment). Fewer former U.S. Attorneys take positions in state judicial posts (3%) or receive some other government job without Senate confirmation requirements (2%). Consistent with the expectation that most U.S. Attorneys are using the position as a stepping stone within a career, only about 1% of U.S. Attorneys immediately retire after leaving office.

In most categories, U.S. Attorneys appointed by Democratic and Republican presidents have the same career trajectories. The one very notable exception is that U.S. Attorneys appointed by Republican presidents are more likely to leave their posts to become a federal judge. As shown in Figure 4.5, U.S. Attorneys appointed by Republican presidents are chosen for Article III federal judgeships at about twice the rate of Democratic-appointed U.S. Attorneys (15% versus 7%). These findings mirror those of Miller and Curry (2019, 130), who argued that the discrepancy may reflect the fact that Democratic presidents have a deeper pool from which to select judges beyond U.S. Attorneys since the legal profession as a whole is relatively liberal (Bonica, Chilton, and Sen 2016). The relative proportion of other categories between the two party's appointees, however, is comparable with most categories within a few percentage points.[23]

Of course, U.S. Attorneys may not seek higher office or appointment immediately upon exiting their position. One way to sidestep this time horizon problem is to look at careers from the other end of the spectrum: among individuals who have achieved important political positions, how many have served as U.S. Attorneys? To this end, we examine Article III judicial appointments since the Reagan era, shown in Table 4.1. Of the individuals newly appointed to an Article III court between the earliest Reagan nominations and midway through 2019 during the Trump Administration, about 6.2% of these new judges had prior experience as a U.S. Attorney while a further 17.8% had experience as an Assistant U.S. Attorney. Overall, almost

[23] Importantly, these data comprise the *immediate* future career paths of U.S. Attorneys. Many of these individuals in our dataset may still go on to have prominent political careers. The Barack Obama appointees in our dataset, for example, have not experienced another Democratic administration in which they could serve in the cabinet or receive a federal judicial nomination. In this way, our data may undercount the percentage of U.S. Attorneys who will go on to serve in politics because their careers are still unfolding.

Table 4.1 Proportion of newly appointed federal judges with experience as a U.S. Attorney, an Assistant U.S. Attorney (AUSA), or either of these categories.

Appointing President	Number	% Prior US Attorney	% Prior AUSA	% With Either
Reagan	347	8.4	12.7	21.0
G.H.W. Bush	169	6.5	10.1	16.6
Clinton	357	5.3	14.0	19.3
G.W. Bush	310	8.4	17.1	25.5
Obama	308	3.9	27.3	31.2
Trump	98	1.0	25.5	26.5
All Cases	1,589	6.2	17.8	23.4

Data come from the Federal Judicial Center's Biographical Directory of Article III Judges. *Note:* Trump Administration numbers contain only data through 2019.

a quarter of these new judges worked in a U.S. Attorney's office, making it a defined career path to the federal judiciary.[24]

Former U.S. Attorneys have also been successful seeking executive and legislative office. In the executive branch, for example, several of the most recent Attorneys General have had prior experience as a U.S. Attorney including Jeff Sessions, Loretta Lynch, and Eric Holder. Experience in a U.S. Attorney's office presents "top-flight congressional recruiting opportunities" according to campaign consultants because many of the traits that make one a successful U.S. Attorney—good public speaking skills, media savvy, and strict personal and financial behavior—also translate well to the campaign trail (Hawkings 2017). As lawyers, U.S. Attorneys are also significantly advantaged by their professional connections in terms of raising early money for congressional campaigns (Bonica 2020). As of 2017, 60 members of Congress (11% of the legislative branch) had prior prosecutorial experience, and eight of them—most notably Senators Richard Blumenthal and Sheldon Whitehouse—had previously served as U.S. Attorneys. As noted in Chapter 3, U.S. Attorneys also tend to have strong ties to the states in which they serve and this can translate into state-level office. Between 1990 and 2020, 11 state governors, including Chris Christie and Janet Napolitano, had prior experience as a

[24] That many U.S. Attorneys today go on to become federal judges is not a new phenomenon. Eisenstein (1978) reports that "about one of every eight U.S. attorneys appointed between 1961 and 1973 and no longer serving in 1975 became a federal judge" (230).

U.S Attorney. In short, many former U.S. Attorneys advance to important positions of power within government.

Moreover, even if these U.S. Attorneys will not seek higher office or receive a judicial appointment, their U.S. Attorney credential may have opened the doors for them to serve in a high-paying private practice position that, in turn, provides them with the resources to influence politics in other ways. Indeed, Bonica, Chilton, and Sen (2016) reports that lawyers donate to political campaigns at a rate 10 times higher than the average citizen. The Center for Responsive Politics (2020a) reports that lawyers and law firms donated more than $216 million to political candidates during the 2016 election cycle; out of more than 80 industries, lawyers and law firms were the top donating industry in 9 of the last 15 biennial election cycles.[25] As a result, even U.S. Attorneys who leave office to join the private sector can continue to significantly influence politics through donations to their party and by aiding in the candidate selection process through their support of candidates who often come from within their own profession.

Ultimately, this means that when a president chooses to nominate someone to be a U.S. Attorney, they are also building the resumes of future judges, elected officials, executive appointments, and influential party members. We have shown that hardly anyone leaves a U.S. Attorney position directly into retirement. How and why these officials depart their office is important because those seeking U.S. Attorney positions may themselves view the post as a steppingstone to future employment. This, consequentially, may alter their behavior while in office.

4.6 Conclusion

How U.S. Attorneys leave their office and what they do next can be as political and important as how they are appointed. Though they serve a statutory four-year term of office, our analysis has revealed that the de facto term of a U.S. Attorney lasts from the day she is confirmed by the Senate until a new president takes office. Though they technically serve at the pleasure of the president, this power has very rarely been used outside of administrations making sweeping personnel changes after a transition.

[25] In the 2018 cycle, lawyers and law firms were the fourth-ranked industry, behind Securities and Investments, Retired, and Real Estate (Center for Responsive Politics 2020b).

Still, forcible removal from office remains an available (if costly) tool for dealing with recalcitrant U.S. Attorneys. Just as presidents need rarely veto to make credible veto threats that alter congressional actions (Cameron 2000), so too might presidents threaten removal for those officials not willing to address the administration's priorities. Thus, the threat of removal can be an effective tool to keep U.S. Attorneys in line even if presidents rarely need to use it.

That U.S. Attorneys are so rarely dismissed from office outside of transitions suggests that the intensive vetting process that potential U.S. Attorneys undergo—by both home state and administration officials—is relatively successful at selecting individuals who will perform their duties in ways that align with administration goals. Because (a) U.S. Attorneys are typically allowed to serve out their full terms and (b) the costs of dismissing a U.S. Attorney in the middle of a presidential term carries with it such high costs, administrations must be careful to select good agents as U.S. Attorneys.

Our findings also highlight the complex role that presidential transitions play in the turnover of U.S. Attorneys. While many U.S. Attorneys resign at the end of an administration, they don't have to. We find that a significant portion of U.S. Attorneys continue to serve some length of time under a new president. As such, new presidents must choose between at least temporarily retaining their predecessor's appointees, who are often from their opposition party, or coming up with a plan for replacements that does not appear to be overly opportunistic or political. We have shown that while the blanket firings of U.S. Attorneys has been used in prior administrations, this choice comes at a significant cost in terms of the logistics of running U.S. Attorney offices as well as the optics in terms of public perceptions.

The fact that U.S. Attorneys often "use their jobs as political steppingstones" provides another practical constraint on their behavior (Liptak 2007). As we note, U.S. Attorneys are often elevated to the federal bench, a higher-level position in the administration, or some other job requiring the favor of a president or a political party including running for elected office themselves. A president's favor can be critical. For example, Jessie Liu served as the U.S. Attorney for the District of Columbia under President Trump until she was offered a Senate-confirmed position within the Treasury Department. After resigning her U.S. Attorney post, her nomination to the Treasury position was withdrawn, which some linked directly to her poorly perceived performance on political cases as a U.S. Attorney (Collins 2020). Such lessons are not lost on other U.S. Attorneys. Liu's immediate replacement took controversial and pro-administration measures to reduce the sentence of Roger Stone and dismiss the case against Michael Flynn (Rosenzweig 2020). To the extent that a U.S. Attorney's future career ambitions align with an administration, it may provide the Department of Justice more leverage over how that individual performs their tasks.

Taken together, our findings in Chapters 3 and 4 demonstrate that, though U.S. Attorneys allegedly act as nonpartisan law enforcement officials, every aspect of their service—from their selection, to their removal, to their future career paths—is tinged in politics. These facts provide U.S. Attorneys' political superiors with important opportunities to control their work and influence the decisions U.S. Attorneys make while in office. In the remainder of this book, we examine how politics affects the immense discretion granted to U.S. Attorneys to enforce the law.

5

Theorizing Political Responsiveness in Prosecutorial Decision-Making

> Law enforcement is not automatic. It isn't blind. One of the greatest difficulties of the position of prosecutor is that he must pick his cases, because no prosecutor can even investigate all of the cases in which he receives complaints. If the Department of Justice were to make even a pretense of reaching every probable violation of federal law, ten times its present staff will be inadequate.
>
> —U.S. Attorney General Robert H. Jackson, 1940

Spoken by the U.S. Attorney General for the Franklin D. Roosevelt Administration and a future Supreme Court justice, these words highlight a critical aspect of the federal prosecutor's job. Resource, time, and staffing limitations mean that federal prosecutors and their offices cannot pursue every federal criminal matter or invest the same level of energy in every case that they do pursue. Tough choices must be made.

Given this, how do federal prosecutors decide where to expend their efforts? While rules and standards govern much of what lawyers do (George 2005), key prosecutorial decisions involving charging, plea bargaining, sentencing, and much more are made "without the safety net of specific rules" (Levenson 1999, 557) or "a neat formula" (George 2005, 743). Instead, federal prosecutors have broad discretion when making the many important decisions inherent in their jobs. This decision-making discretion—or "the power to choose between two or more courses of action each of which is thought of as permissible" (Hart and Sacks 1958, 162)—extends to action and inaction, final and interim decisions, and substantive and procedural choices (Davis 1969, 4).

Vast prosecutorial discretion exists for nearly all decisions, from before criminal cases are filed through the sentencing of offenders. As Robert

The Politics of Federal Prosecution. Christina L. Boyd, Michael J. Nelson, Ian Ostrander, and Ethan D. Boldt, Oxford University Press (2021).
DOI: 10.1093/oso/9780197554685.003.0005

Jackson once warned, "the prosecutor has more control over life, liberty and reputation than any other person in America. His discretion is tremendous" (Jackson 1940). Federal and state courts in the United States have repeatedly ratified this "unfettered discretion" for prosecutors in "crucial areas of decision making" that are "beyond review" and "free of accountability" (Albonetti 1987, 292).[1]

Many, including prosecutors themselves, are quick to argue that prosecutors act in neutral, independent, and unbiased ways while carrying out their discretionary duties. As law professor and former Assistant U.S. Attorney Laurie Levenson (1999, 557) put it, "a prosecutor's individual and independent interest in reaching fair and just decisions is often the only compass pointing to the right procedure." But with discretion comes opportunity for other factors—especially political factors—to tilt prosecutorial behavior during criminal case development. U.S. Attorneys' positions—from their politically driven selection and removal, to other sanction threats, to positive incentives—make them ripe to be subject to and responsive to external political pressure in their decision-making. As Perry (1998, 131) argues, "given the nature of what attorneys for the United States do, they could never be nonpolitical. By definition, the Department's [DOJ's] mission is political—both in the grand sense, but also in terms of responsiveness." Others agree. Justice Scalia once noted that "[u]nder our system of government, the primary check against prosecutorial abuse is a political one" (Justice Scalia, dissenting, in *Morrison v. Olson*, 487 U.S. 654, 728 (1988)). Former Maryland U.S. Attorney Thomas DiBiagio has also argued that "[p]rosecutors are not part of a non-partisan priesthood purified of all base motives" (DiBiagio 2000, 63).

Our overarching expectation is therefore that federal prosecutors, exercising discretion while setting their prosecutorial agendas and making individual case decisions, are likely to be responsive to the priorities and preferences of key political actors in their sphere: the president, Congress, and a U.S. Attorney's local public. In the pages that follow, we explore the reasons why the president and Congress are effective political principals for federal prosecutors and how these principals communicate their criminal justice priorities. Similarly, we examine the ways in which a federal

[1] See Jacoby (1980) for a lengthy discussion of historical case law and its construction of broad prosecutorial discretion.

prosecutor may be constrained by her local public's leanings on criminal justice issues despite being a federal employee.

5.1 The President and Congress as Constraining Principals

U.S. Attorneys serve at the behest of the president and Congress, their political principals. A theoretical framework called principal-agency theory, widely used by political scientists, economists, and others to explain bureaucrats' behavior, can help us understand how political principals like the president and Congress can influence the behavior and policy priorities of local federal prosecutors and incentivize U.S. Attorney decision-making and prosecutorial outcomes that are desirable by the principals. Principal-agency theory is based on the tenet that "one party, the principal, considers entering into a contractual agreement with another, the agent, in the expectation that the agent will subsequently choose actions that produce outcomes desired by the principal" (Moe 1984, 756).

Any effective principal-agent relationship necessarily involves vast delegation of responsibilities and tasks, along with a broad authorization of the agent to act on behalf of the principal (George and Yoon 2003). By empowering agents to act on their behalf, principals can take on a larger and more diffuse workload and achieve a more efficient processing of tasks. Delegation is also necessary for many principals since "gathering complete information is regarded as prohibitively expensive" for them (Miller 2005, 205) given principals' competing obligations on their time and resources.

The federal government now commonly engages in "broad, sweeping" delegation to the bureaucracy (Kiewiet and McCubbins 1991, 11). Various reasons explain why this is the case, including "the vast array of policy issues that come before government, the complexity of these issues, and the resources needed to address them" (Huber and Shipan 2011). In addition, Kiewiet and McCubbins (1991) argue that public pressure to solve problems and a lack of agreement among politicians on how to solve those problems mean that the federal government (and especially Congress) has "repeatedly passed the buck by establishing yet another agency and instructing *it* to solve the problem" (Kiewiet and McCubbins 1991, 11).[2]

[2] As Kiewiet and McCubbins (1991) argue, such broad delegations of policy-making power to the unelected bureaucracy were not anticipated by many Founders. For example, "Jeffersonians insisted

While increasingly common and/or necessary, delegation carries notable risks for principals. One common problem is often referred to as a moral hazard. As Moe (1984) argues, "there is no guarantee that the agent, once hired, will in fact choose to pursue the principal's best interests or to do so efficiently. The agent has his own interests at heart" (756). Brehm and Gates (1997) warn that "[g]iven that supervisors often do not have adequate time for supervision," agents "will occasionally shirk or even sabotage" in their work (41). Agent shirking is a real risk in the federal bureaucracy context since "Congress cannot write statutes that are sufficiently detailed to constrain agencies completely" (George and Yoon 2003, 821).

Principal-agency relationships present principals with several methods to help prevent agents from engaging in undesirable behavior or pursuing their own interests. Such tools are designed to reduce asymmetries, minimize shirking, and incentivize behavior and outcomes that the principals would have produced with the same information (Miller 2005; Moe 1984; Randazzo 2008). Examples include the selection and screening of agents, monitoring, incentives, sanctions, and crafting administrative procedures that are likely to produce future outcomes that the present Congress will be pleased with (something referred to as congressional "deck-stacking") (e.g., Bawn 1995; McCubbins, Noll, and Weingast 1987).

When it comes to the president and Congress as principals to the U.S. Attorneys to whom they delegate federal prosecutorial power, a number of strong *ex ante* controls—that is, those in place prior to an agent's decision-making—exist. Careful screening and selection of agents is often the most direct and effective way for principals to control agents (Houten 2009). While a deliberate hiring process requires a substantial investment on behalf of the principal (Kiewiet and McCubbins 1991; Miller and Moe 1986), "both sides are better off if principals are able to identify those individuals who possess the appropriate talents, skills, and other personal characteristics prior to the establishment of the principal/agent relationship" (Kiewiet and McCubbins 1991). As fully detailed in Chapter 3, the president and Congress expend extensive time and effort in the nomination and appointment of U.S. Attorneys, frequently seeking to control the bureaucracy through "politicized" appointments (Lewis 2008; Miller 2000; Nelson and Ostrander 2016). Presidents, in particular, "generally appoint administrators with preferences

that the [unelected] officials should be allowed the smallest possible room for discretion or interpretation in carrying out the laws of the land" (Kiewiet and McCubbins 1991, 9).

similar to their own and, if anything, this trend has increased over time" (Epstein and O'Halloran 1996, 379). President Reagan, for example, prioritized loyalty and ideology in his bureaucratic appointments to such a degree that he deemphasized the importance of candidate expertise (Moe 1985, 260). Evidence seems to indicate that a similar balance in selection priorities may exist for many of President Trump's bureaucratic and judicial nominees. Trump's judicial selection strategy has been described as a "determined effort to nominate and confirm a steady procession of young conservative jurists" (Kaplan 2018) and focused on finding "hard-wired ideologues" that will be "reliable policy agents" (Ruiz et al. 2020). Coming back specifically to U.S. Attorneys, the result of this politicized appointment process means that many selected U.S. Attorneys share broader prosecutorial preferences with their presidential and congressional principals.

Principals are also likely to use positive, outcome-based incentives to promote good behavior and overcome the issues associated with moral hazard (Miller 2005). For U.S. Attorneys and other prosecutors, these positive incentives include promotions, potential for career advancement, and more general personal reputation-building to induce agent compliance (Kiewiet and McCubbins 1991; Peppers 2006). As we saw in Chapter 4, many U.S. Attorneys frequently seek to use their temporary political appointment as a springboard for future political or legal job opportunities.

With these future career ambitions comes significant emphasis on building and maintaining one's reputation. This, in turn, influences prosecutors' decision-making behavior. Gordon and Huber (2009) note that

> [P]rosecutors . . . may anticipate seeking private sector employment and/or more prestigious government posts (e.g., appointment to the federal bench). In order to develop the personal experience (social capital), track record, peer networks, and social relationships necessary to obtain those positions, these prosecutors may be inclined to consider factors other than the normatively desirable sentence for each defendant. (142)

A federal prosecutor interviewed by Lochner (2002, 277) confirms the presence of this reputation-induced constraint on prosecutorial behavior, explaining that many of the federal prosecutors "want to be judges or Department of Justice officials, and do not want to alienate potential supporters" (277). These ambitions place a high priority on staying in the good graces of Congress and the White House, since both are likely to play a role in the selection of future employment—whether that be a higher-ranking position within the DOJ, a federal judgeship, or something else.[3]

In addition to *ex ante* control via selection and positive incentives, presidents and Congress also have *ex post* controls (post decision-making) available to them to sanction U.S. Attorneys who do not behave as desired. Even when rarely utilized, sanctions (and their threat) can serve as an important agent control mechanism. If the threat of sanctions is credible, agents should be more likely to behave according to their principals' interests (Kiewiet and McCubbins 1991). As we detailed in Chapter 4, presidents have the authority to fire U.S. Attorneys or fail to reappoint them for a second four-year term (Scott 2007). The president and Congress can also utilize other threats of sanctions to incentivize good behavior like threatening the agency with reorganization (such as consolidating prosecution districts via altering 28 U.S. Code §541(a)[4]), reduced discretionary authority, diminished jurisdiction, and budget cutbacks (Epstein and O'Halloran 1999; MacDonald 2013; Shipan 2004). For U.S. Attorneys, their ability to maintain a large and meaningful caseload depends on the size of their office staffs and the resources made available to them, so the threats of these sanctions have teeth to them.

The wide variety of incentives political principals have available to them may reduce or eliminate the need for those principals to closely monitor agents and sanction or even fire them. As Weingast and Moran (1983) argue, "the more effective the incentive system, the less often we should observe sanctions" (769). Weingast (1984) lauded the ability of Congress to dominate bureaucracy in this way, noting that "[t]he mechanisms evolved by Congress over the past one hundred years comprise an ingenious system for control of agencies that involves little direct congressional monitoring of decisions but which nonetheless results in policies desired by Congress" (148). The strength of these *ex ante* mechanisms may help explain why, as we observed in Chapter 4, *ex post* control of U.S. Attorneys through involuntary removal has been so rare.

How do the president and Congress reduce uncertainty and communicate their preferences on behavior and actions to U.S. Attorneys? In the next

[3] While concerns for organizational reputation may moderate U.S. Attorneys' political behavior (Carpenter and Krause 2012; Krause 2009), their short-term political appointee status means that they have less incentive than many other bureaucrats to focus exclusively on building a long-term bureaucratic reputation that is independent of all political influences (Krause 2009).

[4] 28 U.S. Code §541(a) reads "The President shall appoint . . . a United States attorney for each judicial district."

section, we discuss how these principals rely on signaling through rhetoric and hearings to do just that.

5.2 Presidential and Congressional Signaling

Agents like U.S. Attorneys are motivated to do good work for their principals. But even with *ex ante* controls like politicized appointments, threats of sanctions, and plentiful positive incentives, agents seeking to behave faithfully may, in isolation, lack the needed information on their principals' preferred policies and outcomes to be able to implement them. To overcome this agent uncertainty and imperfect information, principals can transmit guidance to the agent through signals (Carpenter 1996; Shipan 2004). Agents will listen and follow these signals. Empirical evidence indicates that presidential and congressional signaling work in affecting political agent decision-making. As Shipan (2004) argues, "agencies are sensitive to a variety of signals that they receive from the political environment" (478). Carpenter (1996) and Olson (1995) find that presidential and congressional signaling affect the outputs of the Food and Drug Administration. Wood (1988) and Wood and Waterman (1991) observe similar patterns when it comes to the effect of congressional budget signals on the Environmental Protection Agency's abatement and inspection activities. Whitford and Yates (2003, 2009) and Eshbaugh-Soha (2008) find that presidential rhetoric provides a strong signaling effect on federal bureaucrats in agencies like the Drug Enforcement Administration and the DOJ.

5.2.1 Presidential Rhetoric

Presidential rhetoric is likely to provide important, meaningful signals regarding presidential law enforcement priorities and how they should translate to federal prosecutorial decision-making. Presidential speeches can serve many functions for the White House, including to increase issue salience in the media (Eshbaugh-Soha and Peake 2011), raise the odds of legislative success (Canes-Wrone 2001; Eshbaugh-Soha 2010), and affect the success of judicial nominations (e.g., Blackstone and Goelzhauser 2014; Holmes 2007; Johnson and Roberts 2004;). Perhaps most importantly, through public speeches, a president can "go public" and emphasize the importance of an issue to his administration (Kernell 1997) relative to other issues (Whitford and Yates 2009). Presidential rhetoric can thus signal to agents what their behavior should be, where their policy priorities should lie, and what their level of commitment to those policies should be (Eshbaugh-Soha 2010). Simply put, for presidents, their rhetoric "is an efficient means of signaling information because speeches can effectively penetrate multiple layers of a thickening federal bureaucracy" (Eshbaugh-Soha 2008, 118).

Rhetoric on crime allows the president to define the area as an important and salient problem facing the country (Oliver 1998). Better termed as anticrime rhetoric, this type of speech helps presidents prioritize "tough on crime" and "law and order" policies (Marion and Oliver 2012). Applied here, the more presidents prioritize specific crimes in their rhetoric, the more likely U.S. Attorneys should respond by also prioritizing their prosecution of those crimes. This means making decisions that are inherently more punitive in relation to cases in those crime areas—whether that behavior is prosecuting a higher percentage of cases referred to them, advancing a more serious set of charges in the cases that they prosecute, using other prosecutorial tools like asset forfeiture to more aggressively attack the broader criminal enterprise in that area, or something else. Whitford and Yates (2009) observed this very thing in their study of drug policy implementation and U.S. Attorney prosecutions, with more presidential rhetoric about drugs leading to higher prosecution rates. We expect that presidential rhetoric provides important policy signals to U.S. Attorneys about other types of crime too, both directly (hearing the president's words) and indirectly (through directives coming from the U.S. Attorney General and her staff) (Whitford and Yates 2009, 28).

Figure 5.1 plots presidential rhetoric relating to violent crime—a crime area that we focus on much more in later chapters—from 1996 to 2011. Federal violent crimes include, for example, murder, assault, bank robbery, and firearm offenses. To compute the presidential rhetoric amounts on violent crime, we coded the number of sentences in presidential public statements each month that contain mentions of violent crime from *Public Papers of the President* (Peters and Woolley 2017). We then standardize this count by dividing it by the total number of presidential statements (of all types) in a month and then multiplying it by 100. To ensure proper temporal ordering, where the U.S. Attorneys are considering presidential statements that have been made in the past, this measure is lagged one month. The resulting quantity reported in each subfigure for each (lagged) month is thus the number of violent crime sentences per 100 statements.

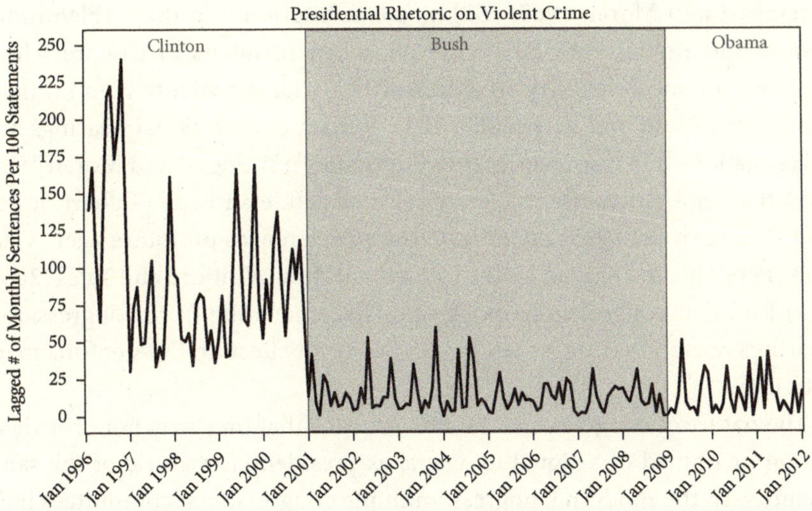

Figure 5.1 Presidential rhetoric on violent crime from 1996 to 2011. Figure plots the number of sentences containing violent crime keywords per 100 presidential public statements in a given month-year.

Figure 5.1 reveals a substantial amount of variation in presidential rhetoric across a number of dimensions. First, there is variation across presidents. The 1996–2011 data plotted here provide coverage of the Bill Clinton, George W. Bush, and Barack Obama Administrations. As the figure reveals, Clinton spoke much more frequently about violent crime issues than Bush or Obama. Second, there are also some notable instances of intra-president rhetoric differences on violent crime. There was a downward trend in violent crime rhetoric during the Clinton Administration years and, to a lesser degree in the Bush years. There was a slight uptick in violent crime rhetoric over the first few years of the Obama Administration relative to the later years of the Bush Administration.

5.2.2 Congressional Hearings

We also anticipate that the frequency of congressional hearings on potential matters for prosecution will provide meaningful signals to U.S. Attorneys regarding congressional priorities. Congressional hearings are generally not used when things in an issue or policy area "are operating smoothly"

(Weingast and Moran 1983, 769) or are unimportant to them (Flemming, Wood, and Bohte 1999, 80). After all, when members of Congress hold hearings on one issue, they are necessarily giving less attention and time to others (Whitford and Yates 2009, 104). Rather, congressional hearings and investigations "are resource-intensive activities" (Weingast and Moran 1983, 769) that legislatures use to clearly raise or define an issue (Talbert, Jones, and Baumgartner 1995) or indicate their preferences on future agency action (Ferejohn and Shipan 1989). In their analysis, Whitford and Yates (2009, 111) find that congressional policy signals, emanating from congressional hearings related to drug issues, have a powerful effect on DEA enforcement activities.

The nature of congressional hearings means that they may not provide as strong or unified of a signal to agents as presidential rhetoric of the same quantity. In the modern Congress, multiple congressional committees have jurisdiction over issue areas and oversee single agencies (Baumgartner and Jones 2015, 110). While this committee redundancy "may promote the discovery of more effective ways of doing things or lead to the detection of agency malfeasance" and increase congressional influence (Clinton, Lewis, and Selin 2014, 388), it can also make it more complicated for Congress to control agency outputs or provide clarity in its communicated preferences. "[I]ncreasing the number of involved committees increases the chances of congressional disagreement," meaning time and effort is needed to reconcile differences (Clinton, Lewis, and Selin 2014, 389). Additionally, since Congress frequently signals with multiple perspectives rather than one single voice, the nature of congressional communication to federal prosecutors may be diluted and lack clarity and consistency.

Figure 5.2 displays congressional hearings on violent crime from 1996 to 2011. We turn to the Baumgartner and Jones (2013) *Policy Agendas Project* to code the congressional hearings by crime area. Using those data, we count the number of hearings per month related to violent crime. As with presidential rhetoric, this measure includes a one-month lag. The resulting variable is calculated as the percentage of total hearings per (lagged) month related to violent crime. The Chapter Data Appendix provides full details on the grouping of congressional hearing subject matters into the violent crime umbrella.

Figure 5.2 provides interesting insight into congressional hearings mentioning violent crime. As it reveals, there is little cross-time stability in how much of the total congressional hearings "docket" they compose. Rather, the

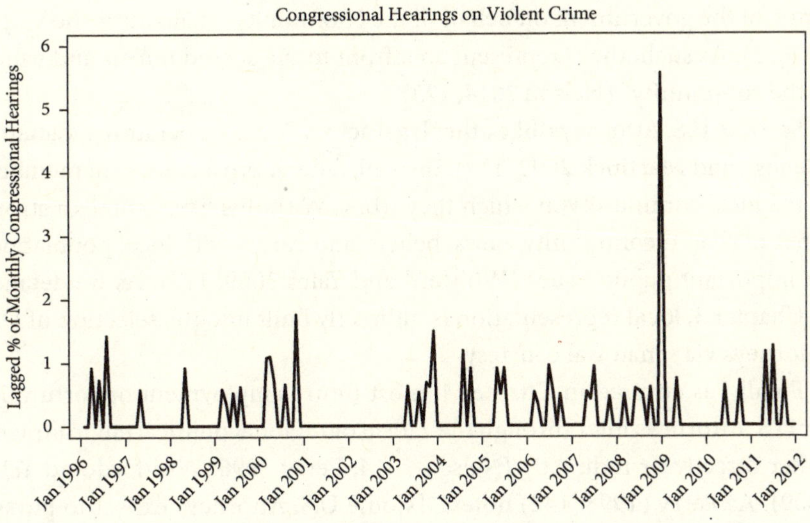

Figure 5.2 Congressional hearings on violent crime from 1996 to 2011. Figure plots the percentage of hearings in a given month-year devoted to violent crime.

patterns ebb and flow, with the numbers reaching their peak in 2009 and nearly disappearing in the first few years following September 11th (surely giving way to more pressing terrorism-related hearings).[5]

5.3 The Local Public Connection

In addition to federal prosecutors being responsive to congressional and presidential signals, we also anticipate that U.S. Attorneys will be mindful of the preferences of their local public when making decisions. Elected state prosecutors must curb their behavior based on their constituents' desired positions or face the prospects of electoral defeat (Gordon and Huber 2002; Nelson 2014). But even appointed prosecutors, like U.S. Attorneys, have good reason to pay heed to their local public and its views toward crime.

For one, the nature of criminal cases means that the community and local public are invested in their resolution. Criminal cases "are brought in the

[5] In another longitudinal analysis, Miller (2010) plots how congressional hearing attention on crime and justice issues like police, guns, prisons, drugs, and riots varied significantly over time from 1971 to 2000. As Miller found, congressional attention allocations frequently shifted on these topics across years.

name of the government on behalf of the community" (Saltzburg and Capra 1996, 2). As such, they "represent an affront to the shared norms and values of the community" (Nelson 2014, 123).

Second, U.S. Attorneys, like other legal actors, "do not operate in a vacuum" (Benesh and Martinek 2002, 112). Instead, federal prosecutors are members of the local community in which they work. With this likely comes a strong sense of shared community views, beliefs, and values with local populations on important public issues (Whitford and Yates 2009, 118). As we detailed in Chapter 3, local representation is indirectly built into the selection of U.S. Attorneys via senatorial courtesy.

Finally, as covered in Chapter 4, most future employment opportunities for U.S. Attorneys filter through their local or regional political environment, either directly or indirectly (Nelson 2014; Perry 1998; Whitford and Yates 2009). As Perry (1998, 142) notes, "[s]ome U.S. Attorneys expect to pursue elected political office after their stint as a U.S. Attorney and campaign throughout their tenure, while others aspire to the federal bench, requiring a different sort of campaigning. Some return to private practice. All, however, are political." And, we would add, nearly all filter through their local and/or regional ties. As such, U.S. Attorneys are likely to be mindful of local prosecutorial preferences even if they themselves do not share them.

This powerful connection between U.S. Attorneys and their local public leads us to anticipate that local public opinion and priorities about the perceived seriousness of crime problems will help drive federal prosecution priorities. The "communication of citizen preferences to public officials" may be the most important component of having responsive government officials (Kuklinski and Stanga 1979, 1099). Prosecutors and judges respond to public opinion when making decisions (Brace and Boyea 2008; Kuklinski and Stanga 1979; Nelson 2014). This holds even for appointed officials, who, although they don't face an electorate, are motivated to bolster legitimacy (Flemming and Wood 1997; Gibson and Nelson 2014). Thus, where the local public views a type of crime as an important negative issue or prioritizes punitiveness, local U.S. Attorneys are likely to respond with more aggressive prosecutions. Similarly, as the local region gets more committed to punitiveness and law and order principles, we expect a higher overall priority among local U.S. Attorneys in pursuing prosecutions (Epstein and Kobylka 1992; Epstein, Walker, and Dixon 1989).

There are three key metrics that federal prosecutors can use to help respond to their local public's preferences and priorities on crime issues. First is public opinion on crime issues. Figure 5.3 displays the public concern regarding violent crime from 1996 to 2011. These data are constructed using General Social Science (GSS) biennial opinion polls for nine geographic regions in the United States. The GSS survey question captures regional mood on the perceived seriousness of the violent crime problem as a matter of policy. It asks survey respondents whether the United States is spending too much, too little, or about the right amount on "halting the rising crime rate." This variable, which is computed as a percentage, has higher values when respondents answer that "too little" is spent on this issue. The Chapter Data Appendix provides further details on the GSS data.

As Figure 5.3 indicates, there are significant differences in local public opinion on violent crime across regions and time. The publics in the "East South Central" (Kentucky, Tennessee, Alabama, and Mississippi) and "West South Central" (Arkansas, Oklahoma, Louisiana, and Texas) regions tend to, on average, believe at a higher rate than other regions that too little is spent on halting crime. Other regions like the "Pacific" (Washington,

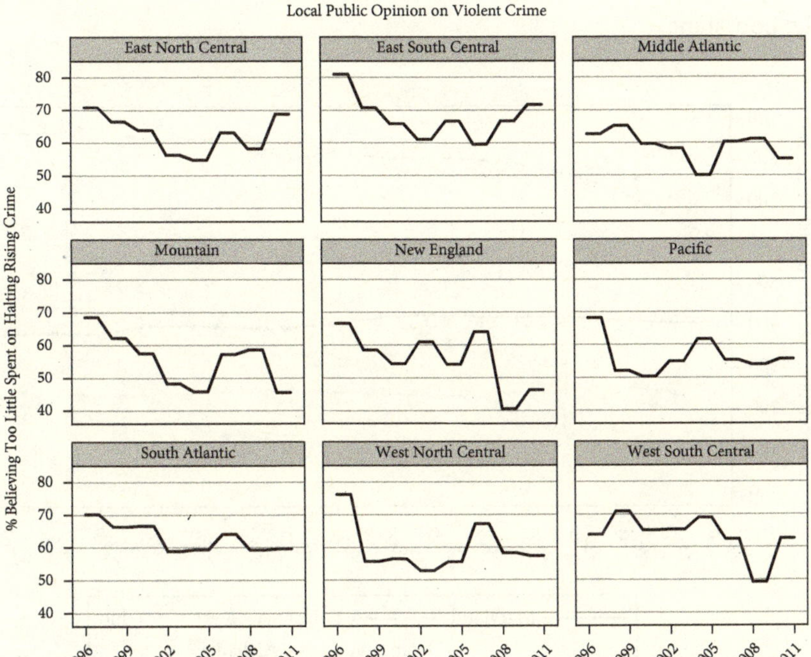

Figure 5.3 Percent of respondents concerned about the seriousness of violent crime from 1996-2011.

Oregon, California, Alaska, and Hawaii) and "Mountain" (Montana, Idaho, Wyoming, Nevada, Utah, Colorado, Arizona, and New Mexico) stand out for having substantially lower rates of concern about what is being spent on crime. These local public opinion numbers are likely to reflect the community signals that federal prosecutors receive on where to place their prosecutorial attention.

Second is local punitiveness toward criminal offenders. States that imprison a large number of convicts relative to the population have more punitive preferences in responding to crime and disorder (Enns 2014, 2016). This harshness provides a signal to federal prosecutors on how aggressive the local public wants them to be in pursuing alleged crimes. To capture this, Figure 5.4 plots the number of incarcerated inmates in state-run prison facilities per 100,000 residents for each state-year (per Bureau of Justice Statistics) from 1996 to 2011. Figure 5.4 displays incarceration statistics for five representative states—Maryland, Ohio, Alabama, Louisiana, and Utah—and shows how varied state incarceration rates are across the country. In short, federal prosecutors in a state like Utah receive a very different message from their community than do those in a state like Louisiana.

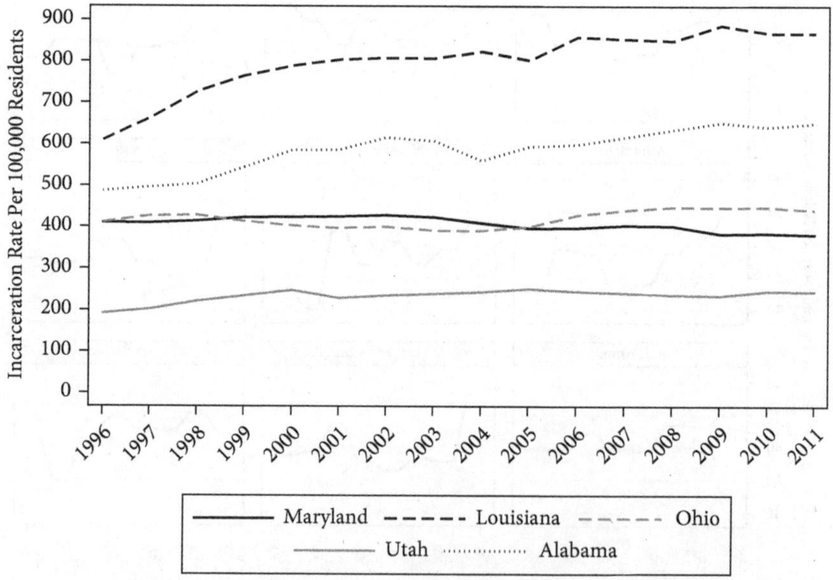

Figure 5.4 Number of incarcerated inmates in state-run prison facilities per 100,000 residents for each state-year for five selected states.

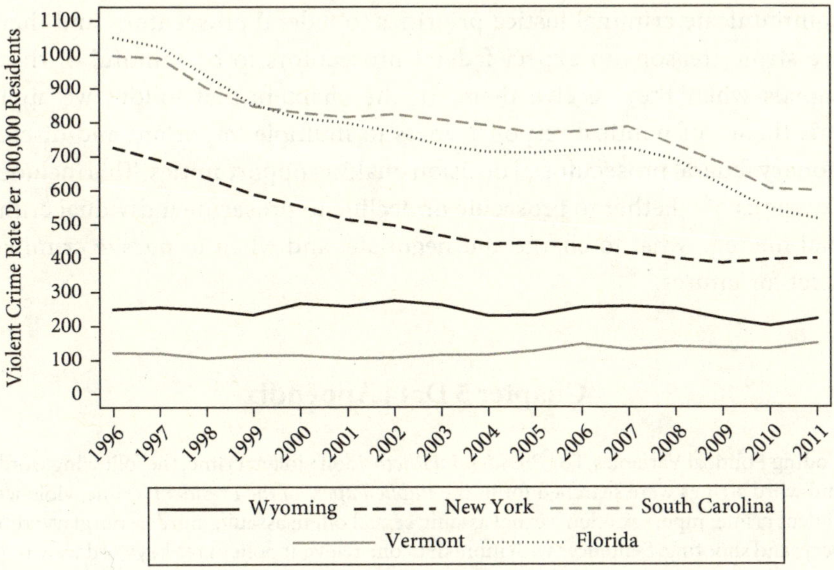

Figure 5.5 Violent crime rate per 100,000 residents for each state-year for five selected states.

Third, we expect that federal prosecutors will be mindful of the local crime rate. As crime grows in a prosecutor's state, there is likely a corresponding increasing pressure on local prosecutors to address an underlying crime problem. Figure 5.5 displays the violent crime rate as reported by the FBI's Uniform Crime Reports for every state-year per 100,000 residents from 1996 to 2011 for five representative states: Wyoming, South Carolina, Florida, New York, and Vermont. Some states, like Vermont and Wyoming, have consistently low violent crime rates across 1996 to 2011. Other states, like Florida and South Carolina, have seen their violent crime rates steadily fall, from higher numbers in the 1990s to more moderate numbers in the early 2010s.

5.4 Up Next: Applying the Theory

Our goal in this chapter has been to provide theoretical insight into how the priorities and preferences of political principals, like the president and Congress, along with the local public, are likely to impact federal prosecutorial behavior. As we have seen, national and local signals are used to communicate criminal justice priorities to federal prosecutors, and there are strong reasons to expect federal prosecutors to be mindful of these signals when they receive them. In the chapters that follow, we apply this theory of political responsiveness to multiple important and discretionary federal prosecutorial decision-making opportunities. This includes decisions of whether to prosecute or decline to prosecute individual criminal matters, what to charge and negotiate, and when to pursue criminal asset forfeitures.

Chapter 5 Data Appendix

Coding Political Variables: For *Presidential Rhetoric* on violent crime, the following words and word strings were searched for in the *Public Papers of the President*: crime; violence; violent crime; rape; sex offen; sexual assault; sexual offen; assault; murder; burglary; robbery; and shooting. Sentences with more than one relevant policy area keyword were only counted once. Filtering took place within the searches for individual keywords to avoid false positives (i.e., uses of the word clearly not related to violent crime). For example, in searching for "violent," we did not include uses of the word related to international, war-type violence. We also excluded certain statements from our calculations both in counting relevant sentences and in computing the denominator for each month (i.e., the total number of presidential statements per month). This included the omission of executive orders (which tend to lack sentences), memorandums and presidential determinations (which are written directly to agencies and thus lack ambiguity or a "signaling" quality),

Table 5.1. States by General Social Survey Region

Region	States
New England	Maine, Vermont, New Hampshire, Massachusetts, Connecticut, Rhode Island
Middle Atlantic	New York, New Jersey, Pennsylvania
East North Central	Wisconsin, Illinois, Indiana, Michigan, Ohio
West North Central	Minnesota, Iowa, Missouri, North Dakota, South Dakota, Nebraska, Kansas
South Atlantic	Delaware, Maryland, West Virginia, Virginia, North Carolina, South Carolina, Georgia, Florida, District of Columbia
East South Central	Kentucky, Tennessee, Alabama, Mississippi West
West South Central	Arkansas, Oklahoma, Louisiana, Texas
Mountain	Montana, Idaho, Wyoming, Nevada, Utah, Colorado, Arizona, New Mexico
Pacific	Washington, Oregon, California, Alaska, Hawaii

States assigned to regions by the U.S. Bureau of the Census.

and any statements that were not made by presidents Clinton, Obama, or Bush during their presidency. Statements made by other speakers (e.g., minority party responses to the State of the Union address) and by former presidents (e.g., Clinton's addresses to the Democratic National Convention in 2004 and 2008) were not included. We do include, however, joint statements where the current sitting president and someone else (usually a foreign leader) co-issue a statement.

For *Congressional Hearings*, we relied on the following hearing topic within the *Policy Agendas Project*: 1211: Riots, Crime Prevention, and Crime Control.

In compiling the *Local Public Opinion* variable, we coded the percentage of GSS respondents answering "too little" to the following query:

> We are faced with many problems in this country, none of which can be solved easily or inexpensively . . .are we spending too much, too little, or about the right amount on . . . Halting the rising crime rate?

This violent crime-related question is available in the GSS from 1996–2010, every two years. Computed percentages exclude non-respondents and those answering "don't know." Table 5.1 provides the region assignment for U.S. states in the GSS data.

6

To Prosecute or Not: Prosecutors as Agenda Setters

In *United States v. Armstrong* (1996), the U.S. Supreme Court addressed the amount of discretion federal prosecutors have when deciding to bring charges in some criminal matters while declining to do so in others. *United States v. Armstrong*'s court history dated back to 1992, when a group of five defendants, including Chris Armstrong and Aaron Hampton, were indicted by federal prosecutors on cocaine distribution charges in the Central District of California, a federal trial court. Shortly after the case proceedings began, the defendants filed a discovery and dismissal motion with the district court, arguing that the prosecutors selected the case for prosecution because of the defendants' race. In a stunning blow to prosecutorial discretion, the district court granted the defendants' motion. The district court ordered the prosecution to provide extensive evidence to justify its indictment of Armstrong, Hampton, and their codefendants including:

- "a list of all cases from the prior three years in which the government charged both cocaine base offenses and firearms offenses"
- "the race of the defendants in those cases"
- "whether state, federal, or joint law enforcement authorities investigated each case"
- "the criteria used by the U.S. Attorney's Office for deciding whether to bring cocaine base cases federally" (quoted in *United States v. Armstrong*, 21 F.3d 1431, 1433 (9th Cir. 1994))

When the Government failed to comply with the district court's detailed order, the resulting sanction included a dismissal of all of the indictments. Although the district court's order was overturned by

The Politics of Federal Prosecution. Christina L. Boyd, Michael J. Nelson, Ian Ostrander, and Ethan D. Boldt, Oxford University Press (2021).
DOI: 10.1093/oso/9780197554685.003.0006

a divided 9th Circuit Court of Appeals panel, the en banc 9th Circuit quickly reinstated it.

In an 8-1 decision, the U.S. Supreme Court reversed the lower courts, holding that selective-prosecution cases would only be successful if defendants can "show that the Government declined to prosecute similarly situated suspects" (458).[1] *United States v. Armstrong* created a "demanding" standard for constitutional violations that places the burden of proof on the defendant rather than the prosecution. More generally, court rulings like that in *United States v. Armstrong* clarify that prosecutorial decisions to bring or decline to bring charges rest in the "'special province' of the Executive" (*United States v. Armstrong* at 464; citing *Heckler v. Chaney*, 470 U.S. 821, 832 (1985)). Or, as stated in similar but even more stark language by the court in *United States v. Flemmi*, "a United States Attorney's decision to prosecute (or, conversely, to forbear) is largely unreviewable by the courts" (225 F.3d 78 (1st Cir. 2000)).

This decision to pursue or decline prosecutions in criminal matters is a critically important "threshold determination" (O'Neill 2003, 222) and "gateway to justice" (Kerstetter 1990, 182) in the criminal justice system. Pursued prosecutions proceed forward toward an indictment and, in over 90% of such federal cases, a conviction via a plea bargain, jury trial, or bench trial (Motivans 2017, Table 4.2). By contrast, declined prosecutions, or declinations, disappear. No charges are advanced, and suspects face no further proceedings or consequences. There is no trial or plea bargain, no sentencing, and no prison time. The initial charging decision thus empowers federal prosecutors to be the agenda setters of criminal courts and for criminal defendants' fates.

Despite the importance of this declination decision and what it means for the ability to "bring justice" for crimes that may have been committed, as *United States v. Armstrong* tells us, prosecutors very rarely have to provide any justification or reasons for why they prosecute some cases and decline to do so in others. As O'Neill (2004) argues, "[u]nderstanding why prosecutors select certain cases for prosecution and disregard others is one of the great

[1] The Supreme Court made the argument that the defendants' evidence, in effect, made a fundamental research design error by failing to "identify individuals who were not black and could have been prosecuted for the offenses for which respondents were charged, but were not so prosecuted" (*United States v. Armstrong*, at 470). The Court provided examples of better evidence that the defendants could have provided: "respondents could have investigated whether similarly situated persons of other races were prosecuted by the State of California and were known to federal law enforcement officers, but were not prosecuted in federal court" (*United States v. Armstrong*, at 470).

enigmas of the criminal justice system . . . A prosecutor's determination to pursue, or to forgo, a criminal matter is as difficult to penetrate as a juror's decision to convict or to acquit" (1439).

Federal and state prosecutors in this country assert that their charging decisions are independent, free from political pressure, and based on the facts before them. After a California police officer fatally shot an unarmed homeless man in 2016, the Los Angeles County District Attorney announced that "[d]ecisions on whether or not to file criminal charges [in this matter] will be based solely on the facts and the law—not on emotion, anger or external pressure" (Mather 2016). And, as we saw at the beginning of Chapter 1, when discussing the potential prosecution of Hillary Clinton regarding her personal email server usage during her time as the U.S. Secretary of State, Attorney General Loretta Lynch noted that the DOJ would independently review the facts and evidence before reaching "an independent conclusion" on how to proceed (Goldman 2016).

While prosecutors may adamantly assert their decision-making independence when it comes to their discretionary decision-making, including whether to bring charges in cases, the political factors pressing on federal prosecutors, described in Chapter 5, give us good reason to expect something quite distinct from independent behavior. The limited empirical evidence that exists on this topic provides preliminary confirmation. Studies examining charging decisions in individual criminal areas like federal drug crimes (Whitford and Yates 2003, 2009), federal regulatory crimes (Whitford 2002), and federal immigration prosecutions in California (Apollonio, Lochner, and Heddens 2013) indicate the important influence of political factors. However, until recently, incredible data availability constraints have hampered our ability to determine whether politics has this effect across other crime categories, into more recent years, and for individual cases.

The stakes for how federal prosecutors exercise their prosecutorial discretion could not be higher, since virtually everything that happens in the criminal justice system stems from this decision. As Frase (1980) notes, "prosecutors can evade even the strictest plea bargaining and sentencing controls by simply not . . . charging certain offenders" (247). This chapter proceeds as follows in its quest to better understand this phase of prosecutorial decision-making. We begin with an in-depth examination of the decision of federal prosecutors to decline or bring prosecutions in criminal matters, detailing the reasons that prosecutors give for their decisions and the openings that exist for political factors to play a role. We then turn to an empirical examination of the effects that politics have on the decision to bring or decline to bring prosecutions in a key federal criminal issue area: violent crime matters. We explain the importance of violent crime matters. From there, we detail our research design and data and provide our statistical results. We conclude the chapter by discussing the bigger picture implications of our results for the role and power of federal prosecutors as agenda setters for criminal cases.

6.1 The Declination Decision

A federal prosecutor is directed by DOJ policies and procedures to "commence or recommend Federal prosecution if he/she believes that the person's conduct constitutes a Federal offense and that the admissible evidence will probably be sufficient to obtain and sustain a conviction" (U.S. Attorneys' Manual §9-27.220).[2] On its face, this prosecutorial guidance suggests an objective evaluation of the case evidence and odds of success on the merits. In other words, if criminal matters meet the evidentiary threshold and are likely to get a conviction, they will be prosecuted. And if they do not, they will be declined.

However, a deeper dive into the DOJ's prosecutorial guidance for U.S. Attorneys reveals this to be a more complex decision-making environment. Prior empirical research confirms that prosecutors' decisions to not bring charges are often based on biased assumptions (Spohn, Beichner, and Davis-Frenzel 2001) and extralegal factors (Albonetti 1986; Spohn and Holleran 2001). The U.S. Attorneys' Manual notes that the "determination to prosecute represents a policy judgment" (§9-27.001), with permissible declinations occurring for a variety of non-evidentiary reasons including that "[n]o substantial Federal interest would be served by prosecution" (§9-27.220). The "no substantial federal interest" rationale for declination is broadly defined to include the seriousness and nature of the offense, federal law enforcement priorities, and the deterrent effect of prosecution, among other factors (§9-27.230).

This focus on policy judgments and evaluating the degree of federal interest in pursuing prosecution vastly reduces the objectiveness of the prosecutorial decision. In its place rests some of the broadest discretion in the

[2] In 2018, the U.S. Attorneys' Manual was renamed the *Justice Manual*.

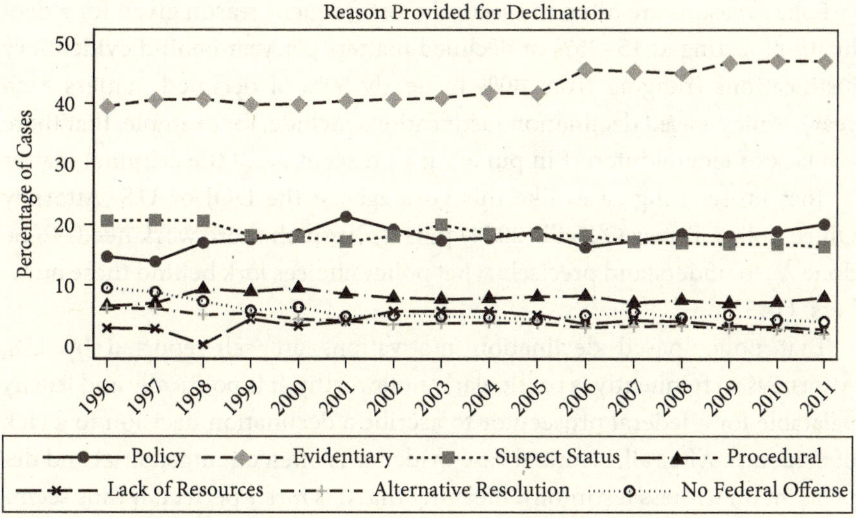

Figure 6.1 Reasons provided by U.S. Attorneys for declining prosecutions, 1996 to 2011. Data Source: Federal Justice Statistics annual reports.

criminal justice system. Prosecutorial discretion at the screening stage of cases, sometimes called the "discretion to be lenient," is nearly invisible to onlookers (Frase 1980). There is also virtually no oversight of individual federal prosecutorial decisions to pursue or decline prosecution; rather, "[i]t is left to the judgment of the attorney for the government" (§9-27.220 Comment). The U.S. Supreme Court has repeatedly endorsed this position, in *United States v. Armstrong* and elsewhere. As Wright and Miller (2002) put it, "[i]t has proven almost impossible to convince judges or legislatures to create meaningful limits on the screening decisions of prosecutors" (53).

U.S. Attorneys' self-reporting for internal DOJ annual records on their reasons for declining to prosecute matters is informative. Figure 6.1 displays these categorized justifications for declination decisions, from 1996 to 2011.[3] As the figure indicates, the distribution of declination justifications is remarkably stable across 1996 to 2011. This is despite the fact that three different presidents, hundreds of U.S. Attorneys, and thousands of Assistant U.S. Attorneys served during that time period.

[3] Data compiled from the annual Federal Justice Statistics reports. Categorization of declination reasons follows O'Neill (2004, Table 10).

Policy reasons are often the second most frequent reason given for a declination, resting at 15–25% of declined matters per year behind evidentiary justifications (ranging from 40% to nearly 50% of declined matters each year). Policy-based declination justifications include, for example, that there is a lack of federal interest in pursuing a prosecution of the criminal matter or that prosecuting cases like this goes against the DOJ or U.S. Attorney Office policy. But as O'Neill (2004) puts it, "[m]uch more work needs to be done . . . to understand precisely what policy choices lurk behind these numbers" (1453).

That policy-based declination motivations are self-reported by U.S. Attorneys so frequently is particularly noteworthy. It is politically and legally palatable for a federal prosecutor to ascribe a declination decision to a lack of evidence. After all, criminal case evidence is often circumstantial and dependent on witness testimony, meaning that it is *rarely* perfect. It thus seems very likely that Figure 6.1's self-reported evidentiary-based declination numbers overreport that motivation and undercount the effects of policy forces on declination decisions.

Other provided declination reasons beyond evidentiary and policy are also nontrivial, including suspect status (10–20% per year; includes cases where the suspect was deceased, deported, or already serving a sentence), procedural (7–10%; includes cases that are stale or removed), lack of resources (1–6%), alternative resolution (2–6%; category includes such areas as restitution, pretrial diversion, and administrative alternatives), and determinations that there was no federal offense (4–10%).

Despite leaning heavily on evidentiary justifications for their declination decisions, federal prosecutors readily admit that they care about national and local priorities when setting their agendas. Descriptive data provided by the DOJ on the priority levels assigned by the U.S. Attorney offices to criminal matters that are referred to them for potential prosecution help illustrate this. The DOJ's five priority levels are (1) National Priority, (2) District Priority, (3) Both National and District Priority, (4) Neither National or District Priority, and (5) Unknown. Figure 6.2 reports the breakdown of priority classifications for declined criminal matters in the U.S. Attorneys offices from 1996 to 2011.[4] The figure reveals that, by far, the most common priority level for declined cases is Neither National or District Priority. National or

[4] Data in this figure compiled by the authors using the DOJ's internal tracking data (Legal Information Office Network System [LIONS]) described in further detail below.

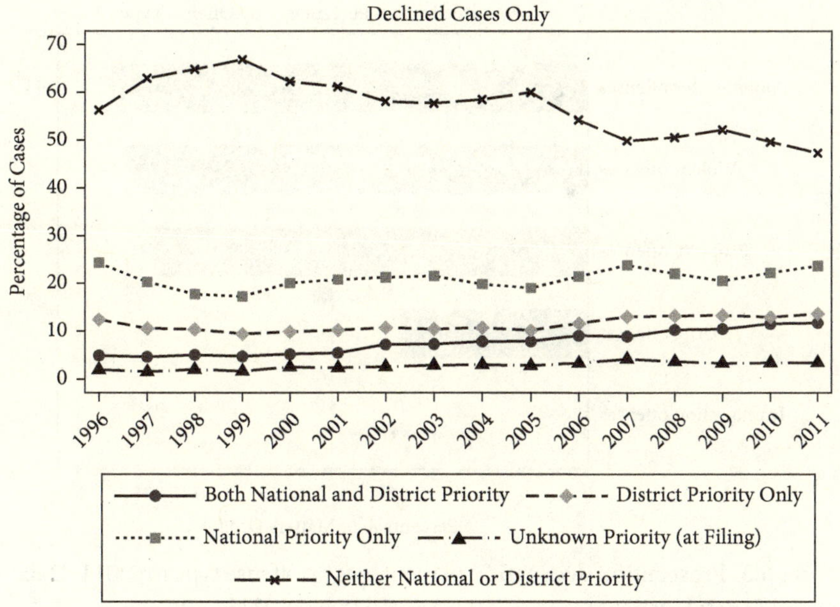

Figure 6.2 Priority level assigned by U.S. Attorney offices for declined prosecutions, 1996 to 2011. Data Source: DOJ LIONS data

District priority cases are much less frequently declined, with this being particularly true for cases that are both national and district priorities (declined only 5–10% of the time).

How does this declination decision play out for different types of criminal matters referred to U.S. Attorneys' offices? Figure 6.3 displays the percentage of criminal matters declined by federal prosecutors, by offense type, for 2011. The declination percentages are very similar for three major offense categories—public-order offenses (37.3%; e.g., regulatory offenses, racketeering, tax law violations), violent offenses (36.2%; e.g., murder, assault, sexual abuse), and property offenses (34.4%; e.g., fraud, embezzlement, arson, motor vehicle theft). Drug offense declinations are significantly lower, at 14.6%.[5] And immigration offenses were very rarely declined, at only 1% in 2011.[6]

[5] The lower percentage of drug offense declinations in 2011 compared to other offenses matches earlier work in this area. O'Neill (2004), in his study of declination percentages from 1994–2000, found that drug offenses were declined 20% of the time.

[6] Immigration accounts for the largest number of criminal matters in the federal system today. This, plus the very low declination rate, likely reflects a combination of norms for the mass (or streamlined) prosecution of migrants by the criminal system, statutory limits on prosecutors' discretion,

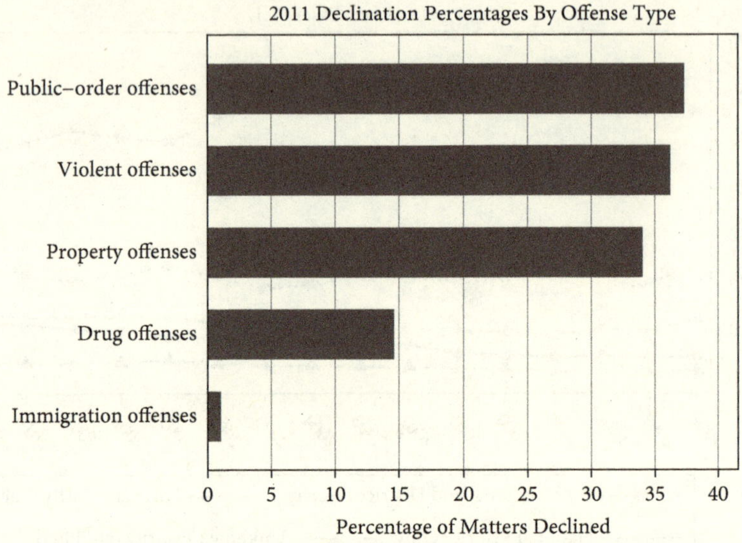

Figure 6.3 Prosecution declination percentages by offense type for 2011. Data Source: Federal Justice Statistics 2011 Annual Report, Table 2.2.

6.2 Violent Crime Prosecutions and Declinations

We now turn to a more in-depth discussion and empirical examination of how declination decisions are made for matters falling in one of these offense categories: violent crime offenses. Since the political pressure on prosecutors to address violent crime in America can be especially pronounced, the examination of the effects of political factors on whether to bring or forgo prosecution in these cases is important.

Several modern presidential administrations have made notable efforts to signal their desire for a tough prosecutorial stance on violent crime. Richard Nixon, for example, famously ran a "law and order" campaign in which he made the safety of Americans a central issue. When accepting the nomination of the Republican Party in 1968, Nixon pledged that he would direct a new Attorney General to "launch a war" against "merchants of crime and corruption in American society" (Nixon 1968). Campaigning on behalf of George H.W. Bush in 1988, President Ronald Reagan explained to a crowd

political support to keep those numbers high, and a particularly high level of deference to the investigating agency's (Department of Homeland Security) recommendations.

of supporters, "Violent crime has fallen significantly since 1981 because George and I put criminals on notice. We said make a false move, and the next sound you hear is the clang of a jail cell door slamming shut" (Reagan 1988). More recently, during his inauguration address in 2017, Donald Trump decried "the crime and gangs and the drugs that have stolen too many lives and robbed our country of so much unrealized potential." He went on to promise that "[t]his American carnage stops right here and stops right now" (Trump 2017).

Congress has also devoted considerable attention to reducing crime in America, passing major legislation such as the Violent Crime Control and Law Enforcement Act of 1994 and maintaining oversight by holding over 100 hearings on violent crime since 1980 (Baumgartner and Jones 2013). And the American public expects prosecutors to prioritize the battle against violent crime. Despite falling national crime rates in recent years, nearly 70% of Americans polled believe that crime is actually rising (Gallup 2015). Given these considerations, prosecutors are incentivized to pursue violent crime on the behalf of their political principals and constituents. Consequently, violent crime has become a centerpiece of federal prosecution, making up roughly 20% of federal criminal case filings annually (Executive Office for U.S. Attorneys 2015).

Based on the theory of political responsiveness developed in Chapter 5, we anticipate that federal prosecutors will be cognizant of and heed the political signals that they receive regarding violent crime. Specifically, the more the president and Congress speak about violent crime relative to other topics, the more likely federal prosecutors should be to prosecute, rather than decline, individual violent crime matters. Similarly, the greater the frequency with which a federal prosecutor's local public is concerned about violent crime and punitiveness, the higher the corresponding prosecution rate should be. In other words, we expect responsiveness in how federal prosecutors allocate their limited agenda space. When punitiveness toward violent crimes is a priority to the president, Congress, and the local public, more space will be given to prosecuting cases of this type (and fewer of them will be declined).

6.3 Data and Variables

To empirically examine the political effects on federal prosecutors' decisions to pursue or decline violent crime prosecutions, we combine case-level data retrieved from the DOJ's internal tracking data, the Legal Information Office Network System (LIONS), with compiled and collected presidential, congressional, local public, judicial, and district variables.[7] As part of the DOJ's compliance with the Freedom of Information Act (FOIA), the agency has made publicly available rich and complex data tracking the entrance, processing, and exit of individual criminal and civil cases (matters). This includes detailed information on multiple aspects of a case including the decision to pursue a case for prosecution.

Here, we direct our attention to criminal matters disposed by U.S. Attorneys in 89 districts[8] from 1996 to 2011 in the DOJ's violent federal crime prosecutorial category.[9] Examples of federal violent crimes within the data include murder, sexual abuse, assault, bank robbery, violence against federal employees, other violent crimes occurring across interstate lines, and violent crimes due to the presence of violence associated with major criminal enterprises like mafia organizations or drug cartels. Another common federal violent crime falls within 18 U.S.C. §922(g)(1), which prohibits the possession of firearms by convicted felons. This charge has been used to vigorously punish members of street gangs and prevent firearm-related homicides in urban areas through a federal prosecutorial strategy known as Project Exile (Crime Solutions 2015; Green 2017). Our data include 194,907 such criminal matters that have been referred by federal agencies to U.S. Attorney offices for potential prosecution.

The unit of analysis for our statistical analysis is the individual criminal matter. The dependent variable is *Prosecuted*. We derive this variable from the DOJ's publicly available FOIA data described earlier. *Prosecuted* is a dichotomous variable coded as 1 if the matter is prosecuted by a U.S. Attorney's

[7] We do not model the grand jury decision to indict an alleged offender following the prosecutors' threshold determination. The U.S. Constitution's Fifth Amendment guarantees the right to a grand jury indictment for federal felony prosecutions. Importantly, grand jury proceedings require a low standard of proof and rarely fail to yield an indictment (a true bill). For fiscal year 2009, for example, the federal government reports that in less than 0.1% of criminal matters did a grand jury not return a true bill of indictment (Bureau of Justice Statistics 2011, 11).

[8] We exclude only four U.S. Attorney offices: District of Columbia, District of Puerto Rico, Districts of Guam and the Northern Mariana Islands (a shared U.S. Attorney office), and District of the Virgin Islands.

[9] We exclude extreme outlier cases terminated more than five years after their receipt by the U.S. Attorneys office. This amounts to approximately 5.3% of the data. We also exclude matters with obscure lead charges (appearing in less than 100 matters between 1996–2011; represent 2.6% of all lead charges in the violent crime data) and those referring agencies that do not have a clear stake in pursuing violent crime (e.g., the IRS, United States Postal Service, and State Department represent less than 5% of agencies in the violent crime data).

Office and 0 if it is declined for prosecution. Nearly 38% of violent crimes within our data are declined.

Following the expectations derived from Chapter 5's theory, we measure independent variables related to the potential effects of political (presidential, congressional, local public) factors on the prosecutorial declination decision. Summary statistics and expected direction of effects for all independent variables are provided in the Chapter Data Appendix. We briefly review our political variables that were introduced in Chapter 5.

First, to consider the potential signaling effect of violent crime-related presidential rhetoric on the decision to prosecute cases in this area, we utilize *Presidential Rhetoric*—the one-month lagged number of sentences in presidential public statements each month that contain policy mentions about violent crime, standardized by dividing that count by the total number of statements in a month and then multiplying it by one hundred. The resulting measure is thus the number of sentences relating to crimes of violence per 100 statements for each (lagged) month.

Related to Congress as a principal to U.S. Attorneys, as fully outlined in Chapter 5, we code *Congressional Hearings*. This variable captures the amount of public attention that Congress pays to violent crime-related policies. With the *Congressional Hearings* variable, we count the number of congressional hearings related to violent crime and lag the measure by one month to account for temporal considerations. The resulting *Congressional Hearings* variable is calculated as the percentage of total hearings per (lagged) month related to violent crimes.

In considering the local public's potential influence on prosecutorial declination decisions, we focus on three variables of interest. First, *Local Public Opinion* measures regional public opinion on violent crime, capturing the percentage of survey respondents who believe that "too little" is spent on "halting the rising crime rate." *Local Punitiveness* toward criminal offenders is our second measure of local public influence. It serves to capture state-level preferences regarding how much the justice system should assert itself in the lives of their citizens by measuring the number of incarcerated inmates in state-run prison facilities per 100,000 residents for each state-year. Third, we measure *State Violent Crime Rate* as the number of violent crimes for every state-year per 100,000 residents. With each of these local measures, we expect that higher values will communicate to U.S. Attorneys the need to prosecute a higher number of the violent crime matters that cross their desks.

Looking beyond variables related to political principals and the local public on U.S. Attorneys' charging behavior, we also take into consideration other factors such as resource constraints, political and strategic aspects, and individual criminal matter characteristics that may affect federal prosecution decisions. First, we control for the average caseload of individual attorneys in local U.S. Attorney offices (*Staff Workload*). While no U.S. Attorney office has the resources and time to pursue every prosecution, we expect that less-burdened attorneys and offices will be more likely to pursue prosecutions in individual cases than those offices facing higher workload constraints. To measure *Staff Workload*, we divide the total number of civil and criminal matters pending in a U.S. Attorney office in a year (as reported in the U.S. Attorneys' Annual Statistical Reports) by the number of Assistant U.S. Attorneys in an office in that year (per Nelson and Ostrander 2016).

We anticipate that prosecutors will be forward looking, accounting for future courts' influence on cases—including the probability of conviction and the length of sentence imposed—and adjust their calculation about whether to pursue prosecutions accordingly. Prior research indicates that litigants and trial court judges engage in this type of strategic behavior (Boyd 2015; Randazzo 2008; Scott 2006), so we expect prosecutors to behave similarly. *District Court Conservatism* measures the ideology of the appropriate federal district court using the median Judicial Common Space score for each district-year (Boyd 2010; Epstein et al. 2007; Giles, Hettinger, and Peppers 2001). These ideology scores range from −1 (most liberal) to +1 (most conservative). We expect that more conservative prospective district courts will serve to encourage more aggressive charging prosecutorial decisions in law and order criminal matters like violent crimes (George 2001).

Third, we account for the political preferences of the U.S. Attorney leading each district. We anticipate that Republican-leaning U.S. Attorneys will be more likely to favor violent crime prosecutions than Democratic-leaning U.S. Attorneys. We measure *Republican U.S. Attorney* using the party of the sitting president at the time the U.S. Attorney commences her work (coded as 1 for Republican, 0 for Democratic). We also control for whether the DOJ is being led by an *Acting Attorney General* instead of a permanent, U.S. Senate-confirmed U.S. Attorney General. The presence of an Acting Attorney General will likely lead to substantial uncertainty for U.S. Attorneys about the overarching preferences and priorities of the DOJ. As a result of this uncertainty, we should expect to see fewer prosecutions.

We also include fixed effects of note in our modeling. This includes case-level factors about the specific type of violent criminal matter in each potential prosecution (*Lead Charge Type*). We develop a variable that captures the lead criminal charge for each criminal matter. To do this, we utilize the lead charge criminal statute's title and section of the United States Code (e.g., 18 U.S.C. §2113, which covers bank robbery and incidental crimes; and 18 U.S.C. §2241, which criminalizes federal aggravated sexual assault) to assign each criminal matter into one of 10 crime types that fall with high frequency within the DOJ's violent crime program: firearm offenses, bank robbery offenses, domestic violence offenses, assault-related offenses, homicide-related offenses, sex-related offenses, burglary and robbery offenses, kidnapping offenses, arson offenses, and other violent crime offenses.[10] This variable naturally controls for crime-specific considerations like the complexity of proving the offense, the substantive nature of the conduct involved, and the potential penalties for the crime.

We also use fixed effects to control for the federal agency that referred the matter to the DOJ for prosecution. The most common federal agencies that refer violent crime matters to the DOJ for prosecution in our data are the Bureau of Alcohol, Tobacco, Firearms and Explosives (ATF); the Federal Bureau of Investigation (FBI); and the Drug Enforcement Administration (DEA). Finally, we include fixed effects for the individual U.S. Attorney offices and year.

6.4 Results

To empirically examine how political factors affect U.S. Attorneys' decisions to prosecute federal violent crimes, we estimate a logistic regression model with robust standard errors. The results are provided in Table 6.1. Four of our five key political variables have a statistically meaningful impact on the decision to prosecute federal violent crimes. Below, we provide a more in-depth examination of the individual political variables and their effects.

[10] We note that a few of the offense categories for these lead charges are considered by some to be property crime offenses instead of violent crime offenses. Since the DOJ has selected to categorize these cases as belonging to the violent crime program, we opt to follow the DOJ's classification.

Table 6.1 Logistic regression estimates for whether a case is Prosecuted.

	Coefficient		RSE
Presidential Rhetoric	0.002*		(0.000)
Congressional Hearings	0.059*		(0.010)
Local Public Opinion	0.001		(0.001)
Local Punitiveness	0.002*		(0.000)
State Violent Crime Rate	0.000*		(0.000)
Staff Workload	−0.008*		(0.001)
District Court Conservatism	0.133*		(0.041)
Republican U.S. Attorney	0.061*		(0.023)
Acting Attorney General	−0.234*		(0.041)
Lead Charge Type			
Firearm Offense	0.837*		(0.054)
Bank Robbery Offense	0.589*		(0.055)
Domestic Violence Offense	−0.763*		(0.092)
Assault-Related Offense	−0.340*		(0.057)
Homicide-Related Offense	−0.302*		(0.073)
Sex-Related Offense	0.452*		(0.113)
Burglary and Robbery Offense	−1.058*		(0.061)
Kidnapping Offense	−0.289*		(0.110)
Arson Offense	−0.497*		(0.188)
Referring Agency Fixed Effects		Included	
District Fixed Effects		Included	
Year Fixed Effects		Included	
Constant	−1.700*		(0.185)
Observations	194,747		

Robust standard errors (RSE) are included in parentheses. Baseline *Lead Charge Type* is the Other Violent Crimes category. * Significant at $p < 0.05$.

We first consider the effects of presidential signals to U.S. Attorneys on violent crime prosecution decisions. *Presidential Rhetoric* has a statistically significant and positive effect in the regression model in Table 6.1. To further delve into the substantive effects of *Presidential Rhetoric*, we estimate predictive margins to calculate the average predicted effect of presidential rhetoric on whether a matter is prosecuted. Figure 6.4 plots the resulting probability of prosecution given the changing levels of a president's rhetoric on violent crime.

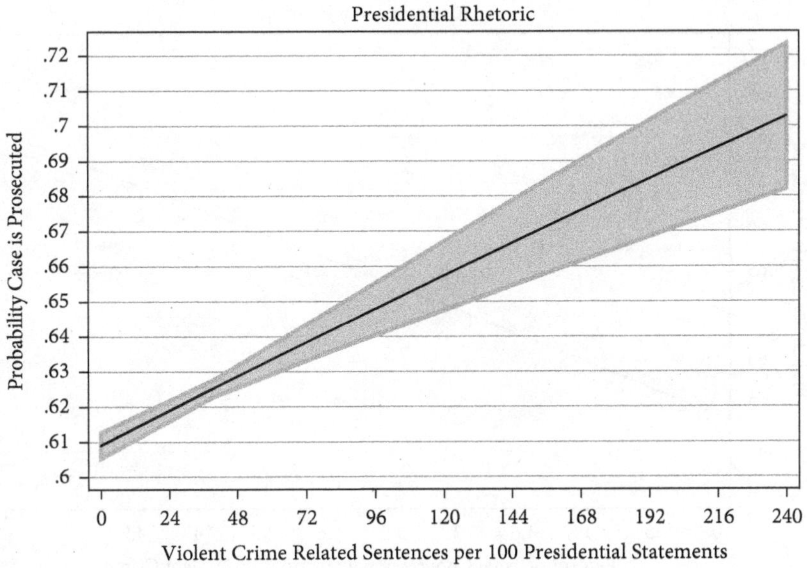

Figure 6.4 Marginal effects of presidential rhetoric on case prosecution.

The effect of presidential rhetoric is positive, meaning that, as expected, the more a president speaks about issues related to violent crime, the more likely U.S. Attorneys and their offices are to pursue prosecutions of those crimes. Presidential rhetoric's effect ranges from a prosecution probability of 0.61 (during low violent crime rhetoric) to nearly 0.7 (during much higher periods of presidential rhetoric on violent crime). This is a substantial increase in the probability of nearly 0.09 across the range of presidential violent crime rhetoric in the data.

To examine whether there is a similarly strong level of responsiveness to signaled congressional prosecutorial priorities, we look to the *Congressional Hearings* variable where we expect to observe a positive effect similar to presidential rhetoric. Table 6.1 again indicates a positive, significant effect for *Congressional Hearings*. Figure 6.5 plots the substantive effects of this variable. As it reveals, the increase in the probability of case prosecution is approximately 0.06 as the percentage of congressional hearings dedicated to violent crime moves from its minimum to maximum value. This is solid evidence that the more Congress discusses issues related to violent crime, the stronger and more effective the signal sent to prosecutors that this area is a prosecutorial priority area.

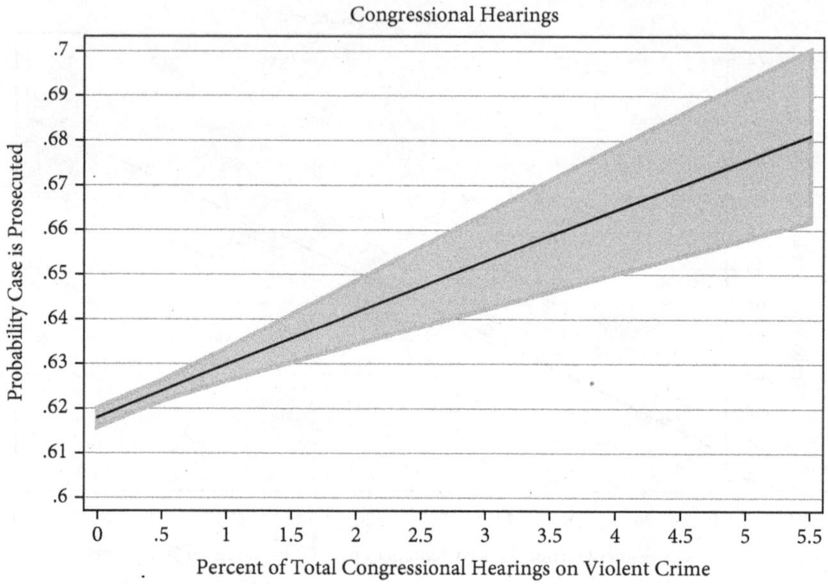

Figure 6.5 Marginal effects of congressional hearings on case prosecution.

For our final set of variables related to the politics of prosecution decisions, we focus on the potential constraining effect of the local public. While *Local Public Opinion* does not have a statistically significant effect on prosecution decisions, *Local Punitiveness* and *State Violent Crime Rate* do.

Prosecutors considering violent crime prosecutions appear to be strongly influenced by the punitiveness of their jurisdiction (*Local Punitiveness*). In those states with significantly more prisoners in state government facilities relative to the population, prosecutors are much more likely to bring a prosecution in a violent criminal matter. Figure 6.6 plots the probability of prosecution across the state imprisonment rate, which serves as a proxy for local views about punishment. We find that local punitiveness has a large impact on how likely federal prosecutors are to pursue violent offenders. From the minimum state incarceration rate to the maximum, the probability that an individual criminal matter is pursued increases in probability by 0.29.

State Violent Crime Rate also has a meaningful impact on federal violent crime prosecutions. As Figure 6.7 depicts, there is a nearly 0.05 increase in the probability of violent crime prosecutions across the range of this variable. Overall, this indicates that federal prosecutors are mindful of whether violent crime is a problem in their state. Where it is, federal prosecutors will respond by vigorously pursuing offenders through federal laws.

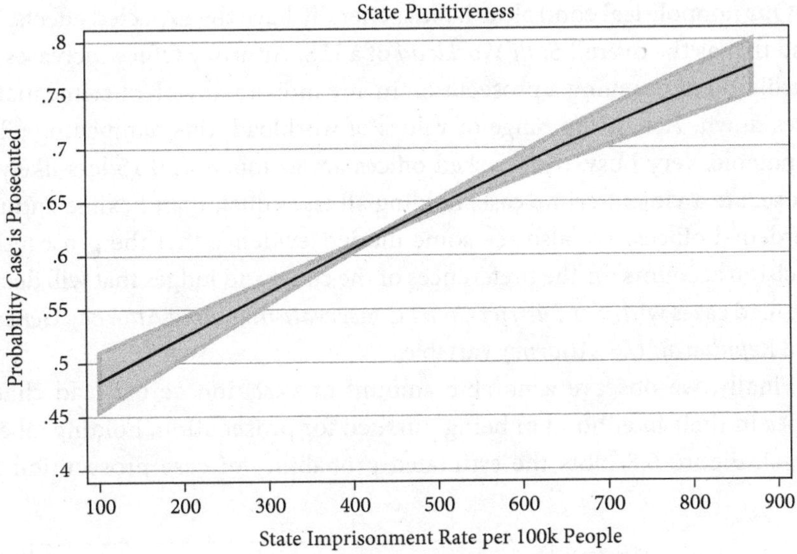

Figure 6.6 Marginal effects of local punitiveness on case prosecution.

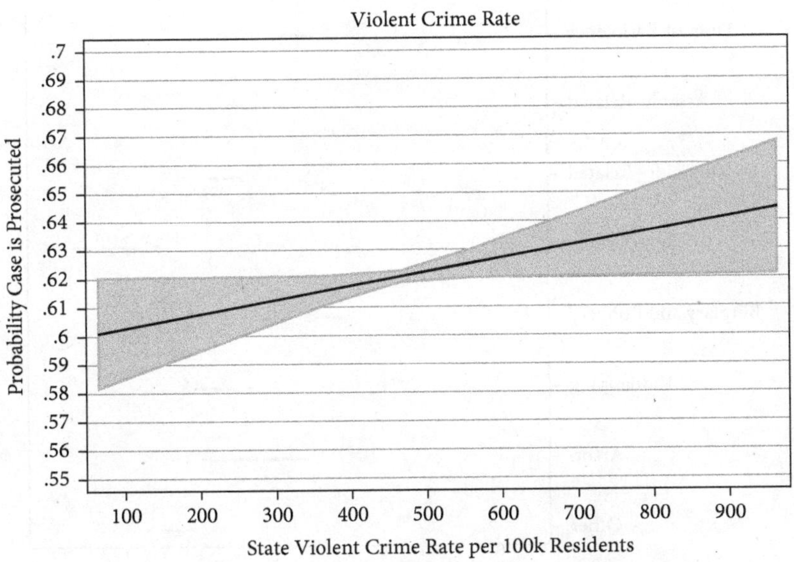

Figure 6.7 Marginal effects of violent crime rate on case prosecution.

Our nonpolitical control variables generally have the expected effects. We find that as the overall *Staff Workload* of a U.S. Attorney Office increases, its likelihood of pursuing a prosecution in any individual violent crime matter goes down. Across the range of values of workload, this dampening effect is notable: very busy, overworked offices are as much as 0.15 less likely to prosecute a violent crime case, holding all else equal, than flexible and unburdened offices. We also see some modest evidence that the prosecution decision accounts for the preferences of the court and judges that will decide the filed cases with our *District Court Conservatism, Acting Attorney General,* and *Republican U.S. Attorney* variables.

Finally, we observe a notable amount of variation across lead charge types in their likelihood of being pursued for prosecution, holding all else equal. Figure 6.8 plots the estimated probability of case prosecution for

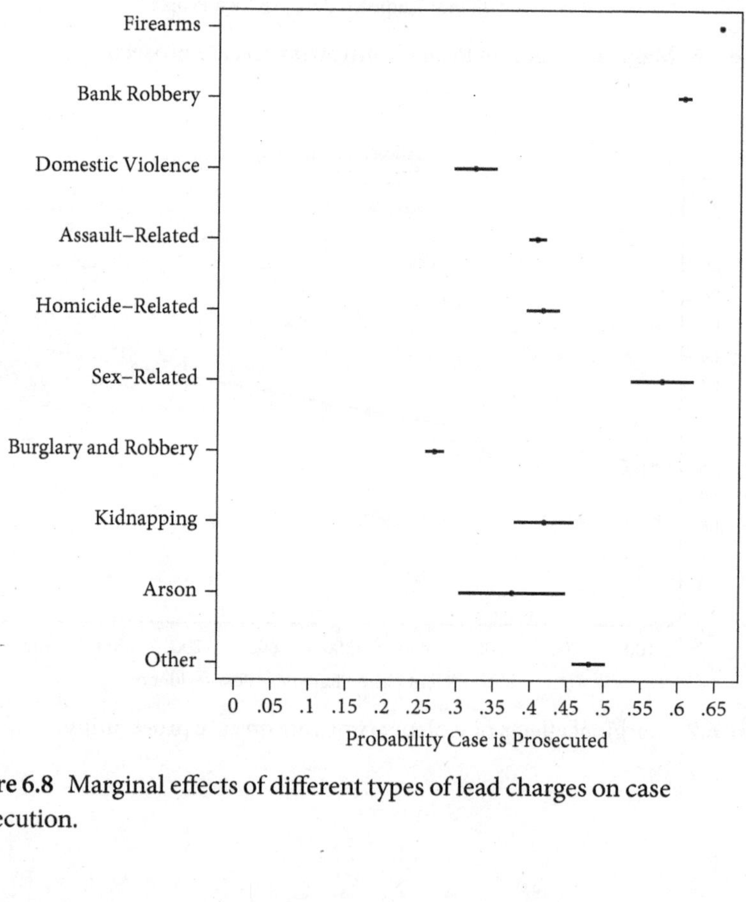

Figure 6.8 Marginal effects of different types of lead charges on case prosecution.

each of the types of lead charges within the DOJ's violent crime program. As it indicates, firearm, bank robbery, and sex offenses are the most likely federal violent crime matters to be prosecuted, while burglary, domestic violence, and arson federal violent crime matters are significantly more likely to be declined.

6.5 Discussion

With the Supreme Court's blessing in cases like *United States v. Armstrong*, federal prosecutors know that the decision to prosecute or decline prosecution in criminal matters rests very much at their discretion. It also gives them substantial criminal justice agenda-setting power. The presence of so much prosecutorial discretion at this stage leaves vast opportunities for the policy preferences of their political principals and local public to affect prosecutors' charging decisions. And as our empirical evidence reveals, the explanatory power of both national and local political factors on the decision to prosecute violent crime matters is indeed quite strong.

In the nearly 200,000 violent crime matters in our data, we observe sizable prosecutorial responsiveness to presidential rhetoric, congressional hearings, and local concerns about violent crime. In the case of presidential rhetoric, our results indicated that federal prosecutors are up to 0.09 more likely to pursue an individual violent crime matter when the president has signaled his commitment to aggressively battling violent crime. Congressional hearings also send a powerful message about the federal legislative branches' desired prioritization of curbing violent crime. All other things equal, our findings indicate that frequent congressional hearings on the issue of violent crime can bring up to a 0.06 increase in the chance that an individual violent crime matter is prosecuted. The strength of the results for *Presidential Rhetoric* and *Congressional Hearings* confirm the power that presidential and congressional signaling on prosecutorial priorities have in the decisions of U.S. Attorney offices, as theorized in full in Chapter 5. Simply put: when U.S. Attorneys' national political principals send strong signals that aggressively fighting violent crime is important, these federal prosecutors respond by allocating their limited resources to that area and pursue individual violent crime prosecutions that they otherwise would not.

We also see notable evidence that federal prosecutors are mindful of their local public's appetite for an aggressive stance toward violent crime. As we discussed in Chapter 5, there are numerous reasons to expect U.S. Attorneys to be responsive to local considerations in addition to national political ones, including shared values on crime with the community and future employment opportunities. Our results showed that a state's punitiveness and levels of violent crime can lead to up to 0.29 and 0.05 increases in the probability of prosecution, respectively. In other words, national and local political signals and political culture matter when it comes to federal violent crime prosecutions, but the size of the effect and the source of the political influence varies.

This chapter's findings make significant strides forward in the study of prosecutors' critical roles as agenda setters for the U.S. criminal justice system's adjudication, sentencing, and corrections institutions. When prosecutors choose to file criminal charges, the wheels of criminal justice are quickly put into motion, with convictions via plea bargains and trials nearly always resulting. But when federal prosecutors decline to bring prosecutions, whether we like it or not, that is the end of the story. The fact that this decision is often affected by political, non-neutral factors and is "largely unreviewable by the courts" (*United States v. Flemmi* (1st Cir. 2000)) may rub many the wrong way. The reality is that this influence of political factors on decision-making is no different than is present for many other legal actors, including federal judges. Whether there is a case to be made that the political effects on prosecutorial decisions are less palatable than those for other legal actors is a more complicated story best left for the reader to ponder.

We move now to Chapter 7 and its examination of a related area of politics and prosecutorial decision-making: the charging and bargaining process prior to criminal case termination.

Chapter 6 Data Appendix

Table 6.2 Summary statistics for dependent and key independent variables.

	Expected Direction	Mean	Standard Deviation	Range
Prosecuted		0.62	0.49	0–1
Presidential Rhetoric	+	28.16	38.59	0–240.60
Congressional Hearings	+	0.21	0.54	0–5.56
Local Public Opinion	+	59.95	6.69	40.54–81
Local Punitiveness	+	435.44	140.08	100–886
State Violent Crime Rate	+	465.17	172.58	66.9–1051
Staff Workload	–	18.33	7.55	7.72–95.89
District Court Conservatism	+	0.08	0.29	–0.52–0.60
Republican U.S. Attorney	+	0.63	0.48	0–1
Acting Attorney General	–	0.02	0.13	0–1
Firearm Offense	+	0.77	.042	0–1
Bank Robbery Offense	+	0.12	0.32	0–1
Domestic Violence Offense	+	0.01	0.08	0–1
Assault-Related Offense	–	0.05	0.21	0–1
Homicide-Related Offense	+	0.01	0.10	0–1
Sex-Related Offense	+	0.003	0.05	0–1
Burglary and Robbery Offense	–	0.03	0.16	0–1
Kidnapping Offense	+	0.003	0.05	0–1
Arson Offense	–	0.001	0.03	0–1
Other Violent Offense	N/A	0.01	0.10	0–1

Expected direction of effects for lead charge types are relative to other violent offenses.

7

The Charging and Bargaining Decisions

In *Bordenkircher v. Hayes* (1978), a divided U.S. Supreme Court affirmed the enormous charging and bargaining powers held by U.S. prosecutors. In the now-famous case, the Kentucky prosecutor threatened to pursue a conviction under the Kentucky Habitual Criminal Act should Paul Hayes, the defendant, refuse to plead guilty to forging a check for $88.30. Hayes was offered a plea deal that came with a recommended prison sentence of five years; if Hayes went to trial and was convicted, he would face a mandatory life imprisonment sentence under the Kentucky repeat offender law (Hayes had two prior felony convictions). Hayes ultimately declined to plead guilty and, as promised, the prosecutor re-indicted Hayes under the Kentucky Habitual Criminal Act. The case went to trial, and the jury convicted Hayes of check forgery. He was sentenced to imprisonment for life.

A battle over the constitutionality of the Kentucky prosecutor's bargaining strategy ensued. On appeal to the Sixth Circuit Court of Appeals, the court issued a blow to the prosecutor, arguing that the "vindictive exercise of [the] prosecutor's discretion" placed Hayes "in fear of retaliatory action for insisting upon his constitutional right to stand trial" (*Hayes v. Cowan*, 547 F.2d 42, 44–45 (6th Cir. 1976)). But the U.S. Supreme Court disagreed. In ratifying the prosecutor's negotiation tactics, the Supreme Court majority characterized the events unfolding between Hayes and the prosecutor as the typical "give-and-take" of plea bargaining without any "punishment or retaliation" because Hayes was free to "accept or reject the prosecution's offer" (*Bordenkircher v. Hayes* at 363).

According to the *Bordenkircher v. Hayes* majority, it was well within the power of the Kentucky prosecutor to pursue tough charges and negotiations with Hayes, even if he didn't do the same with other defendants' files that came across his desk. "[T]he conscious exercise of some selectivity in enforcement," the *Bordenkircher* Court said, "is not in itself a federal constitutional

The Politics of Federal Prosecution. Christina L. Boyd, Michael J. Nelson, Ian Ostrander, and Ethan D. Boldt, Oxford University Press (2021).
DOI: 10.1093/oso/9780197554685.003.0007

violation" (364, quoting *Oyler v. Boles* (1962)). *Bordenkircher*'s approval of prosecutorial "selectivity in enforcement" helps shed light on why many see the prosecutor as "the most powerful [position] in the criminal justice system" (Bishop and Frazier 1984, 387). Among his broad charging and bargaining powers,

> A prosecutor may file charges consistent with the strength of the evidence in a given case, or charge with greater or lesser offenses than the evidence will support. The prosecutor may negotiate with the defense or refuse to do so. In negotiating, he or she may drop counts or reduce initial charges to lesser offenses, which may have the effect of sharply limiting the sentencing discretion of the judge. (Bishop and Frazier 1984, 387)

Why did the *Bordenkircher v. Hayes* prosecutor decide to use his vast discretionary powers to pursue such an aggressive charging and negotiation stance against Hayes? We suspect that political considerations are much to blame. Like many state prosecutors, the Kentucky prosecutor in *Bordenkircher v. Hayes* was elected. As such, he was almost certainly driven by concerns about successfully getting a conviction, maintaining a tough stance on crime that was palatable to his voters, and expeditiously disposing of Hayes's case through a plea bargain, among other things. An uncompromising style of plea agreement negotiations would help him achieve these goals.

As we will see throughout this chapter, prosecutors control this decision-making space nearly alone, with their charging and plea-negotiation decisions unchecked, invisible, and unreviewable (Bishop and Frazier 1984; Hartley, Maddan, and Spohn 2007). This presents the real potential for defendants to be treated differently via "actual and perceived abuses of power, including political favoritism, personal self-interest, undercharging, overcharging, arbitrariness, and bias" (Levine 2016, 4). The result is a "substantial opportunity for disparity and inefficiency in the exercise of discretion" by prosecutors (Forst 1999, 523). Among other negative implications, this practice "poses obstacles to achieving consistency and uniformity in sentencing" outcomes in the U.S. criminal justice system (Hartley, Maddan, and Spohn 2007, 387).

Despite the vast charging and bargaining powers held by prosecutors and the importance of their decisions leading up to a defendant's conviction, there has been limited research on this subject. The discretionary work of prosecutors is the "little understood" (Frederick and Stemen 2012, 1) " 'black box' of contemporary research on courts and sentencing" (Shermer and Johnson 2010, 395) that gets "obscured in many studies of sentencing outcomes" (Piehl and Bushway 2007). Because "records on prosecutorial charging behavior remain elusive" (Shermer and Johnson 2010, 396), "we actually know less today than we did in the 1970s and 1980s" (Forst 1999, 525). What empirical scholarship that does exist on prosecutors' decision-making in charging and bargaining cases focuses largely on defendant characteristics like race, gender, and prior criminal history, leaving political influences on prosecutorial behavior at this stage unexamined in a systematic way.

The discretionary charging and negotiation process can be utilized by federal prosecutors to achieve their political goals. Just as with the decisions to charge or decline to charge certain cases, federal prosecutors are likely to look for opportunities in their charging and bargaining decisions to respond to their political principals and local public. We expect that when federal prosecutors receive political signals that a particular type of crime is a priority, they will treat those cases more seriously and harshly than other, nonpolitical priority cases. We expect this to take place both with the level of charge reductions presented by prosecutors during plea negotiations and the selective offering of downward sentencing departures to defendants for their assistance in prosecuting others.

In this chapter, we provide an in-depth examination of federal prosecutors' charging and bargaining powers and the federal guidance provided to prosecutors deciding how to exercise these powers. We also review the dominant role that plea bargaining has in today's criminal justice system and examine how prosecutorial bargaining and charging decisions leave room for disparity in how different defendants and cases are treated. Next, we directly assess how political responsiveness likely drives the way prosecutors exercise their powers during this stage of cases. Using federal charging and sentencing data, we then empirically test for political effects on charge reduction and downward sentencing departure behavior.

7.1 Charging, Bargaining, and the Prosecutor

Once a prosecutors' office decides to pursue the prosecution of a defendant (Chapter 6's topic), they must quickly turn to an evaluation of what charges to bring[1] and what strategy to pursue to successfully gain a conviction—almost certainly via a negotiated plea agreement. Charging and bargaining are closely intertwined, with prosecutors often setting up their initial charges with an eye toward how they plan to conduct their negotiations and how severe of a conviction they hope to secure.

7.1.1 Prosecutorial Discretion and Power in Charging

While scholars, policy makers, judges, and prosecutors disagree on much about prosecutors' roles in the charging and plea bargaining process—from whether prosecutors engage in systematic overcharging to whether defendants are unfairly coerced into plea bargains (and much more)—one universal point of agreement seems to be on how powerful prosecutors are during this stage of criminal cases. Prosecutors "have the full discretionary power to dismiss criminal charges outright, to reduce initial charges to lesser offenses, and to negotiate sentencing discounts through the process of plea bargaining. Their potential influence over criminal punishments in society is therefore substantial" (Shermer and Johnson 2010, 395). Indeed, prosecutors during this stage of criminal proceedings have been described as "gatekeepers" (Kerstetter 1990), "kings of the courtroom" (Johnson, King, and Spohn 2016, 481), not "advocates" but "rulers" with "near-total power over the resolution" of cases (Rakoff 2017, 1430), "the real policy-maker within the criminal justice system," (Misner 1996, 743) and as holding "virtually absolute power . . . over federal prosecution and sentencing" (Miller 2004, 1252).

Much of the pre-outcome power attributed to prosecutors stems from the nature of the decisions that they make regarding charging and negotiation: they are "largely invisible and unreviewable" (Hartley, Maddan, and Spohn 2007, 386). The decisions are *invisible* because they happen out of an open courtroom and off the record. We have little-to-no information on internal prosecutors' office considerations leading to the decisions to bring certain charges and not others or to offer specific plea deals. "[I]t is rare for

[1] These initial federal charges are contained in the indictment, information, or criminal complaint, each of which also serves to provide formal notice to the defendant of the charges being pursued against him. In federal courts, and in many states, a grand jury ultimately makes the decision whether to issue an indictment based on a one-sided presentation of the case by the prosecutor's office. Grand juries rarely fail to adopt the prosecutor's recommendation to indict (e.g., Bureau of Justice Statistics 2011).

the victims and public observers to hear the full story behind the charges" (Wright and Miller 2003, 1411). The same follows for what ultimately ends up in the signed plea agreement. As Wright and Miller (2003, 1411) note, "the public cannot tell the difference between reasonable and unreasonable charge bargains. Nobody can know after the fact which bargains are 'good' bargains, based on sound reasons, and which ones are 'bad' bargains, reflecting overcharging or sloppiness by the prosecutor or undue pressures created by dramatic plea/trial sentencing differentials" (1411). The nonpublic nature of the process can raise significant "doubts about fairness and equity in the justice system" (Shermer and Johnson 2010, 420).

As we learned from *Bordenkircher v. Hayes*, the charging/bargaining decisions of prosecutors are also almost completely *unreviewable* by the courts. There, the Supreme Court noted that "[i]n our system, so long as the prosecutor has probable cause to believe that the accused committed an offense defined by statute, the decision whether or not to prosecute, and what charge to file or bring before a grand jury, generally rests entirely in his discretion" (364). Other courts have echoed this sentiment:

- "[I]t is not the function of the courts to review the wisdom of the prosecutor's decision to investigate, or to inquire into the prosecutor's motives" (*LaRouche v. Webster*, 566 F. Supp. 415, 418 (S.D.N.Y. 1983)).
- "Of necessity, courts are reduced to expressing concern over the practice [of prosecutorial overcharging] and their inability to do anything about it" (*United States v. Robertson*, 15 F.3d 862, 876 (9th Cir. 1994)).
- "Few subjects are less adapted to judicial review than the exercise by the Executive of his discretion in deciding . . .what precise charge shall be made . . . To say that the United States Attorney must literally treat every offense and every offender alike is to delegate him an impossible task . . . Myriad factors can enter into the prosecutor's decision . . . No court has any jurisdiction to inquire into or review his decision" (*Newman v. United States*, 382 F.2d 479 (D.C. Cir. 1967)).

At the federal level, some attempts have been made to cabin prosecutorial discretion in the charging decision. The modern manual for U.S. Attorneys directs that "[o]nce the decision to prosecute has been made, the attorney for the government should charge and pursue the most serious, readily provable offenses. By definition, the most serious offenses are those that carry the most substantial guidelines sentence, including mandatory minimum sentences"

(§9-27.300). Prior prosecutorial guidance from the DOJ has provided a similar message. The original DOJ prosecution guidelines issued in 1980 read that "the attorney for the government should charge, or should recommend that the grand jury charge, the most serious offense that is consistent with the nature of the defendant's conduct, and that is likely to result in a sustainable conviction" (U.S. Department of Justice 1980). Policy memoranda issued by Attorneys General to federal prosecutors, including a 1989 memorandum from Attorney General Dick Thornburgh and a 2003 memorandum from Attorney General John Ashcroft, have continued to emphasize this prosecutorial language (Miller 2004, 1256).

While it may sound relatively simple and straightforward to charge "the most serious, readily provable offenses," the reality of most criminal prosecutions complicates matters for federal prosecutors. Indeed, it is quite likely that in many cases, no two federal prosecutors will interpret "the most serious, readily provable offenses" in quite the same way.

7.1.2 From Charge to Plea

Charging and plea bargaining are closely linked for prosecutors. Prosecutors seeking to offer plea agreements must have room to negotiate with the defendant. The initial charges brought by the prosecutor are the "asking price in plea bargaining, and the drafting of accusations is therefore an integral part of the negotiating process" (Alschuler 1968, 85). Federal prosecutors know from the moment they initiate a prosecution that the case will almost certainly resolve through a plea bargain. As such, they have "a powerful incentive to begin the inevitable negotiating process from a position of strength" (Caldwell 2011, 65). To do this, a prosecutor may multiply or stack the charges against a defendant or even charge "a single offense at a higher level than the circumstances of the case seem to warrant" (Alschuler 1968, 86).[2] This charging practice gives "the prosecutor added leverage in the plea bargaining process. Because of the threat of prosecution on such charges, defendants may be induced to plead guilty on more unfavorable terms than might otherwise be fair or reasonable. The risk of going to trial may simply become too great, even in cases in which the defendant may arguably be

[2] Alschuler (1968, 85) called the former practice of stacking charges "horizontal overcharging" and the latter practice of charging at a higher level "vertical overcharging."

innocent of some of the charges" (*United States v. Robertson*, 15 F.3d 862, 877 (9th Cir. 1994)). As the case proceeds, the prosecutor can present an offer to the defendant: the initial charges would be reduced and/or the prosecutor will recommend a lower sentence in the case than anticipated by the original charges in exchange for a guilty plea by the defendant. Prosecutors who have started from a "position of strength" in their initial charges are more likely to end up not only with a guilty plea, but one that takes a strong, tough-on-crime stance.

The *U.S. Attorneys' Manual* makes it clear that the DOJ permits federal prosecutors to manage their cases in this way:

> The attorney for the government may, in an appropriate case, enter into an agreement with a defendant that, upon the defendant's plea of guilty or nolo contendere to a charged offense or to a lesser or related offense, he/she will not bring or will move for dismissal of other charges, take a certain position with respect to the sentence to be imposed, or take other action. (§9-27.400)[3]

The comment to §9-27.400 cautions federal prosecutors to be neither too harsh nor too lenient in striking plea agreements: "Charges should not be filed simply to exert leverage to induce a plea; nor should charges be abandoned to arrive at a plea bargain that does not reflect the seriousness of the defendant's conduct."[4]

The vastness of prosecutorial charging and bargaining powers has not gone unnoticed. Justice Blackmun's dissent in *Bordenkircher v. Hayes* lamented the Court's sanctioning of "deliberate overcharging" and its "cynical view of the bargaining process." Years later in *Lafler v. Cooper*, 132 S. Ct. 1376, 1397 (2012), a dissenting Justice Scalia would argue that aggressive plea bargaining "presents grave risks of prosecutorial overcharging that effectively

[3] Similar detail on permissible plea bargaining by prosecutors is provided in Rule 11(c)(1) of the Federal Rules of Criminal Procedure.

[4] The DOJ distinguishes between three types of plea bargains: (1) charge bargaining, where the defendant agrees to plead guilty to a charged or lesser offense in exchange for the government dismissing other charges and not seeking additional charges; (2) sentence bargaining, where the agreement involves a guilty plea and the government seeking a specific sentence either within the United States Sentencing Commission's guideline range or through a departure; and (3) mixed agreements, which are a combination of charge and sentence bargaining. DOJ policies through the years have expressed a "strong preference for the use of charge bargains over sentence bargains" (Miller 2004, 1256), although "[t]he reasons for the Department's more permissive approach to charge bargaining are something of a mystery" (Nagel and Schulhofer 1992, 507).

compels an innocent defendant to avoid massive risk by pleading guilty to a lesser offense." Since "overcharging" is such a subjective term, even given DOJ guidance to prosecutors, it is virtually impossible to accurately measure how often it happens or whether it alters defendant behavior.

Many have also been critical of DOJ efforts to clarify prosecutorial bargaining and charging procedures, like the "most serious, readily provable offenses" language discussed earlier. These critics have argued that the content of the clarifications have been "ambivalent and inconsistent" (Nagel and Schulhofer 1992, 508), "general, malleable, and unhelpful" (Vorenberg 1981, 1544), contain significant loopholes (Nagel and Schulhofer 1992, 509), and "have accomplished little" (Stuntz 2004, 2567). On top of internal issues with the guidelines and memos, Nagel and Schulhofer (1992, 544) find that "some U.S. Attorneys are unfamiliar with guideline provisions, not committed to them, or both." Barkow (2009) has asserted that the sum of this has been a complete failure to constrain federal prosecutors' charging and bargaining decisions: "there are currently no effective legal checks in place to police the manner in which prosecutors exercise their discretion to bring charges, to negotiate pleas, or to set their office policies" (871).

7.1.3 The Dominance of Plea Bargaining

There is no question that federal and state prosecutors in the United States today rely heavily on plea bargaining to manage their criminal caseloads. As Justice Kennedy's majority opinion in 2012's *Lafler v. Cooper* put it, "criminal justice today is for the most part a system of pleas, not a system of trials."[5] The data increasingly bear this out, as illustrated in Figure 7.1. The figure plots the rate of guilty pleas for defendants in federal district courts across the United States from 1963 to 2017. It displays an uptick in the percentage of criminal defendants who plead guilty starting in the early 1980s, when plea rates were lower than 65%. By the late 1990s and early 2000s, the plea rates had plateaued at nearly 90% for defendants.

An abundance of criminal cases filed by prosecutors led to the genesis of plea bargaining. After the U.S. Civil War, prosecutors were charging "far more persons with criminal offenses than U.S. judges and juries could

[5] Settlements similarly dominate outcomes in civil litigation in the U.S. today (Boyd 2013; Boyd and Hoffman 2013; Galanter 2004).

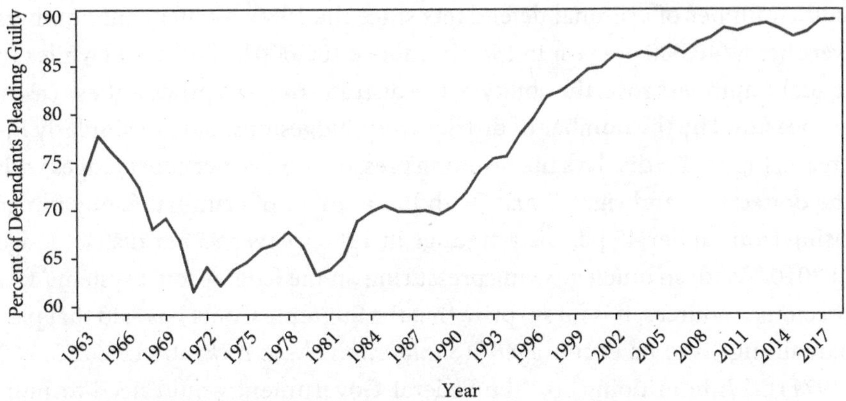

Figure 7.1 Nationwide federal district court guilty plea rate for defendants, by year. Sources: Administrative Office of the U.S. Courts. Judicial Business of the United States Courts and Federal Offenders in the United States District Courts.

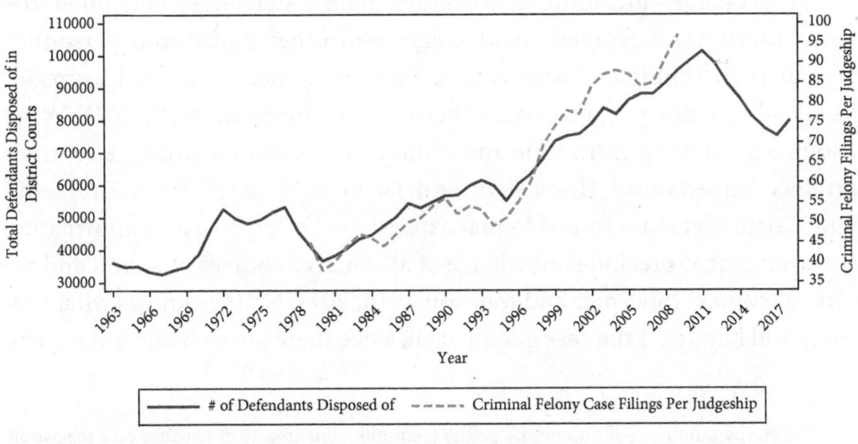

Figure 7.2 Number of defendants disposed of (left side Y-axis) and average number of criminal felony case filings per judgeship (right side Y-axis) in federal district courts by year. Sources: Administrative Office of the U.S. Courts. Judicial Business of the United States Courts, Federal Offenders in the United States District Courts, and Federal Court Management Statistics.

possibly handle. To deal with this overload, prosecutors increasingly offered criminal defendants the opportunity to plead to lesser charges, and the 'plea bargain' was born" (Rakoff 2017, 1430). As Figure 7.2 indicates with the solid black line and left Y-axis, the federal district courts have seen a steady rise in the number of criminal defendants since the 1980s—defendant numbers were below 40,000 per year in 1980 but above 100,000 by 2011. And while defendant numbers rose, the ability of the district courts to process these cases, as measured by the number of district court judgeships, did not similarly increase. Figure 7.2 displays the resulting pressure on district court judges with the dotted line and right Y-axis, with the number of criminal felony filings rising from under 45 per district judge in 1980 to over 95 per district judge in 2010.[6] With so much growing pressuring on the federal court systems' few precious resources, it is no surprise that the Supreme Court has said that plea bargaining "is to be encouraged" (*Santobello v. New York*, 404 U.S. 257, 260 (1971)). Without doing so, "the Federal Government would need to multiply by many times the number of judges and court facilities" (*Santobello v. New York*, 404 U.S. 257, 260 (1971)).

Caseload considerations are just one of many factors that help to incentivize plea bargaining over trials for all actors involved in criminal case processing—including prosecutors, public defenders and other defense attorneys, defendants, and judges and other courtroom personnel. For all such criminal justice actors, there is a "near universal aversion" to allowing cases to go to trial (Shermer and Johnson 2010, 402). Why? Along with costing extra time and money, "more than anything else, trials produce uncertainty" (Eisenstein and Jacob 1977, 27).[7] Prosecutors and public defenders "are forced to make decisions under time and information constraints that preclude knowledge of alternative courses of action and future outcomes" (Shermer and Johnson 2010, 401). Neither knows what precisely will happen if the case goes to trial, since there are so many unknowns.

[6] Data on the number of filings per judgeship are limited due to a 1979 law that gave magistrate judges a great deal of authority to decide criminal misdemeanors. In 2010, federal data collection on criminal felony filings switched from case level to defendant level, meaning that the data pre- and post-2010 are not comparable.

[7] Without a doubt, the attractiveness of plea bargains is complicated for many defendants. Defendants often accept plea bargains without a complete understanding about the serious consequences of doing so. As Chin and Holmes (2002) note, the ramifications of a plea beyond any prison or probation sentence include:

> By virtue of the conviction, the offender may become ineligible for federally funded health care benefits, food stamps and Temporary Assistance for Needy Families, and housing assistance. She is ineligible for federal educational aid. Her driver's license will probably be suspended and she will be ineligible to enlist in the military, receive a security clearance, or possess a firearm. If an alien, she will be deported; if a citizen, she will be ineligible to serve on a federal jury and in some states will lose her right to vote.

Many worry that with the deck stacked against them—poor, racial and ethnic minorities, low education, and with an overburdened public defender as their only legal advocate—defendants are essentially coerced into pleading guilty (Butler 2013; Caldwell 2011).

Who will be selected on the jury? How will prospective witnesses perform in open court? How will the evidence be received by the jury? All of this "uncertainty leads them to search for satisfactory rather than optimal solutions in their decision-making" (Shermer and Johnson 2010, 401). Contrary to trials, many pleas are entered with "a tacit understanding of the likely sentence or with an informal indication by the judge as to the probable sentence" (Mather 1979, 55).

For prosecutors, plea bargaining serves as an efficient and effective way to achieve their goal of obtaining a high rate of convictions. Prosecutors "may further their careers by racking up good win-loss records, in which every plea bargain counts as a win, but trials risk being losses. The statistic of conviction, in other words, matters much more than the sentence. Favorable win-loss statistics boost prosecutors' egos, their esteem, their praise by colleagues, and their prospects for promotion and career advancement. Thus, prosecutors may prefer the certainty of plea bargains" (Bibas 2004, 2471).

7.1.4 Room for Disparity

Not all plea bargains are created equal. With vast discretion to charge cases and craft plea agreements, prosecutors are well-positioned to gain convictions and achieve their other goals. As discussed above, there is little to nothing that constrains federal prosecutors' charging and bargaining decisions or guarantees uniformity in those decisions across prosecutors, offices, cases, and time. As Holmes, Daudistel, and Farrell (1987, 236) put it, "plea bargaining . . . is by nature subject to a substantial element of caprice. Because such negotiations are not ruled by the degree of due process characteristic of more formal proceedings, there is little to prevent status influences from informally entering into them in ways that formally are considered illegitimate." The result is the very real possibility that two defendants, with nearly identical case files including underlying criminal activity and prior criminal history, are treated differently by the system. One defendant may be charged with fewer and less severe crimes and even have some of those charges dropped in the negotiation of the plea agreement. The other defendant may be charged much more harshly, with a much more severe and varied indictment. And on the road to negotiating a plea agreement, that second defendant may have few or none of his initial charges dropped.

This is much more than a hypothetical. Prior research on charging and bargaining indicates that defendants' cases are frequently treated differently during this process, with the differences aligning with measurable defendant characteristics. This includes findings that defendant gender (Farnworth and Teske 1995; Shermer and Johnson 2010) and race (Bernstein et al. 1977; Hartley, Maddan, and Spohn 2007; LaFree 1980; Metcalfe and Chiricos 2018) can affect what initial charges are brought and whether prosecutors offer charge reductions or departures. And, as Spohn and Fornango (2009) find, even after accounting for differences in defendant and case characteristics, interprosecutorial differences in behavior still remain.

The different treatment of otherwise similar cases and defendants presents the potential for disturbing ramifications. When "the same criminal conduct as defined by the statute . . . [is] prosecuted differently based on factors quite divorced from the crime in question," it implies that "the defendant is being punished less for the crime than for these other factors" (Pizzi 1978, 273). The results can be far reaching, including posing "obstacles to achieving consistency and uniformity in sentencing" (Hartley, Maddan, and Spohn 2007, 387) and affecting the political and social legitimacy of the criminal justice system (Shermer and Johnson 2010; Wright and Miller 2003).

Not surprisingly, findings like these about defendant characteristic effects during the charging and bargaining process have led to a call to "future researchers . . . [to] address the importance of decision making at different stages of the criminal justice process to expose areas of potential unwarranted disparity or unfairness so that policy makers can act accordingly" (Wilmot and Spohn 2004, 340). In what follows, we take up this call by exploring how political signals may lead federal prosecutors to treat their prosecuted cases differently from one another.

7.2 What (Political) Prosecutors Want Out of Charging and Bargaining

The discretionary charging and bargaining process that proceeds plea agreements provides opportunities for prosecutors to achieve their political goals. As we have argued consistently in this book, federal prosecutors are likely to look for opportunities throughout their work to respond to their political principals and local public. We expect this to translate to charging and bargaining decisions just as it did with the earlier prosecution-declination stage. Because of this focus on responsiveness, when federal prosecutors receive political signals that a particular type of crime is a priority, they will treat those cases more seriously and harshly than other cases.

At this charging and bargaining stage of a case, we expect that "treating these cases more seriously" means working toward obtaining the harshest sentence possible for a defendant while still getting a conviction. As we have discussed, prosecutors can craft their initial charges and offer plea deals that vary in their generosity. The prosecutorial discretion that characterizes this stage of case processing positions prosecutors well to be selectively aggressive. "[P]ressures and incentives . . . vary depending on the case, the lawyer, and the particular prosecutor's office policies. Prosecutors offer less favorable pleas in strong, high-profile cases than in comparable low-profile cases" (Bibas 2004, 2474).

Responding to political signals on crime also means that prosecutors will prioritize limited prosecutorial time and resources to focus more on these cases of political interest and importance. Burke (2007) puts it like this: "Prosecutors cannot, of course, always indulge their prosecutorial pride. To maximize limited resources, they must prioritize the most important cases throughout each level of their decision making, using discretion to determine which cases warrant charges, which should be plea bargained and under what terms, which should be tried, and, in some instances, which should be dismissed altogether" (188). Anecdotal evidence confirms that this is exactly what happens in prosecutors' offices. A Utah prosecutor was once quoted as saying that the decisions in his office "are being made on economics rather than on what is a just outcome" (Gibeaut 2004). An Oregon prosecutor echoed the same sentiment, noting that they "had to make some awful choices . . . I pleaded out as many nonviolent felonies as I could. You kind of had to hold your nose" (Gibeaut 2004).

We examine two key ways that prosecutors may use charging and bargaining to achieve their goal to treat political priority cases more seriously than other cases: (1) through the likelihood of charge reductions offered by prosecutors during the bargaining leading up to a plea agreement and (2) through prosecutors' willingness to offer discretionary downward sentencing departures in cases.

We begin first with a discussion of considerations relating to offering charge reductions to a defendant.

7.2.1 Charge Reductions

As we know, charge reductions, through the dismissal of individual charges or the replacement of a higher charge with a lower one, are a key way that prosecutors provide "discounts" to defendants willing to plead guilty. These negotiated charge reductions have real impacts on defendants. Shermer and Johnson's (2010) study of federal prosecutorial charge reductions finds that, when present, charge reductions lower sentence lengths by around 20%. This means that a five-year sentence becomes just four years. Other scholars confirm this empirical effect on outcomes for defendants, with Holmes, Daudistel, and Farrell (1987) finding that "[d]efendants receiving reductions . . . received more favorable dispositions" (245) and Piehl and Bushway (2007) arguing that "charge bargaining plays an important role in determining sentencing outcomes" (122).

Graham (2012)'s descriptive examination of federal prosecutors' offices charge reduction behavior from 2003–2009 reveals wide variation across the country. Graham finds substantial differences across the federal districts when comparing how often pled cases retain the most serious charging offense, with some districts retaining at average rates over 95% and a few others retaining, on the low end, below 70%. This observed variation calls for more in-depth inquiry on the causes. In particular, are differences related to prosecutors and political priorities?

There is certainly reason to believe that this might be the case since, as Wright and Engen (2006) argue, "[p]rosecutorial choice is likely to explain a larger part of the charge movement" (1948). Scholars studying charge reductions found notable disparities in treatment across defendants and cases. Shermer and Johnson's (2010) study of U.S. Attorneys and their cases terminated in 2001 found that defendant gender affects charge reductions, with male defendants being less likely than female defendants to have their initial charges reduced. Recent work by Metcalfe and Chiricos (2018) also finds that Black males are significantly less likely to receive charge reductions than white males and white and Black female defendants. Beyond just defendant characteristics, Spohn and Spears (1996) reveal that charge reductions are more likely in less serious and less salient cases (in their study, that is white on white sex assaults).

While we know of no empirical scholarship that examines how political responsiveness affects charge reduction choices by prosecutors, the leap is a small one to make given the above research. For prosecutors there may be "less political risk in reducing initial charges" for certain offenders (Shermer and Johnson 2010, 404–405) because of the nature of the offense or because those charges "conflict with local norms" (Wright and Engen 2006, 1948). However, for other cases, political priorities may necessitate a tough stance on crime, meaning that they will be "particularly unlikely to receive favorable charging treatment from U.S. Attorneys" (Shermer and Johnson 2010, 404–405).

With substantial charging and bargaining discretion, federal prosecutors are likely to seize on charge reductions as an opportunity to respond to the preferences of their political principals, as needed. In particular, when those principals want "tough" treatment of a crime area, we should see less willingness to reduce charges on the road to plea bargains than for other cases. Within our study, we expect that the more the president, Congress, and the local public signal that a crime area is a high priority, federal prosecutors will respond by being less likely to offer charge reductions.

7.2.2 Substantial Assistance Departures

In addition to using charge reductions, federal prosecutors may use other discretionary charging decisions, like requesting departures from the sentencing guidelines, to cement their prioritization of certain types of criminal cases given the political environment that they serve in. One type of departure to the federal sentencing guidelines, the substantial assistance departure, is particularly well-suited to this task.

Departures for substantial assistance, commonly referred to as the §5K1.1 departure because of their location in the federal sentencing guidelines, provide a sentencing discount to defendants who have "provided substantial assistance in the investigation or prosecution of another person who has committed an offense" (Guidelines §5K1.1). Substantial assistance downward departures may only occur "upon motion of the government" (Guidelines §5K1.1)—that is, when the federal prosecutor has requested it of the sentencing judge. In 2017, §5K1.1 substantial assistance departures were granted in drug, robbery, firearm, larceny, fraud, embezzlement, forgery, and immigration cases, among others (USSC 2017, Table 10). When granted, a substantial assistance departure motion substantially affects sentence severity (Kramer and Ulmer 2002), including through the removal of "the mandatory minimum sentence that otherwise would be binding at sentencing" (Hartley, Maddan, and Spohn 2007, 385).

Our common theme of prosecutorial discretion continues with substantial assistance departure motions coming from federal prosecutors. What does *substantial* assistance mean? The Guidelines and *U.S. Attorneys' Manual* provide little-to-no specifics. As Maxfield and Kramer (1998, 3) put it, "[w]hat objective and equitable parameters distinguish between 'substantial' assistance and 'non-substantial' assistance?" The reality is that under this standard, a prosecutor can find one defendant's "assistance" to be substantial while another defendant's, who provides the same exact "assistance," is not considered to be substantial. This §5K1.1 decision unilaterally belongs to the federal prosecutors, meaning it is "not subject to challenge by the defense and is [generally] not reviewable by the court" (Maxfield and Kramer 1998, 3).

It will come as no surprise, then, that scholars have found disparities in the likelihood of substantial assistance departures being provided. A 2003 U.S. Government Accountability Office (GAO) study found a great deal of variation across federal districts in how often substantial assistance departures were provided (U.S. General Accounting Office 2003).[8] This would be confirmed by Hartley, Maddan, and Spohn (2007) in their study of federal sentencing of defendants for cocaine-related offenses in 2000 and Johnson, Ulmer, and Kramer (2008) in their research on 1997–2000 federal sentencing across multiple crime categories. Other work has found that individual defendants' chances of getting these departures is affected by race and sex, among other things (Hartley, Maddan, and Spohn 2007; Johnson and Betsinger 2009; Kramer and Ulmer 2002; Mustard 2001). In short, the research findings in this area "provide evidence that federal prosecutors' discretion surrounding substantial assistance departures is at least as important a locus of individual disparity and between-district variation as judicial discretion" (Ulmer 2012, 23).

We expect that federal prosecutors will use motions for substantial assistance departures to achieve their political goals. We anticipate that fewer such departures will be offered by prosecutors for high political priority crime areas since they represent discretionary leniency being offered to some defendants. As such, we expect that when the president, Congress, and the local public signal that a crime area is a high priority, federal prosecutors will

[8] The U.S. General Accounting Office was renamed the U.S. Government Accountability Office in 2004.

be less likely to offer substantial assistance departures in cases than for other similarly situated cases that do not receive political priority signals.

7.3 Data

To empirically examine the effects of political factors on the likelihood that federal prosecutors offer charge reductions and substantial assistance departures, we utilize two distinct data sources and introduce two new dependent variables. As was the case with Chapter 6, we continue to focus exclusively on violent crime cases for both analyses in this chapter.

7.3.1 Data on Charge Reductions

First, for our study of charge reductions we utilize violent crime-specific data retrieved from the DOJ's internal case tracking database LIONS that was previously used and discussed in Chapter 6. For this chapter's analysis, the data are organized so that the individual charge is the unit of analysis. Our resulting data include 331,678 charges associated with 85,773 defendants who pled guilty in cases identified as being part of the violent crime prosecutorial program by the DOJ. We again combine these DOJ data with variables tracking the priorities and public signals of the prosecutor's political principals (the president, Congress, and local public) as well as a number of control variables. We analyze individual charge outcomes among defendants whose cases were disposed of from 1996 to 2013 across 89 districts.[9]

The dependent variable in our model is Charge Dismissed that captures whether an individual charge is dismissed against a defendant who pleads guilty.[10] *Charge Dismissed* takes the value of 1 when the charge is dismissed and 0 when the defendant pleads guilty to the charge.[11] Just under half of the charges in our data are dismissed pre-plea bargain.

[9] We once again exclude U.S. Attorney offices in the District of Columbia, Puerto Rico, Guam and the Northern Mariana Islands, and the U.S. Virgin Islands.

[10] To borrow the terminology used by Alschuler (1968), our data allow us to assess horizontal charge reductions—i.e., those where a charge is dismissed leading to a plea bargain. We leave it to future research to tackle vertical charge reductions where a higher individual charge is replaced by a lower one. Current data limitations make the empirical study of vertical charge reductions exceptionally complex.

[11] To examine the ability of prosecutors to reduce sentences through charge dismissals, we include only those defendants who were ever charged with two or more offenses. We also exclude all

The independent variables and our expectations about their effects are consistent with Chapters 5 and 6. First, we model the influence of presidential attention to violent crime through *Presidential Rhetoric*, which is the number of sentences relating to violent crime per 100 public presidential statements each month. We also include *Congressional Hearings*, which tracks the percentage of hearings on topics involving violent crime in a given month. Both of these variables are lagged by a single month to ensure proper temporal ordering. We include a measure of *Local Public Opinion* using a question from the General Social Survey capturing the percentage of respondents who indicate that "too little" is being spent to "halt the rising crime rate." *Local Punitiveness* toward criminal offenders tracks the number of incarcerated inmates in state-run prison facilities per 100,000 residents for each state-year. And to account for the prevalence of violent crime in the prosecutor's community, we include the *State Violent Crime Rate*, which is the number of violent crimes for every state-year per 100,000 residents as reported by the Uniform Crime Reports. Across all five political variables, we anticipate that as a prosecutor's principals and local public become more concerned with violent crime (or become more inclined toward punishment), we will be less likely to see dismissal of charges. Summary statistics and hypothesized effects for these independent variables, along with our control variables, are displayed in the Chapter Data Appendix.

In order to account for the substantive nature of each charge in the bargaining process we control for the *Charge Severity* for every count. This variable measures the average base offense level assigned for that offense in the U.S. Sentencing Commission's Offender Datafile.[12] The base offense level is the starting point for calculations under the federal sentencing guidelines and ranges from 1 (least severe) to 43 (most severe) (U.S. Sentencing Commission 2018). As detailed earlier, federal prosecutors who are prone to engage in vigorous charging and bargaining behavior may seek leverage by

defendants who went to trial or had charges dismissed upon the discretion of the judge for some or all of the charges against them. In these cases, the charge bargaining process is likely to be substantially influenced by the choice to go to trial or the rejection of charges by the court. As such, we leave it to future research to further explore these more complicated matters.

[12] To provide stability in our measure of severity, we utilize the average base offense level from a single year: fiscal year 2006. Doing so guards against the statistical noise created by base offense levels changing from year to year as sentencing guidelines are revised and effectively mutes case-specific factual circumstances that can affect base offense levels (U.S. Sentencing Commission 2018). We exclude observations from the LIONS data where no *Charge Severity* measure can be created. This generally occurs for statutes associated with the forfeiture of assets, probation/supervised release, or penalty provisions.

charging serious offenses and then offering to dismiss them later in exchange for defendant agreements to plead guilty to lesser offenses. Consequently, we expect that charges that are more severe will have a higher likelihood of being dismissed to achieve greater control during plea negotiations.

We also continue to include the set of control variables introduced in Chapter 6: *Staff Workload* (total number of civil and criminal matters pending in a given U.S. Attorney office in a year divided by the number of Assistant U.S. Attorneys in that office), *Republican U.S. Attorney* (political preferences of the district's U.S. Attorney measured by the party of the appointing president), *District Court Conservatism* (political leanings of the judges in the relevant federal district court), *Acting Attorney General* (Acting Attorney General leading the DOJ instead of a Senate-confirmed Attorney General), and *District Fixed Effects.*

7.3.2 Data on Substantial Assistance Departures

For our assessment of the provision of substantial assistance departures, we examine individual violent crime offenders and whether they were given a substantial assistance departure in their sentencing based on a request from the prosecution during fiscal years 1997 to 2011. Our dependent variable is thus *Substantial Assistance Departure.* This dichotomous variable is coded as 1 if a defendant receives a downward departure and 0 if the defendant did not receive such a departure. To code *Substantial Assistance Departure,* we utilize the U.S. Sentencing Commission's (USSC) yearly individual offender data. The USSC data include the conviction and sentencing information, along with personal characteristics, of federal offenders. We code a defendant as receiving a *Substantial Assistance Departure* if the USSC data reflects that either reason 1 or reason 2 for a sentencing departure is due to §5K1.1 substantial assistance with the presence of a government motion.

We again use our five standard independent variables related to the expected effects of political (presidential, congressional, public) factors on substantial assistance departure practices. This includes *Presidential Rhetoric, Congressional Hearings, Local Public Opinion: Violent, Local Punitiveness* toward criminal offenders, and *State Crime Rate.*

We continue to control for *Staff Workload, Republican U.S. Attorney, District Court Conservatism,* and *Acting Attorney General.* Additionally, with the aid of the USSC data, we control for offender-specific factors that frequently affect sentencing: race, gender, and criminal history. *Female Offender* is coded as 1 if the sentenced offender is a female, 0 if male. *African American Offender* is coded as 1 if the sentenced offender's race is recorded as Black/African American by the USSC and 0 if race is White/Caucasian. *Low Criminal History* accounts for the offender's criminal history and is coded as 1 if the offender has a final criminal history category of I and 0 if the offender's final criminal history category is II through VI. An offender's criminal history category is assigned by the sentencing judge based on prior convictions and other sentencing guidelines' instructions. Each of these variables' summary statistics and hypothesized effects are further detailed in the Chapter Data Appendix.

7.4 Charge Reduction Results

To test the influence of a federal prosecutor's political environment on her charge bargaining behavior, we estimate a logistic regression model with robust standard errors clustered on the defendant and a linear time trend that counts the number of years that have passed in the data. Recall that we anticipate that when political principals want "tough" treatment of violent crime, we should see less eagerness among prosecutors to reduce charges than in other cases. The results of our statistical estimation are displayed in Table 7.1. Two of our five political variables have statistically significant effects on *Charge Dismissed: Presidential Rhetoric* and *Violent Crime Rate*. We turn now to a more in-depth discussion of each.

As the results in Table 7.1 indicate, presidential signals about violent crime provided to U.S. Attorneys affect behavior in this arena. *Presidential Rhetoric* has a negative and statistically significant effect, as anticipated. Figure 7.3 plots the substantive effects of presidential rhetoric on charge reduction behavior. As it shows, over the range of presidential rhetoric values, the decline in probability of reducing a charge is nearly 0.08. In other words, when the president sends a message that he prioritizes a tough stance on violent crime, federal prosecutors respond by being less likely to reduce a defendant's charges.

We see a similar trend when it comes to the substantive effects for the other statistically significant political variable: *Violent Crime Rate*. Figure 7.4 plots the effects. As the figure indicates, there is a sizable drop in the likelihood of dropping charges against a defendant for federal prosecutors located

Table 7.1 Logistic regression estimates for whether a charge is dismissed.

	Coefficient	RSE
Presidential Rhetoric	−0.001*	(0.000)
Congressional Hearings	0.002	(0.017)
Local Public Opinion	−0.001	(0.001)
Local Punitiveness	−0.000	(0.000)
Violent Crime Rate	−0.001*	(0.000)
Staff Workload	0.005*	(0.002)
Republican U.S. Attorney	0.043*	(0.018)
District Court Conservatism	−0.306*	(0.049)
Acting Attorney General	0.062	(0.061)
Charge Severity	0.007*	(0.001)
Time Trend	−0.029*	(0.003)
District Fixed Effects	Included	
Constant	0.761*	(0.201)
Observations	331,678	

Defendant clustered robust standard errors (RSEs) are included in parentheses. * Significant at $p < 0.05$.

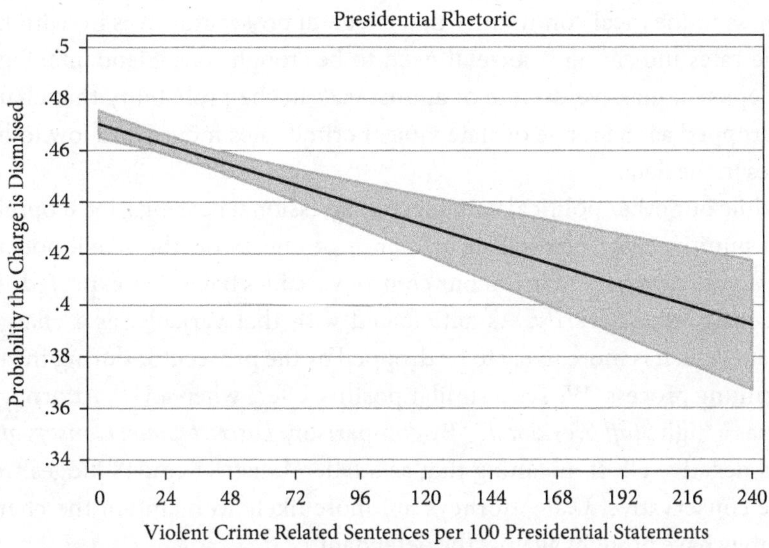

Figure 7.3 Estimated marginal effects of a defendant receiving a charge reduction given the changing values of presidential rhetoric.

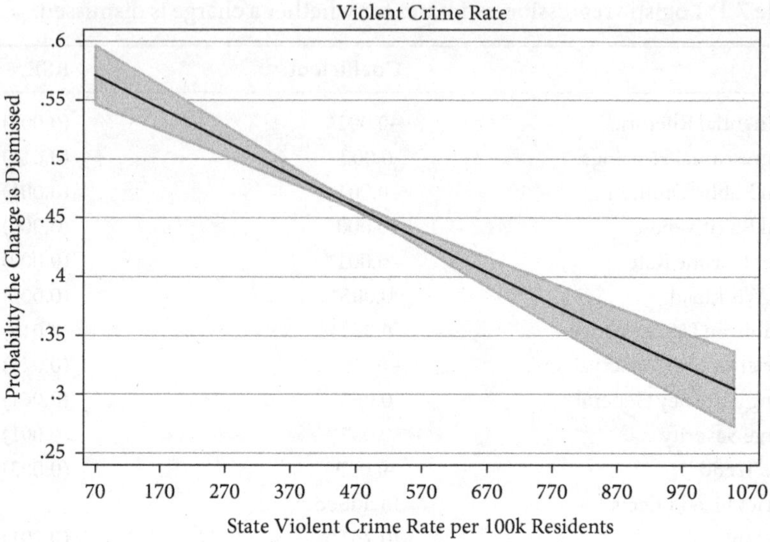

Figure 7.4 Estimated marginal effects of a defendant receiving a charge reduction given the changing values of state violent crime rate.

in states with higher rates of violent crime. We think that this is again responsiveness to the local community that a federal prosecutor lives in, with high crime rates indicating a societal need to be "tough" on defendants. Figure 7.4 depicts a massive decline of almost 0.27 in the probability that charges are dropped as the range of state violent crime rates move from low to high values in the data.

While our other political variables (congressional hearings, local opinion, local punitiveness) provide no evidence of effects on the likelihood that charges are dropped, many of our control variables behave as expected. This includes *Charge Severity*. As anticipated with that variable, as a charge is more severe, it is more likely to be dropped by the prosecutor during the plea bargaining process. We see a similar positive effect when a U.S. Attorney office has a high *Staff Workload*.[13] By comparison, *District Court Conservatism* has a negative effect, meaning that as a federal district court's judges trend more conservative, U.S. Attorneys are more likely to maintain the charges that they have brought against the defendant.

[13] While the *Republican U.S. Attorney* variable has a surprising positive effect on *Charge Dismissed*, that effect is substantively equivalent to 0 at +0.01 in the probability of charges being dropped.

Table 7.2 Logistic regression estimates for whether a defendant receives a Substantial Assistance Departure.

	Coefficient	RSE
Presidential Rhetoric	0.001	(0.00)
Congressional Hearings	−0.285*	(0.13)
Local Public Opinion: Violent Crime	0.009	(0.02)
Local Punitiveness	−0.003*	(0.00)
State Crime Rate	0.001	(0.00)
Staff Workload	−0.018	(0.02)
District Court Conservatism	−0.210	(0.32)
Republican U.S. Attorney	0.213	(0.18)
Acting Attorney General	−0.122	(0.14)
African American Offender	0.433*	(0.19)
Female Offender	0.294	(0.24)
Low Criminal History	−0.086	(0.16)
Time Trend	0.009	(0.03)
Constant	-1.974	(1.14)
Observations	261,419	

District clustered robust standard errors (RSEs) are included in parentheses. * Significant at $p < 0.05$.

7.5 Substantial Assistance Departure Results

While our results indicate that political responsiveness affects charge reduction behavior, does the same hold for when prosecutors offer substantial assistance departures to defendants? To test this, we estimate a logistic regression model of the effects on whether a defendant receives a *Substantial Assistance Departure.* To account for panel effects, we use robust standard errors clustered on the district and control for time via a linear trend that counts the number of years. The regression results are provided in Table 7.2. We again see that two of our five political variables have statistically significant effects on *Substantial Assistance Departures: Congressional Hearings* and *Local Punitiveness.*

As Table 7.2 indicates, *Congressional Hearings* have the expected negative effect on whether prosecutors offer a substantial assistance departure to a defendant. In Figure 7.5, we plot the corresponding substantive effect that congressional hearings have. As Congress prioritizes the fight against violent crime, prosecutors hear the message and avoid providing an excess of these lenient deals that result in lower sentences for defendants. Across the range

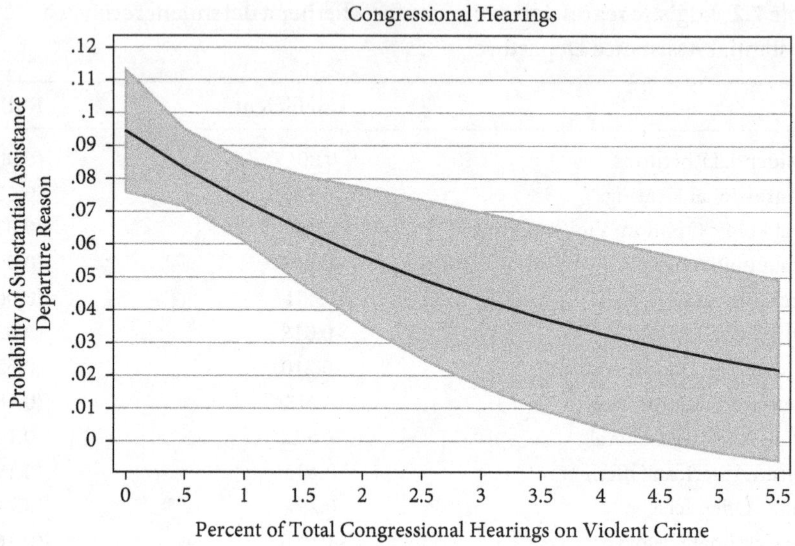

Figure 7.5 Estimated marginal effects of a defendant receiving a substantial assistance departure given the changing values of congressional hearings.

of values for congressional hearings, the drop in the probability of a substantial assistance departure is over 0.07.

Interestingly, we do not see a similar effect for *Presidential Rhetoric* when it comes to substantial assistance departures. What might explain the differences between congressional and presidential signals in this arena? While future research is needed to know with certainty, we suspect that one possible answer lies with the close connection between substantial assistance departures, the sentencing guidelines, and Congress. More so than most things that we have discussed and observed about federal prosecutors, substantial assistance departures are a creature of Congress and not the president. In the 1986 Anti-Drug Abuse Act, Congress directed the U.S. Sentencing Commission to create a downward sentence departure for offenders who assist in the prosecution or investigation of other criminal offenders (Maxfield and Kramer 1998). As directed, the Commission added the §5K1.1 departure to the sentencing guidelines.

The other political factor that has a notable effect on *Substantial Assistance Departure* is *Local Punitiveness.* As expected, as a state's imprisonment rate goes up, a sign of its growing punitiveness, we see less leniency from federal prosecutors in the corresponding district in handing out these discretionary

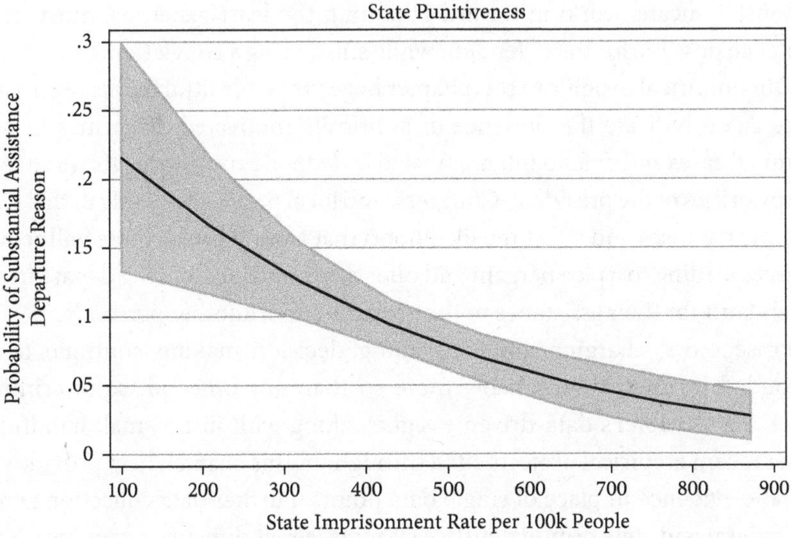

Figure 7.6 Estimated marginal effects of a defendant receiving a substantial assistance departure given the changing values of state punitiveness (measured via state imprisonment rate).

downward departures. Figure 7.6 highlights the notable size of this effect: an over 0.20 decrease in the probability of providing a substantial assistance departure as state punitiveness moves from its minimum to maximum values.

7.6 Discussion

We began this chapter with a discussion of the famous *Bordenkircher v. Hayes* case, where the Supreme Court signed off on the constitutionality of prosecutors' highly discretionary and largely invisible and unchecked role in the bargaining process. With so much discretion and unreviewable power during this stage of decision-making, we suspected that federal prosecutors were likely to again be responsive to their political principals and local forces when shaping their charging and bargaining behavior. In particular, we expected that federal prosecutors would treat certain cases more harshly and seriously than others in the lead-up to striking plea deals with defendants. This differential behavior would be driven, at least in part, by the presence of signals from relevant political forces. We have argued that "treating these cases more seriously" means working toward obtaining the least generous, most harsh sentence possible for the defendant while still getting a conviction.

Our empirical insights in this chapter have proved fruitful in this regard and once again indicate the presence of politically motivated disparities in how criminal cases and defendants are treated by federal prosecutors. As we've seen, the priorities of the president, Congress, and local public play a role in this stage of criminal cases and affect the likelihood that federal prosecutors will reduce charges leading to a plea bargain and offer downward sentencing departures to defendants for their assistance in the prosecution of another person.

Prosecutors' charging and bargaining decision-making continue to be shrouded in mystery—probably more so than any other phase of criminal cases. This chapter's data-driven insights, along with just a small handful of other recent empirical projects cited throughout this chapter, help provide systematic evidence in place of single data points. Further data collection across the federal and state criminal justice systems, albeit difficult to conduct, is essential to our continued efforts to understand these prosecutorial decisions. We turn now to our final empirical inquiry into the politics of prosecutorial decision-making: criminal asset forfeitures.

Chapter 7 Data Appendix

Table 7.3 Expected direction of effects and summary statistics for dependent and key independent variables for charge dismissal modeling.

	Expected Direction	Mean	Standard Deviation	Range
Charge Dismissed		0.46	0.50	0–1
Presidential Rhetoric	–	30.34	38.91	0–240.60
Congressional Hearings	–	0.20	0.53	0–5.56
Local Public Opinion	–	60.26	6.29	40.54–81
Local Punitiveness	–	439.40	132.72	100–886
State Violent Crime Rate	–	462.66	164.87	66.90–1051
Staff Workload	+	18.65	8.00	7.72–95.89
Republican U.S. Attorney	–	0.55	0.50	0–1
District Court Conservatism	–	0.08	0.28	-0.52-0.60
Acting Attorney General	+	0.02	0.13	0–1
Charge Severity	–	20.03	6.68	4–43
Time Trend	–	9.35	4.75	0–17

Table 7.4 Expected direction of effects and summary statistics for dependent and key independent variables for substantial assistance departure modeling.

	Expected Direction	Mean	Standard Deviation	Range
Substantial Assistance Departure		0.09	0.29	0–1
Presidential Rhetoric	–	33.43	44.84	0–240.60
Congressional Hearings	–	0.18	0.51	0–5.56
Local Public Opinion: Violent Crime	–	59.70	7.29	40.54–81
Local Punitiveness	–	466.49	153.58	100–886
State Crime Rate	–	384.10	110.53	103.7–903.2
Staff Workload	–	19.94	8.19	7.72–95.89
District Court Conservatism	–	0.10	0.29	–0.52–0.60
Republican U.S. Attorney	–	0.59	0.49	0–1
Acting Attorney General	–	0.02	0.13	0–1
African American Offender	–	0.40	0.49	0–1
Female Offender	+	0.13	0.34	0–1
Low Criminal History	+	0.38	0.49	0–1
Time Trend	–	8.27	4.45	0–15

8
Criminal Asset Forfeiture as a Political Tool?

In 2008, Daniel Carpenter was convicted by a jury in the District of Massachusetts federal trial court for 19 counts of mail and wire fraud. In the events leading to his conviction, Carpenter had convinced investment clients to mail and wire large funds to his business with a pledge that they would earn between 3% to 6% in escrow account interest. Instead of doing as promised, however, Carpenter used client funds to "trade high-risk stock options" (Brief for the United States 2019, 7). Despite significant losses, Carpenter, over a two-year period, continued to use "the same false and misleading marketing materials" to solicit new clients and acquire additional funds from existing clients (Brief for the United States 2019, 11). All told, Carpenter's victims lost around $9 million.

Following his trial and conviction, Carpenter was sentenced to three years of imprisonment and three additional years of supervised release and was required to pay $310,033.96 in restitution to the victims and an additional fine of $100,000 (*United States v. Carpenter*, 1:04-cr-10029 (D. Mass.)). In addition to the prison sentence, restitution, and a fine, however, the United States Government also asked the district court judge to order a $14,053,715.52 seizure of Carpenter's criminal property through a legal process called criminal forfeiture. The court agreed.

In appealing to the U.S. Court of Appeals for the 1st Circuit, Carpenter argued that the forfeiture order violated multiple provisions of the U.S. Constitution, including the Excessive Fines Clause of the Eighth Amendment. The appellate court panel was convinced that the district judge's forfeiture order was not grossly disproportional to the seriousness of Carpenter's offense.[1] In reaching this conclusion, the 1st Circuit noted that

[1] The "grossly disproportional" standard was created by the U.S. Supreme Court in *United States v. Bajakajian*, 524 U.S. 321 (1998), for determinations of forfeiture-based Eighth Amendment Excessive Fines violations.

The Politics of Federal Prosecution. Christina L. Boyd, Michael J. Nelson, Ian Ostrander, and Ethan D. Boldt, Oxford University Press (2021).
DOI: 10.1093/oso/9780197554685.003.0008

the governing statute, 18 U.S.C. §3571(d), authorized fines up to twice the financial gross loss suffered—in other words, $18 million in this case. Since it agreed that "judgments about the appropriate punishment for an offense belong in the first instance to the legislature" (*United States v. Bajakajian*), Carpenter's appellate court gave "great weight" to Congress's "statutory judgment" that a forfeiture order with monetary value of up to $18 million would be proportional punishment for a criminal conviction of this type (*United States v. Carpenter*, 941 F. 3d 1, 11 (1st Circ. 2019)).

Having secured a prison sentence and hefty restitution and fines for the defendant, why did Carpenter's prosecutor also request a forfeiture of over $14 million? The answer was addressed by Carpenter's appellate court when it noted that forfeiture orders like this "go beyond disgorgement of profits" (10). Rather, they "help to ensure that crime does not pay: [t]hey at once punish wrong doing, deter future illegality, and 'lessen the economic power' of criminal enterprises" (*United States v. Carpenter*, 941 F. 3d 1, 11 (1st Circ. 2019), quoting *Kaley v. United States*, 571 U.S. 320, 323 (2014), quoting *Caplin & Drysdale v. United States*, 491 U.S. 617, 630 (1989)).

In short, then, it appears that politicians, prosecutors, and courts alike agree that forfeiture orders, like the one used in Carpenter's case, can play a powerful role in fighting crime. Like so many criminal justice-related outcomes, whether to pursue forfeiture as a punishment is highly discretionary. Indeed, the *Carpenter* prosecutors could have opted to simply request imprisonment, fines, and supervised release for their defendant. The choice to also motion the court for a massive forfeiture order was almost certainly a calculated one, driven by a desire to send a strong punitive message about the crimes that had been committed. Just a cursory look at U.S. Attorney offices' statistics reveal how massive the asset forfeiture game really is for federal prosecutors. For example, in 2011, there were over 8,500 civil and criminal forfeiture actions pending across the 93 U.S. Attorney offices. And the total federal forfeiture amount for that year alone was over $2 billion.

Forfeiture is another arena ripe for examining how politics affects federal prosecutorial discretionary decision-making. We have already seen how political signals affect federal prosecutors' decisions on whether to file charges and how to negotiate charge reductions and sentence discounts. Just like in those areas, we anticipate that prosecutors and other DOJ officials will be mindful of presidential, congressional, and local political signals on attacking crime and adjust their aggressiveness in pursuing forfeiture options in response. A recent example highlights the clear connection between the DOJ's use of asset forfeiture to fight crime and responsiveness to political signals. In 2017, U.S. Attorney General Jeff Sessions indicated that "President Trump has directed this Department of Justice to reduce crime in this country, and we will use every lawful tool that we have to do that." Sessions continued that, in response to the president's message, his DOJ would encourage "forfeiture whenever appropriate" in order to fight crime and hit it in the wallet (U.S. Department of Justice 2017).

We explore the possibility of this link between criminal asset forfeitures and political responsiveness in greater detail in the pages that follow. We begin by introducing asset forfeiture in law and policy in the United States. We also detail the connection between forfeiture and political motivations and track the evolution of forfeiture policy in federal laws and Supreme Court opinions. We then turn to empirical tests of the effects of politics on criminal forfeiture-seeking behavior. Our data include annual forfeiture numbers for 89 federal districts from 1996 to 2013. Our results are noteworthy, indicating that criminal forfeiture serves as another key way that U.S. Attorneys respond to political signals from the president and Congress on the importance of prioritizing the fight against crime.

8.1 Introducing Federal Criminal Asset Forfeiture

Criminal asset forfeitures are key tools by which federal prosecutors confiscate money, contraband, and property that facilitated crimes or were gained as the proceeds of criminal acts (Department of Justice 2019d). As displayed in the *Carpenter* case discussed before, criminal asset forfeitures are proceedings against an individual (*in personam*) rather than against the property. The confiscation of the property is achieved following the defendant's criminal conviction. If criminal asset forfeiture is pursued, the property must be listed in the indictment or other charging document as being the subject of confiscation. In the *U.S. v. Carpenter* case discussed at the outset of this chapter, the superseding indictment from September 2004 stated the following about the prosecutors' forfeiture intentions:

> As a result of the offenses in violation of Title 18, United States Code, Sections 1341 and 1343 charged in Counts 1-2, 5-6 and 8-19 of this Indictment, the defendant DANIEL E. CARPENTER shall forfeit to the United States of America all property, real and personal, that constitutes, or

> is derived from, proceeds traceable to the commission of the offense. If any of the above-described forfeitable property, as a result of any act or omission of the defendant cannot be located upon the exercise of due diligence, has been transferred to, or sold to, or deposited with a third party, has been placed beyond the jurisdiction of this Court, has been substantially diminished in value, or has been commingled with other property which cannot be divided without difficulty, it is the intent of the United States, pursuant to 21 U.S.C. §853(p), to seek forfeiture of any other property of said defendant up to the value of the above forfeitable property.

With criminal forfeiture, the defendant's property is forfeited as a form of post-conviction punishment (Doyle 2015). A district court judge or jury must first find the defendant guilty, beyond a reasonable doubt, of the charged crime(s). Following conviction, the sentencing district judge must then find that the government has established its right to forfeiture based upon a preponderance of the evidence (*United States v. Patel*, 131 F.3d 1195, 7th Cir. 1997).[2]

Descriptive data from the U.S. Attorney Offices' annual reports indicates the regularity with which criminal forfeitures are used in the federal system. Figure 8.1 plots the total number of completed federal criminal forfeitures from 1992 to 2013. Prior to 1995, criminal forfeitures were significantly less common, sitting at fewer than 1,000 per year.[3] Since 2002, the number of criminal forfeitures per year has been at or above 2,500, with some years extending far above that. The number peaked at 5,131 in 2007.

In addition to a high yearly number of criminal forfeitures, the total values of assets obtained by the federal government through criminal forfeiture each year are significant. While values vary considerably

[2] In addition to criminal asset forfeiture, the DOJ also has civil asset forfeiture powers. Unlike in the criminal forfeiture, civil asset forfeiture is *in rem*, meaning that the property "is proceeded against, and by resort to a legal fiction, held guilty and condemned as though it were conscious instead of inanimate and insentient" (*United States v. Ursery* at 275). Federal civil forfeiture statutes do not require a conviction of the property owner for some crime(s) related to the property. Indeed, "the guilt or innocence of the property owner is irrelevant" for purposes of civil forfeiture so long as the property itself was involved in a criminal violation (Doyle 2013, 5). We return to the topic of civil asset forfeiture, and the controversy surrounding it, in this chapter's conclusion.

[3] While the U.S. Attorney annual report data do not consistently report criminal forfeiture numbers prior to 1992, there is good reason to believe that those numbers are as low (or lower) than those reported in 1992, 1993, and 1994. In a 1992 written statement provided to the House Committee on Government Operations, the DOJ's Director and Chief Counsel of the Executive Office for Asset Forfeiture said that while criminal forfeiture is "relatively new[,] . . . [i]n our training programs, we are encouraging our prosecutors to make greater use of criminal forfeitures" (House Legislation and National Security Subcommittee 1992, 89).

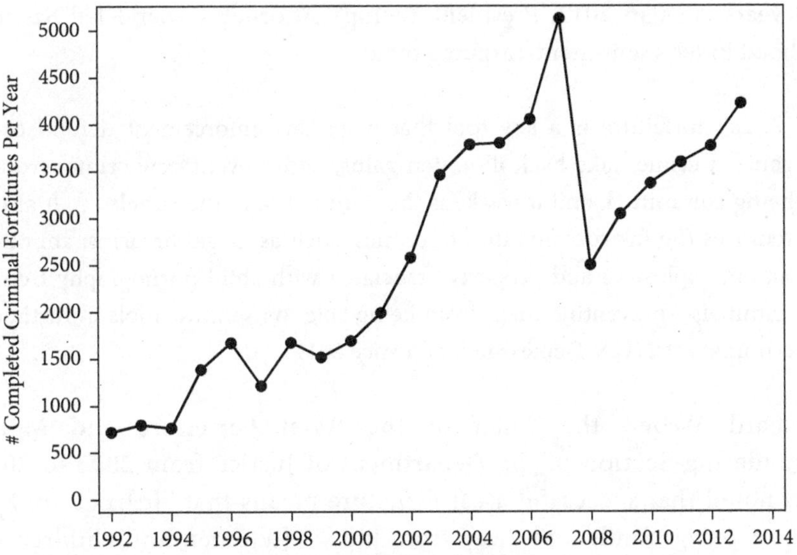

Figure 8.1 Number of criminal forfeitures completed by U.S. Attorney's offices. Source: Yearly United States Attorneys Annual Statistical Reports

from year to year, from 2008 to 2013 the federal government's criminal forfeitures have been valued at a minimum of $400,000,000 each year. Single outlier forfeitures often serve to drive up total numbers in a given year. The large $1,571,153,470 total criminal forfeiture sum in 2013, for example, was driven primarily by the $939,353,852 in criminal forfeitures coming out of just one district: the Eastern District of New York. Similarly, 2010's high total number ($1,244,190,415) is due in large part to the District of Columbia's $500,332,375 criminal forfeiture total for that year.

8.2 Criminal Asset Forfeiture in Law and Policy

Criminal forfeiture procedures can give the federal government broad powers to seize criminal property, fight and deter crime, deprive criminals of illegally obtained property, and punish illegal behavior. In 1980, Senator Joe Biden (D-DE), chair of the Senate Criminal Justice Subcommittee, called asset forfeiture "a major weapon in our attack on" crime and an "absolutely essential tool" (Senate Subcommittee on Criminal Justice 1980, 4). Nearly

30 years later, in 2017, President Trump's Attorney General Jeff Sessions echoed Biden's sentiments, arguing that:

> [A]sset forfeiture is a key tool that helps law enforcement defund organized crime, take back ill-gotten gains, and prevent new crimes from being committed, and it weakens the criminals and the cartels . . . It also removes the instrumentalities of crimes, such as illegal firearms, ammunition, explosives and property associated with child pornography from criminals—preventing them from being able to use these tools in further criminal acts. (U.S. Department of Justice 2017)

Richard Weber, the Chief of the Asset Forfeiture and Money Laundering Section of the Department of Justice from 2005 to 2010, has noted that successful asset forfeiture means that "[d]rugs are kept out of playgrounds and away from kids," "[w]omen and children are safeguarded against forced labor and prostitution by human trafficking gangs," and "[f]unding is kept out of the hands of terrorists and organized crimes" (Weber 2007, 1–2). Another DOJ official argues that asset forfeitures produce multifaceted punishments: "There is an element of simple justice in ensuring that a wrongdoer is deprived of the fruits of illegal acts, but there is also an element of general deterrence as well" (Cassella 2007, 8).

U.S. Attorney's offices in the DOJ work alongside law enforcement investigators from the DEA, ATF, FBI, U.S. Postal Inspection Service, IRS, DHS, Department of Defense, and other federal agencies to investigate and enforce federal criminal laws and seize property as part of broader law enforcement missions (Sessions 2018a, 3). In order to "maximize precision and efficiency," federal forfeiture efforts today are frequently conducted in teams that include "special agents, auditors, accountants and contract data analysts" with specialized training (Department of the Treasury 2004, 21). The U.S. Attorney "is responsible for ensuring that proper and timely pre-seizure planning occurs in asset forfeiture cases" within her district (U.S. Department of Justice 2019a, 26). In addition, U.S. Attorneys' offices "are responsible for the prosecution of criminal and civil forfeitures sought by the federal government, the prosecution and defense of forfeiture-related litigation to which the United States is a party, and the collection of forfeiture-related debts owed to the United States" (Sessions 2018a, 2).

8.2.1 Creature of Statute

Criminal forfeiture in the United States today "is a creature of statute" (Doyle 2013, 16). The federal statutes on triggering crimes, the scope of the property subject to confiscation, and the procedures required for carrying out criminal (and civil) forfeiture "are matters of legislative choice" (Doyle 2007, 3). Up until the early 1980s, Congress chose to give minimal emphasis to forfeiture. Indeed, until 1984, only two federal statutes provided for federal criminal forfeiture powers: 1970's Racketeer Influenced and Corrupt Organization Act (RICO) and Comprehensive Drug Prevention and Control Act (U.S. General Accounting Office 1981, 4).[4] Just the year before their passage, President Nixon spoke to Congress about the need for "new weapons and tools" to battle the Mafia and cut off its revenue sources (Levy 1996, 67). Simply imprisoning Mafia members wasn't enough, Nixon argued, since "[a]s long as the property of organized crime remains, new leaders will step forward to take the place of those we jail" (Levy 1996, 67). Thus, in 1970 Congress and the White House seemed to "suddenly rediscover virtues" in criminal forfeiture with two new pieces of legislation (Levy 1996, 61).[5]

What statutory authority for criminal forfeitures the DOJ had been granted during this period of time largely laid fallow in the 1970s and early 1980s. At the request of Senator Joe Biden, the U.S. General Accounting Office (GAO) issued a report in early 1981 on how little the DOJ had used its forfeiture tools to date. The GAO found that the "Federal Government's record in taking the profit out of crime is not good," with "miniscule" levels of "assets obtained through forfeiture" so far (U.S. General Accounting Office 1981, i). The report's critiques of DOJ forfeiture efforts were scathing and wide-ranging, spanning from its minimal strategy on when and why to pursue forfeitures to its absence of data collection to its lack of incentives for U.S. Attorneys and law enforcement investigators to pursue forfeitures or develop expertise in their use and procedures. It noted:

[4] The GAO reports one earlier criminal forfeiture statute on the books in the United States: the 1862 Confiscation Act that "authorized the President to forfeit the property of Confederate sympathizers" (U.S. General Accounting Office 1981, 4).

[5] Civil forfeiture was similarly slow to develop under federal law. The 1978 Psychotropic Substance Act amended the Drug Enforcement Administration's civil forfeiture authority (21 U.S.C. §881) to extend forfeiture coverage to "proceeds and derivatives of proceeds" (U.S. General Accounting Office 1981, 5)—i.e., "at least the same reach in terms of classes of property subject to forfeiture as the RICO and CCE criminal forfeiture authorizations" (U.S. General Accounting Office 1981, 6). Prior to the 1970s, a notable exception to the use of civil forfeiture was "during Prohibition against automobiles and other vehicles transporting illegal liquor" (Williams et al. 2010, 10).

> Nearly 10 years after the forfeiture statutes were enacted, the Department lacked the most rudimentary information needed to manage the forfeiture effort. No one knew how many forfeiture cases were attempted and why, the disposition of the cases, or why those attempted either failed or succeeded. Investigators and prosecutors lacked incentive and expertise to pursue forfeiture in major drug cases. (U.S. General Accounting Office 1981, 16)

Why had federal forfeiture failed so badly during this decade of legislative rebirth? According to the GAO report, the DOJ was to blame: "The Department of Justice has simply not exercised the kind of leadership and management necessary to make asset forfeiture a widely used law enforcement technique" (U.S. General Accounting Office 1981, 16).

The GAO Report and related political oversight seemed to set a spark in the DOJ's federal forfeiture efforts.[6] By late 1981, both the House and the Senate were holding hearings about the potential for new, more expansive forfeiture legislation to address the many shortcomings highlighted in the GAO Report (Levy 1996, 107, 109). The Reagan Administration's support for fighting the War on Drugs from many angles meant that it too favored expanding civil and criminal asset forfeiture powers and jurisdiction in legislation (Vecchi and Sigler 2001, 45). While criminal justice-related legislative efforts from 1982 and 1983 were not successfully enacted, "Congress persisted in attacking the forfeiture problem" (Levy 1996, 116).

That persistence paid off with the successful passage of sweeping legislation in 1984 that included provisions on sentencing and creating the U.S. Sentencing Commission; increased penalties for drug crimes; and, of course, extensive expansion of federal criminal and civil forfeiture programs. The Comprehensive Crime Control Act of 1984 (CCCA) gave the U.S. Attorney General and federal prosecutors broader asset forfeiture powers by "providing forfeiture provisions that allowed the seizure of all real property, which was used or intended to be used in furtherance of drug trafficking" (Vecchi and Sigler 2001, 46). The CCCA also established an Assets Forfeiture Fund where the proceeds of federal forfeitures are deposited. The Fund "allowed federal enforcement agencies to retain and use the proceeds from asset forfeitures" (Blumenson and Nilsen 1998, 50). Additionally, the CCCA devised an "equitable sharing" program where forfeitures can be tackled

[6] In its response to the GAO Report, the DOJ, while admitting many of the GAO's charges against its forfeiture record, noted that its forfeiture numbers and training efforts were starting to gear up, with "notable progress" being made in 1980 (Levy 1996, 100–101).

as joint investigations between federal and state or local law enforcement agencies. Through shared proceeds among the participating agencies, equitable sharing was designed to incentivize additional forfeitures under the federal umbrella (Williams et al. 2010).

Since the passage of the CCCA in 1984, Congress has continued to broadly define and continually expand the scope of forfeiture. A *Wall Street Journal* story in 2011 reported over 400 federal statutes authorizing forfeiture (Emshwiller and Fields 2011). Federal crimes punishable by forfeiture include drug crimes, motor vehicle theft, credit card fraud, immigration crimes, identity theft, bank fraud, terrorism, firearm smuggling, organized crime, and much more. While civil forfeiture had broader statutory authority than criminal forfeiture for many years, Congress enacted a "bridge statute" in 2000 (28 U.S.C. §2461(c)) that "allows the government to confiscate any property in a criminal proceeding that is forfeitable under the civil forfeiture provisions" (Congressional Research Service 2015, 7).

8.2.2 Supreme Court Acquiescence

In the modern era, the U.S. Supreme Court has largely signed off on the significant and growing powers of criminal forfeiture as a law enforcement and prosecutorial tool, albeit reluctantly at times. The Court has noted favorably its many "prior decisions sustaining" the constitutionality of forfeiture (*Calero-Toledo v. Pearson Yacht Leasing Co.*, 416 U.S. 663, 680 (1974)). The Supreme Court's deference to Congress in its crafting of forfeiture laws has meant that serious intrusions on individual liberties pose a threat only to the scope of forfeiture rather than to the wholesale practice.

In *United States v. Bajakajian*, the Court found that a criminal forfeiture "violates the Excessive Fines Clause if it is grossly disproportional to the gravity of a defendant's offense" (334). In Bajakajian's case, that offense was attempting to transport $357,144 in legal but unreported currency from the United States on an international flight. The Supreme Court said that requiring a forfeiture of all $357,144 went too far given that the defendant's "crime was simply failing to report the wholly legal act of transporting his currency" (338). The decision in *Honeycutt v. United States*, 581 U.S. __ (2017), struck a similar note by limiting criminal forfeiture's reach to only those defendants who could have personally benefited from the crime in question.

While federal prosecutors must take care that criminal forfeitures are not excessive, the Supreme Court has approved of prosecutorial pre-trial preparations for a forfeiture to take place if the defendant is convicted. For example, in *United States v. Monsanto*, 491 U.S. 600 (1989), the Supreme Court noted that when seeking a post-conviction criminal forfeiture, the Government may prevent a defendant from "dissipating his assets prior to trial." Similarly, in *Caplin & Drysdale v. United States*, 491 U.S. 617 (1989), the Court found that the Fifth and Sixth Amendments do not require that a defendant's assets be exempted from forfeiture. As the Court's 5-justice majority noted:

> A defendant has no Sixth Amendment right to spend another person's money for services rendered by an attorney, even if those funds are the only way that that defendant will be able to retain the attorney of his choice. A robbery suspect, for example, has no Sixth Amendment right to use funds he has stolen from a bank to retain an attorney to defend him if he is apprehended. The money, though in his possession, is not rightfully his; the Government does not violate the Sixth Amendment if it seizes the robbery proceeds and refuses to permit the defendant to use them to pay for his defense. (626)

8.3 Data and Methods

Because criminal forfeiture occurs in connection with traditional prosecution efforts, it represents a relatively clean test of our political theories. For federal prosecutors to successfully carry out a criminal forfeiture, they must meet exacting standards—beyond a reasonable doubt for conviction and then preponderance of the evidence for the forfeiture-subject property—that serve as barriers against abuse by officials who might be seeking to pad the DOJ coffers or deny defendants constitutional protections. And, as noted before, prosecutors must frequently coordinate with other agency officials—"special agents, auditors, accountants and contract data analysts" (Department of the Treasury 2004, 21) in order to make the case for when and what should be seized and forfeited. As a result, criminal forfeiture is a costly and burdensome endeavor that is likely to only be pursued by U.S. Attorneys when it is important to do so.

Despite the difficulties in obtaining a criminal forfeiture, when executed, it provides a powerful punishment against a convicted defendant that extends beyond and often in addition to incarceration, community supervision, and fines. Criminal forfeiture thus presents an opportunity for U.S. Attorneys and their staff, seeking to selectively and responsively dole out punitiveness in their prosecutorial behavior, to do so. We anticipate that when political principals (president, Congress, local public) signal their desire for the harsh treatment of crime, U.S. Attorneys will respond accordingly by exerting the effort required to utilize criminal forfeitures to a greater extent.

To examine the political and other constraining effects on federal prosecutors' criminal asset forfeiture pursuit practices, we combine district-level asset forfeiture data derived from the annual reports of the U.S. Attorney's Offices with presidential, congressional, public, and district variables. Our dependent variable is the number of *Criminal Asset Forfeiture* matters pending in each district-year across 89 U.S. districts from 1996 to 2013.[7]

Consistent with Chapters 5, 6, and 7, we measure a variety of independent variables related to the expected effects of political (presidential, congressional, public) factors on asset forfeiture strategies. This includes *Presidential Rhetoric*, measured here as the number of sentences in presidential public statements each year that contain policy mentions of white-collar crime, violent crime, or drugs, then standardized by dividing by the number of presidential statements per year and multiplying by 100. Narcotics, white-collar, and violent crime offenses are types of crime that are closely connected to asset forfeiture. They represent efforts to profit from criminal activity or make "ill gotten gains," which are a crucial target for governmental seizures. We also code *Congressional Hearings*, again focusing on the percentage of hearings related to drugs, violent crime, or white-collar crime in a given year. This variable captures the amount of public attention that Congress pays to white-collar crime, violent crime, and drug-related policies.

In considering the local public's potential influence on asset forfeiture decisions, we focus on public opinion, punitiveness, and crime rate factors. For local public opinion we utilize three GSS survey questions to capture regional mood on crime relevant to forfeiture. These variables are constructed using GSS opinion data on drugs, white-collar crime, and violent crime. The first of these, *Local Public Opinion: Drugs*, measures public opinion on illegal drugs.

[7] We exclude from the data the U.S. Attorneys' office for the District of Columbia and those designated for U.S. territories (U.S. Attorney's Office for the District of Puerto Rico, U.S. Attorney's Office for the Districts of Guam and the Northern Mariana Islands, and U.S. Attorney's Office for the District of the Virgin Islands).

The GSS survey question captures regional mood on the perceived seriousness of the drug problem and is computed as a percentage, with higher percentages reflecting respondents answering that "too little" is spent on "dealing with drug addiction." The second, *Local Public Opinion: White Collar*, measures public opinion on white-collar and fraud-related crime. It computes the percentage of respondents responding "greater" to the question of whether "stealing U.S. advanced technology and trade secrets" is a greater, about the same, or less threat today than it was 10 years ago. The third, *Local Public Opinion: Violent*, computes the percentage of respondents answering "too little" to whether the U.S. is spending the right amount of money to halt the rising crime rate. Further details on these measures are provided in the Chapter Data Appendix.

Second, we again account for *Local Punitiveness* toward criminal offenders. This harshness provides a signal to federal prosecutors on how aggressive the local public wants them to be in pursuing alleged crimes and criminals. We expect that as local punitiveness rises, U.S. Attorneys will respond with an increase in criminal forfeiture activity as a prosecutorial tactic. Third, to capture the influence that the prevalence of crime in a state has in pressuring local prosecutors to address an underlying crime problem, the *State Crime Rate* is included in the model. We measure state crime rate in this chapter as the combined violent crime and property crime rates for every state-year per 100,000 residents (as reported by the Uniform Crime Reports). As the incidence of crime in a state increases, we anticipate that U.S. Attorneys will be more prone to pursue criminal asset forfeiture.

In addition to the variables capturing the potential effects of political principals on U.S. Attorneys' asset forfeiture behavior, we also account for resource constraints (internal staff size and workload) in district offices via the average workload of individual attorneys in local U.S. Attorney offices (*Staff Workload*). While no U.S. Attorney's office has the resources and time to pursue every potential matter, we expect that, all other things equal, less individually burdened attorneys and offices will be more likely to pursue asset forfeiture than other offices facing higher workload constraints. Additionally, we control for the political preferences of the U.S. Attorney leading each district with *Republican U.S. Attorney*. We expect that Republican-leaning U.S. Attorneys will be more likely, as a baseline matter, to favor asset forfeiture as an aggressive way to combat crime than Democratic-leaning U.S. Attorneys.

Because indicting federal prosecutors are likely to be forward looking when deciding whether to pursue a criminal forfeiture, we expect them to account for their future district court's influence on whether to order that forfeiture. Previous research suggests lower court judges and litigants engage in this strategic, forward-looking behavior (Boyd 2015; Randazzo 2008; Scott 2006). We capture this potential in our variable *District Court Conservatism*. Finally, we account for the broadened criminal forfeiture jurisdiction following the enactment of 28 U.S.C. §2461(c)'s "bridge statute" in late 2000 and its potential effect on increasing the overall quantity of criminal forfeitures. *Bridge Statute* is coded as 1 in 2001 and after and 0 otherwise.

We report expected variable effects and summary statistics in Table 8.2 in the Chapter Data Appendix.

8.4 Results

We turn now to an empirical test of the effects of political factors on U.S. Attorneys' criminal asset forfeiture decision-making. We estimate a negative binomial regression model to assess the effects of our factors of interest on the number of criminal asset forfeiture matters filed by the U.S. Attorneys per district-year. The results are displayed in Table 8.1. To

Table 8.1 Negative binomial regression estimates for the number of Criminal Asset Forfeiture matters pending per district-year.

	Coefficient	**RSE**
Presidential Rhetoric	0.003*	(0.001)
Congressional Hearings	0.181*	(0.027)
Local Public Opinion: Drugs	0.022*	(0.011)
Local Public Opinion: White Collar	−0.006	(0.017)
Local Public Opinion: Violent Crime	−0.009	(0.010)
Local Punitiveness	−0.001	(0.001)
State Crime Rate	0.000	(0.000)
Staff Workload	0.027	(0.015)
Republican U.S. Attorney	0.205	(0.147)
District Court Conservatism	−0.721*	(0.332)
Bridge Statute	0.440*	(0.212)
Time Trend	0.128*	(0.029)
Constant	0.234	(1.445)
Observations	1,602	

District clustered robust standard errors (RSEs) are included in parentheses. * Significant at $p < 0.05$.

account for panel effects, we use robust standard errors clustered on the district and control for time via a linear trend that counts the number of years.

As Table 8.1 displays, many of our key independent variables related to the politics of federal prosecution have statistically significant and positive effects, as expected, on the number of criminal asset forfeitures pursued. But how much of an effect? To better understand the substantive effects of these political factors, we again move to a graphical assessment of the predictive marginal effects—here, the average predicted effect for a variable on the count of criminal forfeitures across the remaining independent variables' real values.

First, we examine the marginal effects of *Presidential Rhetoric*. Figure 8.2 plots the mean and 95% confidence intervals for these effects across the values of presidential rhetoric (X-axis) and the count of criminal forfeitures (Y-axis). As the figure reveals, there is a notable upward trajectory in U.S. Attorneys' criminal forfeitures the more presidents talk about and prioritize forfeiture-relevant crime. Specifically, during times when the president has relatively little to say about crime, criminal forfeitures average just 47 per district-year. However, this criminal forfeiture number rises to nearly

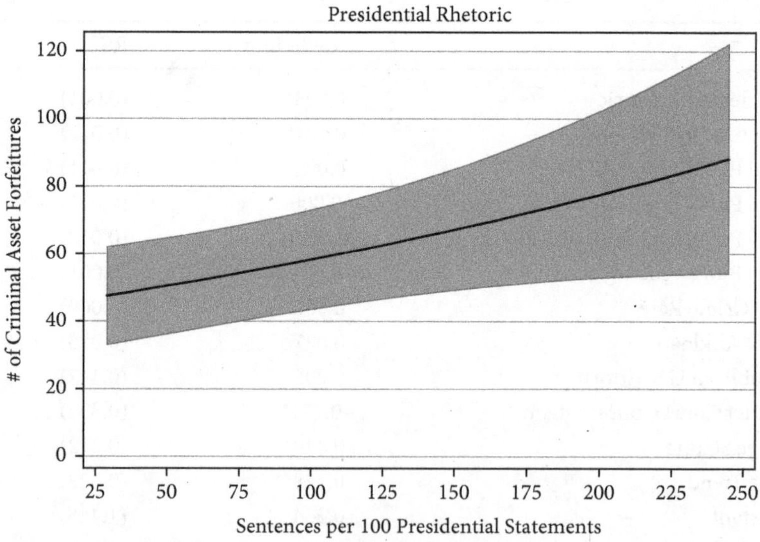

Figure 8.2 Marginal effects of presidential crime rhetoric on the number of criminal forfeitures pursued per district-year.

88 when the president prioritizes crime in his speeches. This amounts to a sizable change of 41 criminal forfeitures per district-year across the span of presidential rhetoric values.

The substantive effects are nearly as strong for *Congressional Hearings*, plotted in Figure 8.3. There, the results indicate that low levels of congressional attention to violent, drug, and white-collar crimes yield about 44 criminal forfeitures per district and year. As congressional hearings on relevant crimes become more common, so do criminal forfeitures, with the maximum level of congressional hearings on the subject associated with about 69 criminal forfeitures per district-year, on average.

We look to the marginal effects of our one statistically significant measure relating to the local public: *Local Public Opinion: Drugs*. As Figure 8.4 reveals, there is again a sharp increase in attention to criminal forfeitures in response to movement in this variable. Indeed, we see the number of criminal forfeitures more than double across the range of public opinion on drugs. Specifically, when a low percentage of the local public responds that they think "too little" is being done about drug addiction, U.S. Attorneys focus their attention elsewhere and pursue only 34 criminal forfeitures per district-year. However, as more and more think

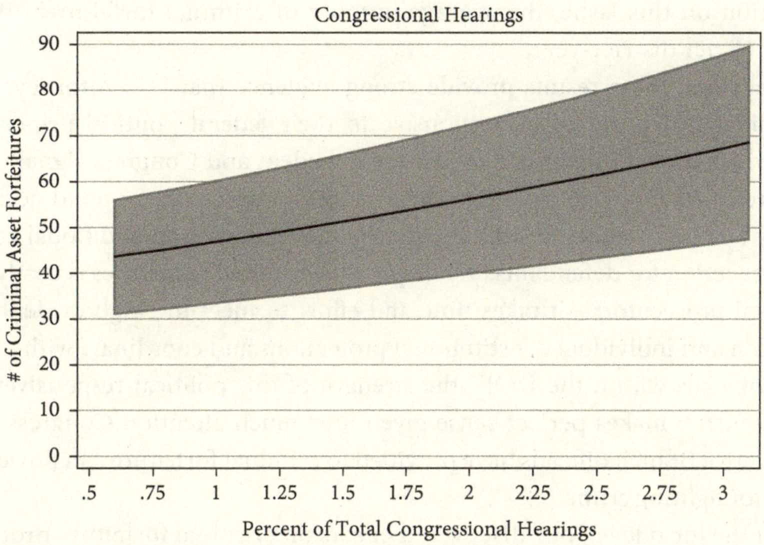

Figure 8.3 Marginal effects of congressional hearings about crime on the number of criminal forfeitures pursued per district-year.

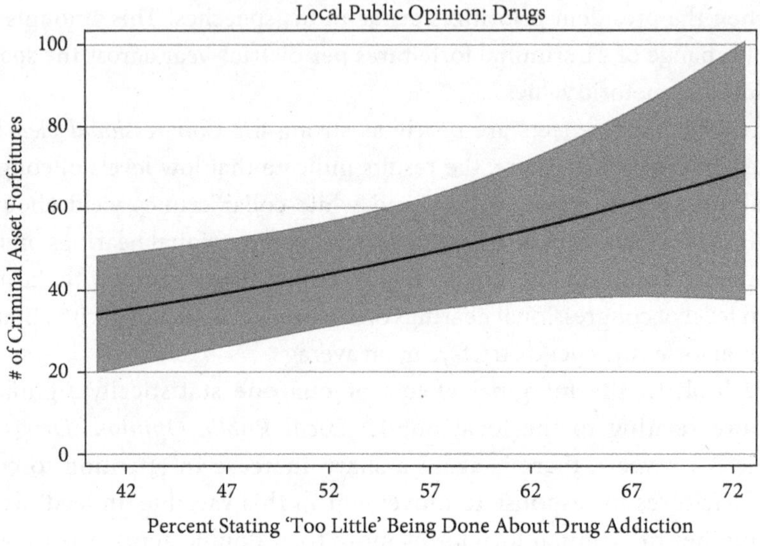

Figure 8.4 Marginal effects of regional public opinion about drugs on the number of criminal forfeitures pursued per district-year.

that "too little" is being done about drug problems, the U.S. Attorneys respond with more criminal forfeitures. At the maximum level of public opinion on this issue, the average number of criminal forfeitures sits at over 69 per district-year.

Together, these results provide strong evidence that U.S. Attorneys use criminal forfeitures to be responsive to their federal political principals' priorities on fighting crime. When the president and Congress signal their desire to be tough in fighting crime, federal prosecutors respond accordingly by more frequently adding criminal forfeitures as an additional criminal sanction for defendants. While pursing criminal forfeitures is costly for federal prosecutors—it takes time and effort to meet the high evidentiary burden and individual constitutional protections and coordinate with other key officials within the DOJ—the strength of this political responsiveness relationship makes perfect sense given how much attention Congress and Executive Branch officials have provided to criminal forfeiture as a powerful tool for fighting crime.

At the local level, our discovered effects on criminal forfeiture propensity are also of note. Local public opinion on what the government is doing for drug addictions, in particular, provides a clear message to federal prosecutors on how those in their region believe government efforts and resources should be placed. We can imagine that U.S. Attorneys later seeking election or appointment in a location that prioritizes fighting drug problems will likely benefit from being able to itemize their concrete efforts to address local drug problems. Citing specific accomplishments on criminal forfeitures relating to drugs—both in terms of the sheer number of increased forfeitures and the monetary value—will almost certainly help in this regard.

8.5 Concluding Thoughts on Asset Forfeiture and Politics

In his statement to Congress in 1992, Cary Copeland, the DOJ's Director and Chief Counsel in the Executive Office for Asset Forfeiture gave a wide-ranging endorsement of federal asset forfeiture:

> [T]he Department of Justice believes in asset forfeiture and we appreciate the strong support which the Congress has given the forfeiture program over the years . . . We in the forfeiture program are engaged in an exciting and challenging mission. We are building a new law enforcement sanction. Ten years ago we had only the three historic sanctions for crime: incarceration, supervised release (parole or probation), and criminal fines. Today there is a fourth sanction—asset forfeiture. And in less than eight years, asset forfeiture has far surpassed criminal fines in importance and effectiveness. The future of asset forfeiture is virtually unlimited and we are committed to ensuring that this powerful and promising new weapon is used prudently and responsibly. (House Legislation and National Security Subcommittee 1992, 91–92)

Our analysis of the years following Copeland's statement confirm that asset forfeiture has indeed become a very powerful sanction for the DOJ's crime fighting and deterrence efforts. Our findings indicate that criminal forfeiture, in particular, is used by U.S. Attorneys' offices to respond to presidential and congressional signals on crime. In other words, when federal politicians prioritize fighting crime, so do U.S. Attorneys, and criminal forfeitures are one of the major ways that they do so (along with incarceration, supervised release, criminal fines, and via other techniques discussed elsewhere in this book). We suspect that the president and

Congress would agree that the DOJ's use of criminal forfeiture has largely been "prudent" and "responsible."

This may not be the case with civil forfeiture where there is no requirement that the property owner be convicted of a crime. Many would argue that civil forfeitures are "virtually unlimited," but in the most negative way possible. The practice of civil forfeiture has come under fire from the scholarly and political community for incentivizing nefarious and profit-seeking motivations among law enforcement officials who utilize it. The charge is that because many state and federal civil forfeiture laws permit law enforcement agencies to retain many or all forfeiture proceeds, these agencies are likely to aggressively employ civil forfeitures (Holcomb, Kovandzic, and Williams 2011; Williams 2002) for reasons that have nothing to do with political responsiveness. Civil forfeiture has been criticized for being a "cash cow" (Levy 1996, 153) and "legalized bounty hunting" (Malcolm 2013). At the federal level, in 2015, Obama's Attorney General Eric Holder gutted the civil forfeiture equitable sharing program, arguing that doing so would help prevent the DOJ from unintentionally incentivizing asset seizures (O'Harrow Jr., Horwitz, and Rich 2015). While this appeared to be a step away from one of the major components of civil forfeiture-for-profit in the DOJ that many have worried about, Attorney General Sessions restored the program to its former state upon taking office in 2017.

Critics have actively encouraged the replacement of abuse-prone civil forfeitures with criminal forfeitures. Here's why:

> [C]riminal proceedings are valuable. Criminal forfeiture reduces the perception of law enforcement as revenue collection agents, provides the wrongdoer with full legal protection not available under administrative or civil forfeiture, can reduce instances of abuse and criticism of the program, and if successful, can result in the incapacitation of both the offender and the property . . . Only criminal forfeiture can effectively incapacitate the offender and the asset in one proceeding. Initiating a shift in emphasis to criminal forfeiture proceedings should provide the government the ability to focus effectively on its objectives, protect the rights of the accused and innocent owners, and allay the criticism directed at this policy. (Warchol, Payne, and Johnson 1996)

While the DOJ has not often acknowledged many of the concerns relating to profit motivations driving its civil forfeiture practices, the overall data do appear to indicate a shift away from civil forfeitures and toward criminal forfeitures. Figure 8.5 plots the annual number of federal completed criminal and civil forfeitures from 1992 to 2018—that is, a full five years beyond the end of our analyzed data.

As the figure indicates, overall civil asset forfeiture numbers have dropped considerably since the 1990s while criminal forfeiture numbers have gone up. Doyle (2013) confirms this observation, indicating that "[o]nce less frequently invoked than civil forfeiture, criminal forfeiture appears to have become the procedure of choice when judicial proceedings are required" (14). Those trends continue today and, at least based on these national-level descriptive data, appear unaffected by the beginning of the Trump Administration. What is clear is that there is much left to learn and contemplate about the use and future of federal asset forfeiture, including whether federal criminal forfeitures will someday fully supplant civil forfeitures. From this book's theoretical lens, if that were to happen, it would only better position U.S. Attorneys and their staff to be politically responsive to the crime-fighting priorities of their principals and local public.

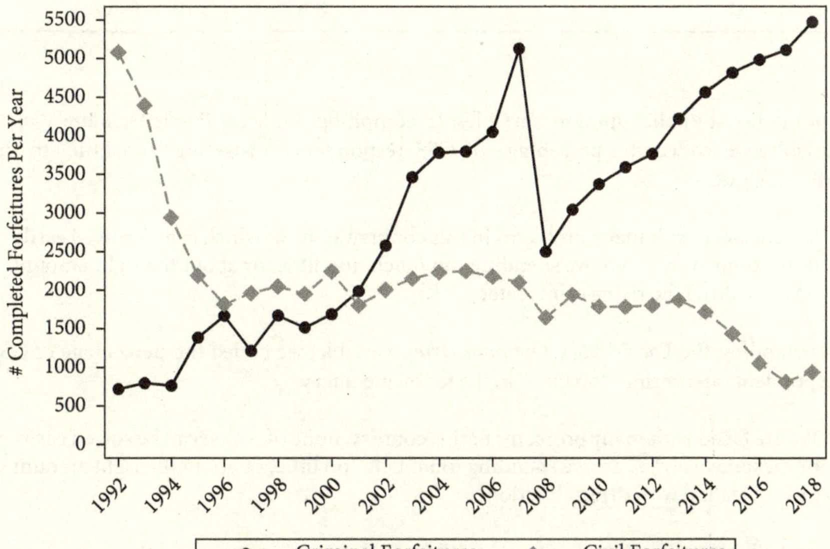

Figure 8.5 Number of criminal and civil forfeitures completed by U.S. Attorney's offices from 1992 to 2018. Source: Yearly United States Attorneys Annual Statistical Reports.

Chapter 8 Data Appendix

Table 8.2 Expected direction of effects and summary statistics for dependent and key independent variables.

	Expected Direction	Mean	Standard Deviation	Range
Criminal Asset Forfeiture Matters		48.79	83.34	0–847
Presidential Rhetoric	+	66.46	56.03	28.57–246.29
Congressional Hearings	+	1.58	0.65	0.67–3.13
Local Public Opinion: Drugs	+	58.85	5.42	40.54–72.73
Local Public Opinion: White Collar	+	59.73	6.11	51.11–71.58
Local Public Opinion: Violent Crime	+	60.97	7.01	40.54–81
Local Punitiveness	+	426.07	154.35	100–886
State Crime Rate	+	3899.02	1013.67	1946–7497
Staff Workload	–	17.37	7.47	7.72–95.89
Republican U.S. Attorney	+	0.47	0.50	0–1
District Court Conservatism	+	0.08	0.29	−0.52–0.60
Bridge Statute	+	0.72	0.45	0–1
Time Trend	+	8.5	5.19	0–17

Coding Local Public Opinion Variables: In compiling the *Local Public Opinion: Violent* variable, we coded the percentage of GSS respondents answering "too little" to the following query:

> We are faced with many problems in this country, none of which can be solved easily or inexpensively. . . .are we spending too much, too little, or about the right amount on . . . Halting the rising crime rate?

In compiling the *Local Public Opinion: Drugs* variable, we coded the percentage of GSS respondents answering "too little" to the following query:

> We are faced with many problems in this country, none of which can be solved easily or inexpensively . . . are we spending too much, too little, or about the right amount on . . . Dealing with drug addiction?

In compiling the *Local Public Opinion: White Collar* variable, we coded the percentage of GSS respondents answering "greater" to the following query:

> Are the following threats to the United States greater, about the same, or less today than they were 10 years ago? . . . Stealing U.S. advanced technology and trade secrets by foreigners.

The violent crime and drug questions are available in the GSS from 1996–2010, every two years. The white-collar question is available only in 2000. Computed percentages exclude non-respondents and those answering "don't know." Region assignment for U.S. states in the GSS data are provided in Chapter 5's Data Appendix.

9

Conclusion: The Political Prosecutor Today and Tomorrow

> As long as I'm attorney general, the criminal justice system will not be used for partisan political ends.
>
> —U.S. Attorney General William Barr, May 2020[1]

In this unequivocal statement, Trump-appointed Attorney General Barr's words echo the sentiments of his predecessors in the DOJ, including those of Obama's Attorney General Loretta Lynch featured at the outset of this book. While the messaging from the DOJ and its attorneys general has been consistent—independence and the rule of law dominate the federal criminal justice system—the pages of this book have worked to weave history, theory, and empirical evidence together to provide a more honest account of the business of federal prosecution.

As we have seen (and despite Attorney General Barr's words), the consistent thread running through this tale is the fact that politics permeates every facet of federal prosecution. Over the historical evolution of the role of the federal prosecutor, we have seen the emergence and persistence of political markers (Chapter 2). From the very beginning, U.S. Attorneys have been an integral part of the U.S. federal government, yet these positions have long been treated as "political plums" for up-and-coming and loyal party members (Huston 1967, 64). Befitting their importance, the selection of U.S. Attorney positions occurs through an explicitly political process where presidents, Congress, and "home state" forces all affect the selection, nomination, and confirmation of new federal prosecutors (Chapter 3). Indeed, though the

[1] Barr's words came during a press conference where he addressed the ongoing DOJ investigation into the handling of the Russian meddling in the 2016 presidential election (Benner and Goldman 2020).

The Politics of Federal Prosecution. Christina L. Boyd, Michael J. Nelson, Ian Ostrander, and Ethan D. Boldt, Oxford University Press (2021).
DOI: 10.1093/oso/9780197554685.003.0009

president formally nominates federal prosecutors, the influence of the home state senators has historically been so strong that the senators, rather than the president, actually select the nominees (Bell 1977). Politics often plays an equally important role at the end of a U.S. Attorney's time in office and beyond, as many U.S. Attorneys resign when a new president takes office (even if their term has not yet expired) and go on to use the position as a springboard to higher political office (Chapter 4).

We have also revealed that politics and political responsiveness play major roles in affecting federal prosecutorial behavior. Chapter 5 theorizes why that should be the case—a combination of high levels of discretion and clear incentives for responsiveness mean that U.S. Attorneys will be mindful of the criminal preferences and priorities communicated to them by their political principals (the president and Congress) and their local communities. The theory bears empirical fruit in a variety of prosecutorial decision-making contexts, including whether to bring or decline a prosecution (Chapter 6), how to charge and bargain with defendants (Chapter 7), and how aggressively to pursue criminal asset forfeitures (Chapter 8). In each of these contexts, we find that the behavior of federal prosecutors systematically tracks the signals coming from Washington and local communities relating to crime. As stronger political signals emerge, federal prosecutors become more likely to prosecute a given case, less likely to reduce a given charge or offer a sentencing discount, and more likely to use their powers to seize the assets of criminal enterprises. Our consistent results are made all the more meaningful since U.S. Attorneys "represent a hard test" for political influence on the bureaucracy (Whitford and Yates 2009, 117), "do not have all the rational capacity and time necessary to choose the best course of action" in all situations (Maor 2010, 154), and are surely cognizant of organizational reputation and legitimacy considerations (Carpenter and Krause 2012; Krause 2009) cautioning them against behaving in an extremely political way.

The implications of the strong connection between politics and prosecution are vast. Federal prosecutors sit in an incredibly important position as the true agenda setters for much of the federal criminal justice system. This means that everything that comes after the prosecutor—from sentencing, to incarceration, to community corrections—depends on (politically tinged) prosecutorial behavior. While federal criminal law has grown in scope in recent years, the federal prosecutor's decision-making has remained largely free from judicial oversight or legislative guidelines. This means that the potential avenues for checking the influence of politics are minimal without the introduction of reforms.

9.1 The Trump Administration and Beyond

While our prior chapters have included some anecdotes, data, and analysis related to the Trump DOJ and U.S. Attorneys, the Trump Administration warrants additional attention and reflection. From his first few months in office, President Trump's relationship with the Department of Justice, and, by extension, U.S. Attorneys, was front page news. Some of the most high-profile headlines from Trump's time in office relate to the DOJ, from Attorney General Jeff Sessions' decision to recuse himself from involvement with the Department's investigations into the 2016 presidential election to the firing of Acting Attorney General (and long-time DOJ official) Sally Yates for her decision to refuse to defend Trump's executive order banning travel from Muslim-majority countries into the United States (Gerstein 2018; Shear et al. 2017). Specifically, what can this administration tell us about the state of the politics of federal prosecution today and in the years to come? How has DOJ and U.S. Attorney staffing compared to prior administrations? What prosecutorial priorities have dominated during the Trump years?

Chapters 3 and 4 provided some important insights into the how President Trump's staffing compares to prior administrations and what that may imply for the future. From the start, the Trump Administration's actions with regard to staffing U.S. Attorneys stood in stark contrast to the relatively placid transitions overseen by George W. Bush and Barack Obama. The Trump Administration fired all remaining Obama-nominated U.S. Attorneys after Trump had been in office for just two months. These tactics were not isolated to the transition. Years later the Trump Administration controversially fired its own interim U.S. Attorney for the Southern District of New York, Geoffrey Berman, who at the time was leading several politically prominent investigations. Importantly, since violations of rules or norms generally makes future violations easier (Shepsle 2017), the Trump Administration's actions may serve to encourage similar behavior in future administrations.

Acting against prior norms, the Trump Administration also sometimes pushed career prosecutors aside in order to install their own chosen officials to run U.S. Attorneys' offices until the Senate confirmed President Trump's nominees (Hauser 2018; Stefansky and Makarechi 2017). And, in some cases, nominations from the Trump Administration never came, enabling a Trump appointee to serve without Senate confirmation for years (Weiser 2018). This follows a Trump Administration trend of relying more on "actings" than prior administrations (O'Connell 2020), which may be calculated to gain policy advantages (Kinane 2019). Once President Trump's nominees reached the Senate, however, they were quite successful; in his first two years in office, Trump's U.S. Attorney nominations were confirmed, on average, in less than 80 days. And, nearly 99% of the individuals Trump submitted to the Senate were confirmed by the end of the 115th Congress. If these trends continue, future presidents may similarly rely on acting officials for controversial cases/positions while reserving Senate confirmation for easy victories.

The Trump Administration was also marked by high-profile roles for long-term DOJ employees, including Robert Mueller, James Comey, and Rod Rosenstein. Mueller is most known in recent years for his service as the Special Counsel for the DOJ from 2017 to 2019 to investigate potential links between Trump's 2016 campaign and Russia. However, his complete record of service with the DOJ is extensive and bipartisan, including U.S. Attorney (1998–2001), United States Assistant Attorney General for the Criminal Division (1990–1993), U.S. Deputy Attorney General (2001), and Director of the FBI (2001–2013). Rosenstein was a very visible U.S. Deputy Attorney General during the Trump Administration (2017–2019), but before this role he served as the U.S. Attorney for the District of Maryland under both presidents George W. Bush and Barack Obama. Rosenstein had long before earned a reputation in the DOJ as "a non-political public servant" (Strohm 2019).[2] And while Comey is best known for his role as FBI Director during the Obama Administration and the start of the Trump Administration, he had served prior as an Assistant U.S. Attorney (1996–2001), U.S. Attorney (2002–2005), and U.S. Deputy Attorney General (2003–2005).

As we move forward in time, it seems likely that U.S. Attorney nominees will face heightened scrutiny before the Senate, especially when the presidency and the Senate are controlled by two different parties. The U.S. Senate under Mitch McConnell's leadership during Trump's time in office was remarkable in the sheer number of federal judgeships it filled (Ruiz et al. 2020).

[2] Many have echoed this sentiment about Rosenstein. For example, Jason Weinstein, a former colleague of Rosenstein's at the DOJ, said that Rosenstein "is not political at all. In every decision he makes—and I've seen him make some very difficult ones—the only question he really cares about is what is right and what is just" (Horwitz 2017b). A *Vanity Fair* article noted that his longevity as a U.S. Attorney meant that he was "either highly competent or blandly unexceptional" (Smith 2017).

Still, in recent years, the amount of delay experienced by nominees has increased, and the Senate's eventual confirmation votes on key presidential nominations have become closer (Ostrander 2017; U.S. Senate 2020). Given the extent to which the Trump Administration's high-level DOJ officials became national news, it seems natural to expect that senators will give these officials—and perhaps U.S. Attorneys for key offices nationwide—closer scrutiny in the coming years. Part of this increased scrutiny may come at the expense of the power of home state senators, whose picks for U.S. Attorney have been typically honored by a copartisan president. In line with the breakdown of the blue slip process for other types of nominations the Senate has already experienced, the power of home state senators to more-or-less unilaterally select U.S. Attorneys may soon be a thing of the past (McMillion 2017).[3]

On the question of Trump-era prosecutorial priorities, DOJ Attorney General policy choices have been informative, and draw a stark contrast between the Obama DOJ and the Trump DOJ. Despite a publicly strained relationship between Attorney General Sessions and President Trump, Sessions acted aggressively in Trump's name in numerous capacities in DOJ policy. We have seen substantial focus on violent crime issues, including Sessions' strong support for Project Exile and asset forfeiture, with Sessions announcing his intentions in mid-2017 to "develop policies to increase forfeitures" (Stillman 2017). Sessions also mirrored the broader Trump Administration's emphasis on ending illegal immigration from Mexico to the United States. In April 2018, Sessions wrote a policy memo announcing a strict "no tolerance" policy for immigration-related criminal offenses:

> I direct each United States Attorney's Office along the Southwest Border to the extent practicable, and in consultation with DHS, to adopt immediately a zero-tolerance policy for all offenses referred for prosecution under section 1325(a). This zero-tolerance policy shall supersede any existing policies. If adopting such a policy requires additional resources, each office shall identify and request such additional resources.

[3] Specifically, the use of the nuclear option in 2013 and later violations of rules and norms during the Trump Administration (Binder 2018) may erode traditions such as senatorial courtesy, especially without the implicit threat of the filibuster as a mechanism for enforcement. The reduction of home state senators' rights would be consistent with a recent cycle in the Senate of minority obstruction followed by majority restrictions (Smith 2014).

> You are on the front lines of this battle. I respect you and your team. Your dedication and insight into border reality is invaluable. Keep us informed, and don't hesitate to give us suggestions for improvement. Remember, our goal is not simply more cases. It is to end the illegality in our immigration system. (Sessions 2018b)

Sessions' successor as Attorney General, William Barr, has continued and even extended this legacy for the Trump Administration. As we saw in Chapter 2, Barr issued a controversial policy memo in early 2020 barring the initiation of investigations into candidates for president, vice president, or senior campaign staff without his approval. The COVID-19 pandemic of 2020 also saw Barr issuing powerful instructions to his local U.S. Attorneys on redirecting their efforts and prioritizing attention to the crisis:

> Every U.S. Attorney's Office is thus hereby directed to prioritize the detection, investigation, and prosecution of all criminal conduct related to the current pandemic . . . Your Office is also encouraged to work closely with state and local authorities to both ensure that we hear about misconduct as quickly as possible and that all appropriate enforcement tools are available to punish it. (Barr 2020b)

A month later, in late April 2020, Barr would further, and more controversially, direct the U.S. Attorneys:

> If a state or local ordinance crosses the line from an appropriate exercise of authority to stop the spread of COVID-19 into an overbearing infringement of constitutional and statutory protections, the Department of Justice may have an obligation to address that overreach in federal court. (Balsamo 2020)

The annual data for U.S. Attorney offices provide another mechanism to examine how the Trump Administration's prosecutors have prioritized their efforts and resources and how these things compare to the immediate years prior during the Obama Administration and the transition from Obama to Trump. Table 9.1 provides key DOJ statistics from fiscal years 2015 to 2018 to enable this comparison. Fiscal year 2018, which ran from October 2017 to September 2018, is the first full year of Trump Administration data available.

Table 9.1 Department of Justice filing statistics (2015–2018)

	2018	2017	2016	2015
Defendants Filed—All Crime	81,888	71,229	72,006	73,316
Defendants Filed—Immigration Only	28,741	21,272	21,921	22,525
Defendants Filed by Referring Agency				
Border & Customs Protection	19,919	14,001	15,537	15,228
Immigration & Customs Enforcement	12,261	11,732	10,981	12,126
Drug Enforcement Administration	10,973	10,266	10,483	10,660
Alcohol, Tobacco, Firearms & Explosives	9,596	8,144	7,304	6,607
Internal Revenue Service	874	1,079	1,310	1,563

Source: Department of Justice United States Attorneys' Annual Statistical Reports for Fiscal Years 2018, 2017, 2016, and 2015.

The statistics provide a number of insights. First, we see that fiscal year 2018 has a notable uptick of around 10,000 in the number of defendants with criminal matters filed against them by U.S. Attorneys relative to 2015, 2016, and 2017. Compared to 2016, 2018 had a nearly 14% increase in defendant filings. As Table 9.1 indicates, much of this increase in defendant filings came from immigration matters, where 2018 saw a 6,820 immigration defendant increase—or 31%—relative to 2016. This immigration prosecution focus will likely come as little surprise to even the most casual observers of the Trump Administration and its policy priorities.

The table's statistics on defendant filings by referring agency further highlight comparative prosecutorial priorities. Nearly all of the Trump Administration's increased focus on immigration defendants results from referrals from the U.S. Customs and Border Protection—the agency charged with the law enforcement aspects of immigration at the border such as preventing entry—and not the U.S. Immigration and Customs Enforcement (ICE)—the agency that operates largely in the interior of the United States to find and remove unlawful aliens. Along with immigration, the Trump Administration's U.S. Attorneys in 2018 filed more cases against defendants coming out of the Bureau of Alcohol, Tobacco, Firearms and Explosives (ATF) than the Obama Administration's prosecutors did. The increase of 2,292 from 2016 to 2018 amounts to a 31% increase in ATF-referred prosecutions. Interestingly, no such increase occurred for Drug Enforcement Administration (DEA) referrals. Prosecutions stemming from Internal Revenue Service (IRS) referrals, while relatively small in number each year, have declined during the start of the Trump Administration, falling 33% from 2016 to 2018.

Just as the Trump Administration had a number of criminal justice priorities that differed from the Obama and even Bush Administrations, we should expect the next presidential administration to shift its policy focus to fit its political agenda and the pressures occurring at that time. That shift will, in turn, likely affect the number of criminal defendants in federal courts and the distribution of defendants coming from the different law enforcement agencies, among other things. In other words, the politics *of the moment* will be relevant for federal prosecution decision-making and staffing well into the future.

9.2 Onward to the States and Beyond

Our study focuses solely on federal prosecutors and prosecutions. We think this is a critical place to begin given the uniform nature of the federal criminal justice system, the salience and importance of many federal criminal cases, and the interplay between federal and local politics in the staffing and decision-making of federal prosecutors. However, as any criminal attorney will attest, federal matters represent just a small slice of criminal proceedings in the United States. Most criminal prosecutions occur in the states and under state law.

Expanding research like ours to the states, while a critical next step, is no small task. One major hurdle lies with the vast amount of variability in the states and their criminal justice systems. Criminal laws and procedures vary significantly from state to state. The position of the prosecutor is also not the same across state lines. Unlike in the federal system, many state prosecutors are elected, but the specifics of the election systems differ considerably. Other examples of interstate variability that likely affect the study of state prosecutors—and the potential influences of politics of state prosecutions—abound.

But with these institutional differences come tantalizing opportunities to expand our collective knowledge about how prosecutors wield the immense powers they are given. The fact that so many prosecutors are directly responsible to the public in the states means that these offices are ripe for formal tests of responsiveness to electoral conditions. Does, for example, the relationship between the punitiveness of a prosecutor's constituency and her charging decisions change with the likelihood that the prosecutor will face steep competition in the next election? Do more competitive electoral conditions encourage prosecutors to act more punitively? These are just two exciting research questions that await scholars who examine state prosecutors.

Another major hurdle in the study of state prosecutions centers around data. Data collection and access issues continue to make the empirical study of state- and local-level prosecutions challenging to conduct. Many states and local jurisdictions lag far behind the federal DOJ in their administrative organization and digital record keeping. Only a small slice of the state-level data that researchers might need are posted on the Web, and FOIA-style requests are often met with delays and mixed results. Local budget shortfalls will likely continue to make data accessibility a challenge.

Researcher have begun to close this gap with large-scale data collection efforts and examinations of individual state prosecutions. Recent studies of individual state prosecutions and prosecutors have covered states like Washington (Boerner 2012), North Carolina (Wright 2012), Colorado (Nelson 2014), and Arizona (Miller and Caplinger 2012). Also notable are large-scale data collection efforts on civil asset forfeiture laws and practices in the states (Carpenter II et al. 2015; Williams et al. 2010), prosecutorial elections and campaign contributions (Hessick 2018, 2020), and various useful state court data and statistics made available by the National Center for State Courts. These data collection efforts, combined with government records, present an enormous opportunity to expand our understanding of the state criminal justice systems (e.g., Ash, Fagan, and Harris 2020; Baumgartner, Epp, and Shoub 2018). With more research and data collection along these lines, we will soon be able to assess the politics of state prosecution.

Additionally, the theoretical argument we advance in this book—that prosecution is political—can be tested in contexts outside the United States. Every country around the world relies on some law enforcement official to determine which potential violations of law should be pursued in the judicial system and which suspected crimes will not be addressed in court. Like their U.S. counterparts, many of these prosecutors have large amounts of unchecked power (Choe 2014; De Federico 1998; Ma 2002). Just as scholars of

U.S. politics have been slow to examine the behavior of prosecutors in this country, so have scholars of law and courts in other countries been reluctant to scrutinize the behavior of prosecutorial actors with the tools of social scientific inquiry.

9.3 Injustice or Politics as Usual?

Some may argue that the presence of ongoing political prosecution, rather than objective and law-based prosecution, may "have serious and prolonged consequences on the criminal process" (DiBiagio 2000, 66) and affect the public's confidence in the criminal justice system and government. Writing about this very thing in 2000 as a former Assistant U.S. Attorney for the District of Maryland, Thomas DiBiagio argued that having prosecutors factor politics and public opinion in their decision-making would:

> [D]emonstrate a fecklessness inappropriate to the responsibilities of a prosecutor. It would signal the acceptance of a false equation between the political and criminal process and legitimate role for political polls, approval ratings and periodic elections in the criminal process. The next step would be for prosecutors to rely on image-makers and focus groups to see what kind of crimes and criminals the public wants prosecuted. The result would be, a culture of corruption and complacency and a criminal process, once conceived as a matter of paramount seriousness, will become just another trivial precinct of raw and partisan politics in service of the vagaries of public sentiment.[4] (DiBiagio 2000, 66–67)

The U.S. criminal justice system already faces an ever-growing legitimacy deficit from issues that are only partially related to prosecutors—from race relations with police to outcries regarding mass incarceration (Enns 2016; Gibson and Nelson 2018; Peffley and Hurwitz 2010). This means that adding

[4] DiBiagio would go on to be appointed by President George W. Bush as the U.S. Attorney for the District of Maryland in 2001. Ironically, DiBiagio was asked to resign from the position in 2005 after investigating officials in Maryland Governor Ehrlich's administration for corruption. According to DiBiagio, he had to resign in 2005 because "I believe it was that investigation that played an integral role in what was done to me . . . I clearly got the message that I had alienated my political sponsor" (Rich 2007). While DiBiagio claimed his forced resignation was political in nature, David Margolis, an associate deputy attorney general in the DOJ argued that he had "lost confidence" in DiBiagio's abilities and that there were "absolutely no political shenanigans" in the removal (Rich 2007).

concerns about political prosecutions being equivalent to injustice and corruption could be crippling to the already fragile criminal justice system. We have highlighted how much discretion prosecutors have as agenda setters for the federal criminal justice system. That discretion opens the door for politically tinged injustice, in the form of political factors, to affect federal prosecutors' decision-making and staffing. In his classic work, Davis (1969, 25) may have captured the intertwined dangers of politics and discretion best:

> [E]very truth extolling discretion may be matched by a truth about its dangers: Discretion is a tool only when properly used; like an axe, it can be a weapon for mayhem or murder. In a government of men and of laws, the portion that is a government of men, like a malignant cancer, often tends to stifle the portion that is a government of laws. Perhaps nine-tenths of injustice in our legal system flows from discretion and perhaps only one-tenth from rules.

Tyler and Huo (2002) have argued that gaining public deference to legal authorities and acceptance of legal decisions depends, at least in part, on the public judging officials' motives as trustworthy. In fact, many studies show that the American people understand that the decisions of political elites are discretionary; they are willing to accept decisions with which they disagree so long as the *process* used to make the decision is fair.

The vast literature on the public's support for the U.S. Supreme Court is instructive. Hibbing and Theiss-Morse (1995) demonstrate that, as the public associates a political institution with "politics," they tend to support it at lower rates. That the public dislikes politicking explains the Supreme Court's comparatively high level of public support as a historical matter:

> [T]he Court is associated with the constitutional system but is viewed as being above the Washington system; decisions seem firm and clear, with bickering and deal making sheltered from the public view, notwithstanding an occasional aberration or expose.[5] (Hibbing and Theiss-Morse 1995, 148)

More broadly, when people think that the judicial branch of government makes its decisions based on principle, rather than politics, they are likely

[5] This suggestion has a long history. Lipset and Schneider (1987) argue that confidence in the U.S. Supreme Court is high because the Court is "perceived as 'above politics'" by Americans (69).

to support the judiciary at higher levels. By contrast, when Americans believe that the judiciary engages in the politicking that they believe to be pervasive in Washington, their support for the judiciary drops sharply (Gibson and Caldeira 2009). The judicial branch, in other words, garners much of its public support from a belief that it is a "different" type of political institution (Gibson and Nelson 2017).

The public generally thinks highly of the Supreme Court even when they are disappointed with its decisions (cf. Bartels and Johnston 2013; Christenson and Glick 2015; Gibson and Nelson 2015). Indeed, as Gibson and Nelson (2014) argue:

> [T]he American people seem to accept that judicial decision making can be discretionary and grounded in ideology, while simultaneously principled and sincere. Judges differ from ordinary politicians in acting sincerely, and their sincerity adds tremendously both to their legitimacy and the legitimacy of their institution. (211)

So long as the public believes that judges are not "ordinary politicians," they trust it to perform its important role in the American political system (Gibson and Nelson 2017).

This research suggests that a public that prefers an aggressive approach to fighting certain types of crimes will approve of a prosecutorial agenda that does the same. Still, the key element of prosecutor's public support lies not necessarily in making decisions that are congruent with public preferences but rather in ensuring the public that they are making their decisions in a fair and straightlaced manner. This fact perhaps goes a long way toward explaining the quotations that opened both this chapter and Chapter 1: Attorneys General take pains to emphasize the formally nonpartisan nature of their Department's work in an effort to maintain the public's support for that institution. To be sure, additional research is needed to assess whether this link between the fairness of prosecutorial process and approval of decisions holds in the federal prosecutorial context.

It is important to note that our empirical results do not suggest that *all* federal prosecution choices are political. There are numerous easy, nondiscretionary prosecution decisions where we should expect virtually all U.S. Attorneys to proceed in the same way, no matter the political signals emanating from their environment or the identity of the president in office. And, in many highly salient prosecutions, intense political and media scrutiny can help ensure that federal prosecutors have the independence they need to enforce the law. The room for political effects comes from the criminal matters that lie between the extremes, where sizable discretion exists on whether and how to proceed with a prosecution.

In a similar optimistic vein rests the nature of the politics that we see in federal prosecutors' work. While we have all heard about the high-profile criminal matters in the DOJ that involve political actors and consequences—whether they be Hillary Clinton, Roger Stone, or Michael Flynn—these are not representative of the typical files that come across U.S. Attorneys' desks. Most federal criminal matters do not involve well-known political figures. Ultimately, the politics that we see federal prosecutors engage in and that have been highlighted throughout this book's empirical analysis is, in the vast majority of cases, much closer to political responsiveness than political nepotism or political injustice.

And this political responsiveness can have important positive effects for the American legal and political systems. To the extent that independence provides opportunities for individual prosecutors to enforce the law as they see fit, prosecutorial independence divorced from political responsiveness would likely bring the American legal system back to the decentralized and chaotic system that characterized the country's federal law enforcement apparatus before the Civil War. In such a system, individual prosecutors would be free to bring cases that helped them advance personally through the political ranks with little regard to the legal arguments and law enforcement priorities that are important across districts and at the federal level. For this reason, political responsiveness can help enhance the uniformity and consistency of American law and its enforcement.

Still, to the extent that some worry that federal prosecution is too political, potential solutions can be found, perhaps ironically, in the political process. In particular, one notable reform option would be to alter staffing mechanisms and reduce decision-making discretion through federal law. Institutional designs that insulate the positions from politics can make offices less responsive to presidential control (Lewis 2003, 2008). These features are often used to insulate activities such as central banking (like the Federal Reserve Board), where the temptation to play politics with the policy at hand is high (North and Weingast 1989). U.S. Attorney positions were created by Congress through statute, and the method of selection and removal is thus amendable through the passage of new laws. While President Carter failed to gain congressional passage for the merit selection of U.S.

Attorneys, it, or a similar plan, remains a possibility given enough political support. Congress could equally amend law to insulate U.S. Attorneys from presidential removal. Similarly, federal criminal laws can curtail prosecutorial decision-making discretion—and the potential for ongoing political responsiveness—in ways that perhaps mirror efforts over the past 40 years to reduce judicial discretion in sentencing (via, e.g., mandatory sentencing laws and sentencing guidelines). Alterations of federal law may change who becomes a U.S. Attorney and the decisions that they make in a way that reduces some of the politics of federal prosecution. But, unquestionably, such changes would surely create new and complex concerns of their own that need to be carefully calculated and considered before any reforms take place.

9.4 Final Thoughts

In the end, prosecutors are important political actors because of their vast power. Their decisions are a fundamental part of "who gets what, when, and how" (to say nothing of who gets *away* with what, when, and how) (Lasswell 1936). When a prosecutor decides whether to pursue a charge against a suspect, they, virtually alone, decide who faces punishment for a potential violation of federal law and who does not. When a prosecutor decides what plea bargain or sentence recommendation to offer a defendant, they, with minimal oversight, decide whether a defendant should face lenient or severe ramifications for violating federal law. These decisions raise fundamental concerns about inequality, fairness, and justice; political scientists and the public have, to date, not given these important political actors a level of attention and scrutiny commensurate with the level of political power they have at their disposal. That should change.

Cases Cited

Berger v. United States, 295 U.S. 78 (1935)
Bordenkircher v. Hayes, 434 U.S. 357 (1978)
Calero-Toledo v. Pearson Yacht Leasing Co., 416 U.S. 663 (1974)
Caplin & Drysdale v. United States, 491 U.S. 617 (1989)
Hamlett v. Dep't of Justice, 20 M.S.P.R. 674 (2002)
Hayes v. Cowan, 547 F.2d 42 (6th Cir. 1976)
Heckler v. Chaney, 470 U.S. 821 (1985)
Honeycutt v. United States, 581 U.S. (2017)
Kaley v. United States, 571 U.S. 320 (2014)
Lafler v. Cooper, 132 S. Ct. 1376 (2012)
LaRouche v. Webster, 566 F. Supp. 415 (S.D.N.Y. 1983)
Morrison v. Olson, 487 U.S. 654 (1988)
Newman v. United States, 382 F.2d 479 (D.C. Cir. 1967)
Oyler v. Boles, 368 U.S. 448 (1962)
Santobello v. New York, 404 U.S. 257 (1971)
United States v. Armstrong, 21 F.3d 1431 (9th Cir. 1994)
United States v. Armstrong, 517 U.S. 456 (1996)
United States v. Bajakajian, 524 U.S. 321 (1998)
United States v. Carpenter, 941 F. 3d 1, 11 (1st Cir. 2019)
United States v. Carpenter, 1:04-cr-10029 (D.MA)
United States v. Flemmi, 225 F.3d 78 (1st Cir. 2000)
United States v. Monsanto, 491 U.S. 600 (1989)
United States v. Patel, 131 F.3d 1195 (7th Cir. 1997)
United States v. Robertson, 15 F.3d 862 (9th Cir. 1994)
United States v. Ursery, 518 U.S. 267 (1996)

References

ABC News. 2007. "What Happened in the U.S. Attorneys Firing Controversy?" March 29, 2007.

Albonetti, Celesta A. 1986. "Criminality, Prosecutorial Screening, and Uncertainty: Toward a Theory of Discretionary Decision Making in Felony Case Processings." *Criminology* 24: 623–44.

Albonetti, Celesta A. 1987. "Prosecutorial Discretion: The Effects of Uncertainty." *Law & Society Review* 21: 291–313.

Alexander, Keith L., Spencer S. Hsu, and Matt Zapotosky. 2020. "President Trump to Nominate New Top Prosecutor for the District." *Washington Post* May 18, 2020.

Alschuler, Albert W. 1968. "The Prosecutor's Role in Plea Bargaining." *University of Chicago Law Review* 36: 50–112.

Alschuler, Albert W. 1991. "The Failure of Sentencing Guidelines: A Plea for Less Aggregation." *University of Chicago Law Review* 58: 901–51.

Apollonio, Dorie, Todd Lochner, and Myriah Heddens. 2013. "Immigration and Prosecutorial Discretion." *California Journal of Politics and Policy* 5: 232–51.

Ash, Elliott, Jeffrey Fagan, and Allison P. Harris. 2020. "Local Public Finance and Discriminatory Policing: Evidence from Traffic Stops in Missouri." *Journal of Race, Ethnicity, and Politics*, 1-28. doi:10.1017/rep.2020.8.

Ashcroft, John. 2003. "Department Policies and Procedures Concerning Sentencing Recommendations and Sentencing Appeals" Official Memorandum. U.S. Department of Justice. July 28, 2003.

Asmussen, Nichole. 2011. "Female and Minority Judicial Nominees: President's Delight and Senators' Dismay?" *Legislative Studies Quarterly* 36(4): 591-619.

Associated Press. 1993. "Briefs Column; Kansas City U.S. Attorney Assails Call for Resignation." *St. Louis Post-Dispatch* March 28, 1993.

Associated Press. 1996. "U.S. Attorney Resigns Amid Turmoil." *Tulsa World* May 18, 1996.

Associated Press. 2006. "Interim U.S. Attorney Post Subject of Legal Fight." *Associated Press* January 5, 2006.

Associated Press. 2008. "Prosecutor Named as New US Attorney for New Mexico." *Associated Press State & Local Wire* January 26, 2008.

Atkins, Burton, and Mark Pogrebin. 1982. "Discretionary Decision-Making in the Administration of Justice" in *The Invisible Justice System: Discretion & Law*, edited by Burton Atkins and Mark Pogrebin, 3–15. Anderson Publishing Co.

Bailey, Michael A., Brian Kamoie, and Forrest Maltzman. 2005. "Signals from the Tenth Justice: The Political Role of the Solicitor General in Supreme Court Decision Making." *American Journal of Political Science* 49: 72–85.

Balsamo, Michael. 2020. "Barr to Prosecutors: Look for Unconstitutional Virus Rules." *Associated Press* April 27, 2020.

Barkow, Rachel E. 2009. "Institutional Design and the Policing of Prosecutors: Lessons from Administrative Law." *Stanford Law Review* 61: 869–921.

Barr, William. 2020a. "Additional Requirements for the Opening of Certain Sensitive Investigations" Official Memorandum. U.S. Department of Justice. February 5, 2020.

Barr, William. 2020b. "COVID-19—Department of Justice Priorities" Official Memorandum. U.S. Department of Justice. March 16, 2020.

Bartels, Brandon L., and Christopher D. Johnston. 2013. "On the Ideological Foundations of Supreme Court Legitimacy in the American Public." *American Journal of Political Science* 57: 711–81.

Baumgartner, Frank R., Derek A. Epp, and Kelsey Shoub. 2018. *Suspect Citizens*. Cambridge University Press.

Baumgartner, Frank R., and Bryan D. Jones. 2013. "Policy Agendas Project." Available at: http://www.comparativeagendas.net.

Baumgartner, Frank R., and Bryan D. Jones. 2015. *The Politics of Information: Problem Definition and the Course of Public Policy in America*. University of Chicago Press.

Bawn, Kathleen. 1995. "Political Control Versus Expertise: Congressional Choices about Administrative Procedures." *American Political Science Review* 89: 62–73.

Beale, Sara Sun. 1996. "Federalizing Crime: Assessing the Impact on the Federal Courts." *Annals of the American Academy of Political and Social Sciences* 543: 39–51.

Beale, Sara Sun. 2009. "Rethinking the Identity and Role of United States Attorneys." *Ohio State Journal of Criminal Law* 6: 369.

Bell, Griffin B. 1977. "Address by Griffin B. Bell to the American Law Institute" Washington, D.C. May 18, 1977.

Bell, Griffin B., and Daniel J. Meador. 1993. "Appointing United States Attorneys." *Journal of Law & Politics* 9: 247–56.

Bell, Lauren Cohen. 2002. "Senatorial Discourtesy: The Senate's Use of Delay to Shape the Federal Judiciary." *Political Research Quarterly* 55(3): 589–608.

Benesh, Sara C., and Wendy L. Martinek. 2002. "State Supreme Court Decision Making in Confession Cases." *Justice System Journal* 23: 109–34.

Benner, Katie, and Adam Goldman. 2020. "Barr Dismisses Trump's Claim That Russia Inquiry Was an Obama Plot." *New York Times* May 18, 2020.

Benner, Katie, and Sharon LaFraniere. 2020. "For Barr, Standoff with Prosecutor Adds to String of Miscues." *New York Times* June 21, 2020.

Berman, Geoffrey S. 2020. "Statement of U.S. Attorney Geoffrey S. Berman on Announcement by Attorney General Barr" Press Release. U.S. Attorney's Office for the Southern District of New York. June 19, 2020.

Bernac, Nancy. 1993. "Clinton Defends Calling for U.S. Attorneys to Resign." *Associated Press* March 25, 1993.

Bernstein, Ilene Nagel, Edward Kick, Jan T. Leung, and Barbara Schulz. 1977. "Charge Reduction: An Intermediary Stage in the Process of Labeling Criminal Defendants." *Social Forces* 56: 362–84.

Bibas, Stephanos. 2004. "Plea Bargaining Outside the Shadow of Trial." *Harvard Law Review* 117: 2464–547.

Binder, Sarah. 2018. "Dodging the Rules in Trump's Republican Congress." *Journal of Politics* 80: 1454–63.

Binder, Sarah A., and Forrest Maltzman. 2002. "Senatorial Delay in Confirming Federal Judges." *American Journal of Political Science* 46(1): 190–9.

Binder, Sarah A., and Forrest Maltzman. 2009. *Advice & Dissent: The Struggle to Shape the Federal Judiciary*. Brookings Institution Press.

Bishop, Donna M., and Charles E. Frazier. 1984. "The Effects of Gender on Charge Reduction." *Sociological Quarterly* 25: 369–85.
Bishop, Tricia. 2009. "Under Obama, No Purge of U.S. Attorneys." *Baltimore Sun* March 9, 2009.
Black, Ryan C., Anthony J. Madonna, Ryan J. Owens, and Michael S. Lynch. 2007. "Adding Recess Appointments to the President's 'Tool Chest' of Unilateral Powers." *Political Research Quarterly* 60: 645–54.
Black, Ryan C., and Ryan J. Owens. 2012. *The Solicitor General and the United States Supreme Court: Executive Branch Influence and Judicial Decisions*. Cambridge University Press.
Blackstone, Bethany, and Greg Goelzhauser. 2014. "Presidential Rhetoric Toward the Supreme Court." *Judicature* 97: 179–87.
Bloch, Susan Low. 1989. "The Early Role of the Attorney General in Our Constitutional Scheme: In the Beginning There Was Pragmatism." *Duke Law Journal* 1989: 561–653.
Blumenson, Eric, and Eva Nilsen. 1998. "Policing for Profit: The Drug War's Hidden Economic Agenda." *University of Chicago Law Review* 65: 35–114.
Boerner, David. 2012. "Prosecution in Washington State." *Crime and Justice* 41: 167–210.
Bond, Jon R., Richard Fleisher, and Glen S. Krutz. 2009. "Malign Neglect: Evidence That Delay Has Become the Primary Method of Defeating Presidential Appointments." *Congress & the Presidency* 36: 226–43.
Bonica, Adam. 2020. "Why Are There so Many Lawyers in Congress?" *Legislative Studies Quarterly* 45: 253–89.
Bonica, Adam, Adam S. Chilton, and Maya Sen. 2016. "The Political Ideologies of American Lawyers." *Journal of Legal Analysis* 8: 277–335.
Box-Steffensmeier, Janet M., and Bradford S. Jones. 2004. *Event History Modeling: A Guide for Social Scientists*. Cambridge University Press.
Boyd, Christina L. 2010. "Federal District Court Judge Ideology Data." Available at: http://cLboyd.net/ideology.html.
Boyd, Christina L. 2013. "She'll Settle It?" *Journal of Law and Courts* 1: 193–219.
Boyd, Christina L. 2015. "The Hierarchical Influence of Courts of Appeals on District Courts." *Journal of Legal Studies* 44: 113–41.
Boyd, Christina L., and David A. Hoffman. 2013. "Litigating Toward Settlement." *Journal of Law, Economics, and Organization* 29: 898–929.
Boylan, Richard T. 2005. "What Do Prosecutors Maximize? Evidence from the Careers of U.S. Attorneys." *American Law and Economics Review* 7: 379–402.
Brace, Paul, and Brent D. Boyea. 2008. "State Public Opinion, the Death Penalty, and the Practice of Electing Judges." *American Journal of Political Science* 52: 360–72.
Brehm, John, and Scott Gates. 1997. *Working, Shirking, and Sabotage*. University of Michigan Press.
Brief for the United States. 2019. *United States of America v. Daniel E. Carpenter*, 14-1641 (United States Court of Appeals for the First Circuit, Filed July 3, 2019).
Briggs, Michael, and Basil Talbott. 1993. "Clinton Defends U.S. Attorneys' Removal; Rosty Denies Roll in Dismissal." *Chicago Sun-Times* March 25, 1993.
Broach, Drew. 2017. "Trump Nominating U.S. Attorneys at Brisk Pace—Louisiana Excepted." *The Times-Picayune* August 14, 2017.
Brown, Pamela, Laura Jarrett, Kevin Liptak, and Theodore Schleifer. 2017. "Anger Mounts over Handling of US Attorney Firings." *CNN* March 10, 2017.
Bureau of Justice Statistics. 2011. "Federal Justice Statistics 2009—Statistical Tables."

Burke, Alafair S. 2007. "Prosecutorial Passion, Cognitive Bias, and Plea Bargaining." *Marquette Law Review* 93: 183–211.

Burke, John P. 2018. "'It Went Off the Rails': Trump's Presidential Transition and the National Security System." *Presidential Studies Quarterly* 48: 832–44.

Butler, Paul D. 2013. "Poor People Lose: *Gideon* and the Critique of Rights." *Yale Law Journal* 122: 2177–2204.

Caldwell, H. Mitchell. 2011. "Coercive Plea Bargaining: The Unrecognized Scourge of the Justice System." *Catholic University Law Review* 61: 63–96.

Cameron, Charles M. 2000. *Veto Bargaining: Presidents and the Politics of Negative Power*. Cambridge University Press.

Canes-Wrone, Brandice. 2001. "The President's Legislative Influence from Public Appeals." *American Political Science Review* 45: 313–29.

Carney, Jordain. 2020. "Schumer Says He Won't Return Blue Slip if Trump Nominates Clayton as US Attorney." *The Hill* June 22, 2020.

Carpenter, Daniel P. 1996. "Adaptive Signal Processing, Hierarchy, and Budgetary Control in Federal Regulation." *American Political Science Review* 90: 283–302.

Carpenter, Daniel P., and George A. Krause. 2012. "Reputation and Public Administration." *Public Administration Review* 72: 26–32.

Carpenter II, Dick M., Lisa Knepper, Angela C. Erickson, and Jennifer McDonald. 2015. "Policing for Profit: The Abuse of Civil Asset Forfeiture. 2nd Edition." Institute for Justice.

Carter, Stephen L. 1994. *The Confirmation Mess: Cleaning Up the Federal Appointments Process*. Basic Books.

Cassella, Stefan D. 2007. "Forfeiture of Property Involved in Money Laundering." *The United States Attorneys' Bulletin* 55: 36–50.

Center for Responsive Politics. 2020a. "Lawyers/Law Firms: Long-Term Contribution Trends" https://www.opensecrets.org/industries/totals.php?cycle=2020&ind=k01.

Center for Responsive Politics. 2020b. "Top Industries" https://www.opensecrets.org/overview/industries.php.

Chin, Gabriel J., and Richard W. Holmes Jr. 2002. "Effective Assistance of Counsel and the Consequences of Guilty Pleas." *Cornell Law Review* 87: 697–742.

Chiou, Fang-Yi, and Lawrence S. Rothenberg. 2013. "Executive Appointments: Duration, Ideology, and Hierarchy." *Journal of Theoretical Politics* 26: 496–517.

Choe, D. H. 2014. "Discretion at the Pre-Trial Stage: A Comparative Study." *European Journal on Criminal Policy and Research* 20: 101–19.

Chozick, Amy. 2016. "Bill Clinton's Fondness for Tarmac Talk Gets Him into Trouble." *New York Times* July 1, 2016.

Christenson, Dino P., and David M. Glick. 2015. "Chief Justice Roberts's Health Care Decision Disrobed: The Microfoundations of the Supreme Court's Legitimacy." *American Journal of Political Science* 59: 403–18.

Clinton, Joshua D., David E. Lewis, and Jennifer L. Selin. 2014. "Influencing the Bureaucracy: The Irony of Congressional Oversight." *American Journal of Political Science* 58: 387–401.

Clinton, William J. 1993. "Exchange with Reporters Prior to a Meeting with Dorsey High School Students." *American Presidency Project* March 25, 1993. https://www.presidency.ucsb.edu/node/219379.

Clymer, Steven D. 1997. "Unequal Justice: The Federalization of Criminal Law." *Southern California Law Review* 70: 643–740.

Coats, Sanford C., and Chris M. Stephens. 2015. "U.S. Attorney: The Servant of the Law." *Federal Lawyer* March: 46–57.

Cole, James M. 2013. *Guidance Regarding Marijuana Enforcement*. U.S. Department of Justice. August 29, 2013.

Collins, Kaitlan. 2020. "Decision to Pull Liu's Nomination Directly Linked to Her Oversight of Stone and McCabe Cases." *CNN* February 12, 2020.

Collinson, Stephen. 2020. "Firing of Powerful NY Prosecutor Appears to Be Latest Move to Protect Trump." *CNN* June 20, 2020.

Congressional Research Service. 2015. "Asset Forfeiture: Selected Legal Issues and Reforms."

Crime Solutions. 2015. "Program Profile: Project Exile."

Cummings, Homer, and Carl McFarland. 1937. *Federal Justice: Chapters in the History of Justice and the Federal Executive*. MacMillan.

Dangel, Stephanie A. J. 1990. "Is Prosecution a Core Executive Function? *Morrison V. Olson* and the Framers' Intent." *Yale Law Journal* 99: 1069–88.

Davis, Kenneth Culp. 1969. *Discretionary Justice: A Preliminary Inquiry*. University of Illinois Press.

De Federico, Guiseppe. 1998. "Prosecutorial Independence and the Democratic Requirement of Accountability in Italy." *British Journal of Criminology* 38: 371–87.

Department of the Treasury. 2004. *Treasury Forfeiture Fund Accountability Report*.

DiBiagio, Thomas M. 2000. "Politics and the Criminal Process: Federal Public Corruption Prosecutions of Popular Public Officials Under the Honest Services Component of the Mail and Wire Fraud Statutes." *Dickinson Law Review* 105: 57–92.

Dienst, Jonathan, and Tracy Connor. 2018. "Sessions Uses Executive Authority to Appoint Interim U.S. Attorneys." *NBC News* January 3, 2018.

Doyle, Charles. 2007. *Crime and Forfeiture*. Congressional Research Service. May 9, 2007.

Doyle, Charles. 2013. *Crime and Forfeiture*. Congressional Research Service. May 13, 2013.

Doyle, Charles. 2015. *Crime and Forfeiture*. Congressional Research Service. January 22, 2015.

Easby-Smith, James S. 1904. *The Department of Justice: Its History and Functions*. W.H. Loudermilk & Company.

Eggen, Dan. 2007. "Prosecutor Firings Not Political, Gonzales Says." *Washington Post* January 19, 2007.

Eisenstein, James. 1978. *Counsel for the United States: U.S. Attorneys in the Political and Legal Systems*. Johns Hopkins University Press.

Eisenstein, James. 2008. "The U.S. Attorney Firings of 2006: Main Justice's Centralization Efforts in Historical Context." *Seattle University Law Review* 31: 219–63.

Eisenstein, James, and Herbert Jacob. 1977. *Felony Justice: An Organizational Analysis of Criminal Courts*. Little, Brown and Company.

Emshwiller, John R., and Gary Fields. 2011. "Federal Asset Seizures Rise, Netting Innocent with Guilty." *Wall Street Journal* August 22, 2011.

Engstrom, Richard L. 1971. "Political Ambitions and the Prosecutorial Office." *Journal of Politics* 33: 190–94.

Enns, Peter K. 2014. "The Public's Increasing Punitiveness and Its Influence on Mass Incarceration in the United States." *American Journal of Political Science* 58: 857–72.

Enns, Peter K. 2016. *Incarceration Nation: How the United States Became the Most Punitive Democracy in the World*. Cambridge University Press.

Epstein, David, and Sharon O'Halloran. 1996. "Divided Government and the Design of Administrative Procedures: A Formal Model and Empirical Test." *Journal of Politics* 58: 373–97.

Epstein, David, and Sharyn O'Halloran. 1999. *Delegating Powers: A Transaction Cost Politics Approach to Policy Making Under Separate Powers*. Cambridge University Press.

Epstein, Lee, and Jack Knight. 1998. *The Choices Justices Make*. CQ Press.

Epstein, Lee, and Joseph F. Kobylka. 1992. *The Supreme Court and Legal Change: Abortion and the Death Penalty*. University of North Carolina Press.

Epstein, Lee, Andrew D. Martin, Kevin M. Quinn, and Jeffrey A. Segal. 2008. "Circuit Effects: How the Norm of Federal Judicial Experience Biases the Supreme Court." *University of Pennsylvania Law Review* 157: 833–80.

Epstein, Lee, Andrew Martin, Jeffrey A. Segal, and Chad Westerland. 2007. "The Judicial Common Space." *Journal of Law, Economics & Organization* 23: 303–25.

Epstein, Lee, Thomas G. Walker, and William J. Dixon. 1989. "The Supreme Court and Criminal Justice Disputes: A Neo-Institutional Perspective." *American Journal of Political Science* 33: 825–41.

Eshbaugh-Soha, Matthew. 2008. "The Impact of Presidential Speeches on the Bureaucracy." *Social Science Quarterly* 89: 116–32.

Eshbaugh-Soha, Matthew. 2010. "How Policy Conditions the Impact of Presidential Speeches on Legislative Success." *Social Science Quarterly* 91: 415–35.

Eshbaugh-Soha, Matthew, and Jeffrey S. Peake. 2011. *Breaking Through the Noise: Presidential Leadership, Public Opinion, and the News Media*. Stanford University Press.

Executive Office for U.S. Attorneys. 1989. *Bicentennial Celebration of the United States Attorneys*. U.S. Department of Justice.

Executive Office for U.S. Attorneys. 2009. "Annual Statistical Report 2009" https://www.justice.gov/sites/default/files/usao/legacy/2010/10/13/09statrpt.pdf.

Executive Office for U.S. Attorneys. 2010. "Annual Statistical Report 2010" https://www.justice.gov/sites/default/files/usao/legacy/2011/09/01/10statrpt.pdf.

Executive Office for U.S. Attorneys. 2015. "Annual Statistical Report 2015" https://www.justice.gov/usao/file/831856/download.

Farnworth, Margaret, and Raymond H. C. Teske Jr. 1995. "Gender Differences in Felony Court Processing: Three Hypotheses of Disparity." *Women and Criminal Justice* 6: 23–44.

Federal Judicial Center. 2012. "Federal Judges Biographical Database" http://www.fjc.gov/public/home.nsf/hisj.

Feinstein, Dianne. 2017. "Feinstein Statement on Firing of U.S. Attorneys" Press Release. March 10, 2017.

Ferejohn, John, and Charles Shipan. 1989. "Congressional Influence on Administrative Agencies: A Case Study of Telecommunications Policy" in *Congress Reconsidered*, 4th ed., edited by Lawrence C. Dodd and Bruce I. Oppenheimer. CQ Press.

Feuer, Alan, Katie Benner, Ben Protess, Maggie Haberman, William K. Rashbaum, Nicole Hong, and Benjamin Weiser. 2020. "Trump Fires U.S. Attorney in New York Who Investigated His Inner Circle." *New York Times* June 20, 2020.

Flemming, Roy B., and B. Dan Wood. 1997. "The Public and the Supreme Court: Individual Justice Responsiveness to American Policy Moods." *American Journal of Political Science* 41: 468–98.

Flemming, Roy B., B. Dan Wood, and John Bohte. 1999. "Attention to Issues in a System of Separated Powers: The Macrodynamics of American Policy Agendas." *Journal of Politics* 61: 76–108.

Forst, Brian. 1999. "Prosecution" in *Crime: Public Policies for Crime Control*, edited by James Q. Wilson and Joan Petersilia, 509–36. ICS Press.

Fox News Sunday. 2016. "Exclusive: President Barack Obama on 'Fox News Sunday.'" *Fox News Sunday* April 10, 2016.

Frase, Richard S. 1980. "The Decision to File Federal Criminal Charges: A Quantitative Study of Prosecutorial Discretion." *University of Chicago Law Review* 47: 246–330.

Frederick, Bruce, and Don Stemen. 2012. *The Anatomy of Discretion: An Analysis of Prosecutorial Decision Making—Technical Report*. Final Report to the National Institute of Justice.

Freed, Daniel J., and Marc Miller. 1994. "Guiding the Discretion of U.S. Attorneys: Department of Justice Policies, 1980–1994." *Federal Sentencing Reporter* 6: 299–301.

Galanter, Marc. 2004. "The Vanishing Trial: An Examination of Trials and Related Matters in Federal and State Courts." *Journal of Empirical Legal Studies* 1: 459–570.

Gashko, John M. 1977. "A Question of Politics and the Law." *Washington Post* June 26, 1977.

George, Sandra Caron. 2005. "Prosecutorial Discretion: What's Politics Got to Do with It?" *Georgetown Journal of Legal Ethics* 18: 739–58.

George, Tracey E. 2001. "Court Fixing." *Arizona Law Review* 43: 9–62.

George, Tracey E., and Albert H. Yoon. 2003. "The Federal Court System: A Principal-Agent Perspective." *St. Louis University Law Journal* 47: 819–34.

Gerstein, Josh. 2018. "Justice Department Confirms Sessions' Recusal from Election Inquiries." *Politico* April 24, 2018.

Gerstein, Josh, and Josh Dawsey. 2017. "Trump Team Ousts Obama-Appointed U.S. Attorneys." *Politico* March 10, 2017.

Gibeaut, John. 2004. "The Good Fight Gets Harder." *American Bar Association Journal* February: 41–46.

Gibson, James L. 1978. "Race as a Determinant of Criminal Sentences: A Methodological Critique and a Case Study." *Law and Society Review* 12: 455–78.

Gibson, James L., and Gregory A. Caldeira. 2009. *Citizens, Courts, and Confirmations: Positivity Theory and the Judgments of the American People*. Princeton University Press.

Gibson, James L., and Michael J. Nelson. 2014. "The Legitimacy of the U.S. Supreme Court: Conventional Wisdoms, and Recent Challenges Thereto." *Annual Review of Law and Social Science* 10: 201–19.

Gibson, James L., and Michael J. Nelson. 2015. "Is the U.S. Supreme Court's Legitimacy Grounded in Performance Satisfaction and Ideology?" *American Journal of Political Science* 59: 162–74.

Gibson, James L., and Michael J. Nelson. 2017. "Reconsidering Positivity Theory: What Roles Do Politicization, Ideological Disagreement, and Legal Realism Play in Shaping U.S. Supreme Court Legitimacy?" *Journal of Empirical Legal Studies* 14: 592–617.

Gibson, James L., and Michael J. Nelson. 2018. *Black and Blue: How African Americans Judge the U.S. Legal System*. Oxford University Press.

Giles, Micheal W., Virginia A. Hettinger, and Todd Peppers. 2001. "Picking Federal Judges: A Note on Policy and Partisan Selection Agendas." *Political Research Quarterly* 54: 623–41.

Glaberson, William. 2011. "A Surplus of 'a Few Good Men.'" *New York Times* September 15, 2011.

Goldman, Adam. 2016. "Justice Department Grants Immunity to Staffer Who Set Up Clinton Email Server." *Chicago Tribune* March 2, 2016.

Goldman, Sheldon. 1997. *Picking Federal Judges: Lower Court Selection from Roosevelt Through Reagan*. University of California Press.

Gordon, Sanford C., and Gregory A. Huber. 2002. "Citizen Oversight and the Electoral Incentives of Criminal Prosecutors." *American Journal of Political Science* 46: 334–51.

Gordon, Sanford C., and Gregory A. Huber. 2009. "The Political Economy of Prosecution." *Annual Review of Law and Social Science* 5: 135–56.

Graham, Kyle. 2012. "Crimes, Widgets, and Plea Bargaining: An Analysis of Charge Content, Pleas, and Trials." *California Law Review* 100: 1573–1630.

Gray, Jeremy. 2018. "Jeff Sessions Resigns: What's Next for Mueller Investigation? Alabama Senate Race? What We Know." *AL.com* November 8, 2018.

Graybiel, Ginny. 2001. "U.S. Attorney to Resign, Try Again for Job." *Pensacola News Journal* April 25, 2001.

Green, Frank. 2017. "In Richmond, Attorney General Jeff Sessions Says He Will Expand Project Exile Nationwide." *Richmond Times-Dispatch* March 15, 2017.

Groer, Anne. 1994. "Colleton Resigns as U.S. Attorney, Gets Another Post." *Orlando Sentinel* July 30, 1994.

Gullo, Karen. 2001. "Ashcroft: Bush Will Keep Federal Prosecutor in New York—for Now." *Associated Press* March 27, 2001.

Haberman, Maggie, and Charlie Savage. 2017. "U.S. Attorney Preet Bharara Says He Was Fired After Refusing to Quit." *New York Times* March 11, 2017.

Hannity, Sean. 2017. "Sean Hannity: Trump Must Purge Deep-State Bureaucracy Now." *Fox News* March 10, 2017.

Hart, Henry M., and Albert M. Sacks. 1958. "The Legal Process: Basic Problems in the Making and Application of Law." Foundation Press.

Hartley, Richard D., Sean Maddan, and Cassia C. Spohn. 2007. "Prosecutorial Discretion: An Examination of Substantial Assistance Departures in Federal Crack-Cocaine and Powder-Cocaine Cases." *Justice Quarterly* 24: 382–407.

Hauser, Jeff. 2018. "How Jeff Sessions Is Sneaking Trump Allies into Key DOJ Positions That Normally Require Senate Confirmation." *Slate* March 14, 2018.

Hawkings, David. 2017. "Yesterday's US Attorneys May Be Tomorrow's Congressional Candidates." *Roll Call* March 16, 2017.

Heller, Robert. 1997. "Selective Prosecution and the Federalization of Criminal Law: The Need for Meaningful Judicial Review of Prosecutorial Discretion." *University of Pennsylvania Law Review* 145 (May): 1309–58.

Hendershot, Marcus E. 2010. "From Consent to Advice and Consent: Cyclical Constraints within the District Court Appointment Process." *Political Research Quarterly* 63(2): 328–42.

Henning, Peter J. 2017. "Bharara's Firing Echoes Furor over Past Prosecutors' Dismissals." *New York Times* March 13, 2017.

Hessick, Carissa Byrne. 2018. "Campaign Contributions in Prosecutorial Elections, 2014–2017." University of North Carolina School of Law. https://doi.org/10.15139/S3/D2GBVQ.

Hessick, Carissa Byrne. 2020. *The Prosecutors and Politics Project: National Study of Prosecutor Elections*. University of North Carolina School of Law. https://law.unc.edu/wp-content/uploads/2020/01/National-Study-Prosecutor-Elections-2020.pdf.

Hettinger, Virginia A., Stefanie A. Lindquist, and Wendy L. Martinek. 2004. "Comparing Attitudinal and Strategic Accounts of Dissenting Behavior on the U.S. Courts of Appeals." *American Journal of Political Science* 48: 123–37.

Hettinger, Virginia A., Stefanie A. Lindquist, and Wendy L. Martinek. 2006. *Judging on a Collegial Court*. University of Virginia Press.

Hibbing, John R., and Elizabeth Theiss-Morse. 1995. *Congress as Public Enemy: Public Attitudes Toward American Political Institutions*. Cambridge University Press.

Hinkle, Rachael K., Andrew D. Martin, Jonathan David Shaub, and Emerson H. Tiller. 2012. "A Positive Theory and Empirical Analysis of Strategic Word Choice in District Court Opinions." *Journal of Legal Analysis* 4: 407–44.

Holcomb, Jefferson E., Tomislav V. Kovandzic, and Marian R. Williams. 2011. "Civil Asset Forfeiture, Equitable Sharing, and Policing for Profit in the United States." *Journal of Criminal Justice* 39: 273–85.

Holder, Eric H. 2010. "Department Policy on Charging and Sentencing" Official Memorandum. U.S. Department of Justice. May 19, 2010.

Holder, Eric H. 2013. "Department Policy on Charging Mandatory Minimum Sentences and Recidivist Enhancements in Certain Drug Cases" Official Memorandum. U.S. Department of Justice. August 12, 2013.

Holmes, Lisa M. 2007. "Presidential Strategy in the Judicial Appointment Process: 'Going Public' in Support of Nominees to the U.S. Courts of Appeals." *American Politics Research* 35: 567–94.

Holmes, Malcolm D., Howard C. Daudistel, and Ronald A. Farrell. 1987. "Determinants of Charge Reductions and Final Dispositions in Cases of Burglary and Robbery." *Journal of Research in Crime and Delinquency* 24: 233–54.

Hoogenboom, Ari. 1961. *Outlawing the Spoils: A History of the Civil Service Reform Movement 1865–1883*. University of Illinois Press.

Horwitz, Sari. 2017a. "A Month After Dismissing Federal Prosecutors, Justice Department Does Not Have Any U.S. Attorneys in Place." *Washington Post* April 18, 2017.

Horwitz, Sari. 2017b. "With Sessions's Recusal, Official Poised to Oversee Probe into Russian Interference in 2016 Race." *Washington Post* March 3, 2017.

Horwitz, Sari, and Devlin Barrett. 2017. "Justice Department Tells All Remaining Obama Administration U.S. Attorneys to Resign." *Washington Post* March 10, 2017.

House Judiciary Committee. 2009. *Department of Justice with Attorney General Eric Holder*. Hearing before the Committee on the Judiciary House of Representatives. May 14, 2009. 111th Congress. 1st Session.

House Legislation and National Security Subcommittee. 1992. *Department of Justice Asset Forfeiture Program*. Committee on Government Operations, House of Representatives, 102nd Congress.

Houten, Pieter van. 2009. "Multi-Level Relations in Political Parties." *Party Politics* 15: 137–56.

Howard, Robert M, Richard E. Chard, Joel T. Kaji, and Jeffrey Davis. 2000. "Pre-Trial Bargaining and Litigation: The Search for Fairness and Efficiency." *Law & Society Review* 34: 431–56.

Huber, John D., and Charles R. Shipan. 2011. "Politics, Delegation, and Bureaucracy" in *The Oxford Handbook of Political Science*, edited by Robert E. Goodin, 849–865. Oxford University Press.

Hurwitz, Jon, and Mark Peffley. 2005. "Explaining the Great Racial Divide: Perceptions of Fairness in the U.S. Criminal Justice System." *Journal of Politics* 67: 762–83.

Huston, Luther A. 1967. *The Department of Justice*. Frederick A. Praeger.

Jackson, Andrew. 1830. "Second Annual Message." *The American Presidency Project.* December 6, 1830 https://www.presidency.ucsb.edu/documents/second-annual-message-3.

Jackson, Robert H. 1940. "Remarks at the Second Annual Conference of United States Attorneys Held in the Department of Justice Building, Washington, D.C. (April 1, 1940)."

Jacoby, Joan E. 1980. *The American Prosecutor: A Search for Identity.* Lexington Books.

Jansen, Mart, and Gregory D. Keisch. 2007. "Attorney Unaware Her Post 'Vacant.'" *Portland Press Herald* March 25, 2007.

Jefferson, Thomas. 1816. "Extract from Thomas Jefferson's Note for Destutt de Tracy's Treatise on Political Economy."

Johnson, Brian D., and Sara Betsinger. 2009. "Punishing the 'Model Minority': Asian-American Criminal Sentencing Outcomes in Federal District Courts." *Criminology* 47: 1045–90.

Johnson, Brian D., Ryan D. King, and Cassia Spohn. 2016. "Sociolegal Approaches to the Study of Guilty Pleas and Prosecution." *Annual Review of Law and Social Science* 12: 479–95.

Johnson, Brian D., Jeffrey T. Ulmer, and John H. Kramer. 2008. "The Social Context of Guidelines Circumvention: The Case of Federal District Courts." *Criminology* 46: 737–84.

Johnson, Timothy R., and Jason M. Roberts. 2004. "Presidential Capital and the Supreme Court Confirmation Process." *Journal of Politics* 66: 663–83.

Johnston, David. 1993. "Attorney General Seeks Resignations from Prosecutors." *New York Times* March 24, 1993.

Johnston, David. 2007a. "A U.S. Attorney Was Removed Without Cause, Official Says." *New York Times* February 7, 2007.

Johnston, David. 2007b. "Dismissed U.S. Attorneys Praised in Evaluations." *New York Times* February 25, 2007.

Johnston, David, and Eric Lipton. 2007. "'Loyalty' to Bush and Gonzales Was Factor in Prosecutors' Firings, E-Mail Shows." *New York Times* March 14, 2007.

Joynt Kumar, Martha. 2008. "Getting Ready for Day One: Taking Advantage of the Opportunities and Minimizing the Hazards of a Presidential Transition." *Public Administration Review* 68: 603–17.

Joynt Kumar, Martha, George C. Edwards, James P. Pfiffner, and Terry Sullivan. 2000. "Meeting the Freight Train Head On: Planning for the Transition to Power." *Presidential Studies Quarterly* 30: 754–69.

Kaplan, Thomas. 2018. "Trump Is Putting Indelible Conservative Stamp on Judiciary." *New York Times* July 31, 2018.

Kernell, Samuel. 1997. *Going Public: New Strategies of Presidential Leadership.* 3rd ed. CQ Press.

Kerstetter, Wayne. 1990. "Gateway to Justice: Police and Prosecutorial Response to Sexual Assaults Against Women." *Criminology* 81: 267–313.

Key, Sewall. 1938. "The Legal Work of the Federal Government." *Virginia Law Review* 35: 165–201.

Kiewiet, D. Roderick, and Mathews D. McCubbins. 1991. *The Logic of Delegation: Congressional Parties and the Appropriations Process.* Chicago: University of Chicago Press.

Kim, Seung Min, and John Bresnahan. 2017. "Trump Personally Interviewed U.S. Attorney Candidates." *Politico* October 19, 2017.

Kinane, Christina. 2019. *Control Without Confirmation: The Politics of Vacancies in Presidential Appointments.* (Doctoral Dissertation). Retrieved from https://deepblue.lib.umich.edu/handle/2027.42/151381.

King, Jonathan M., and Ian Ostrander. 2020. "Prioritizing Judicial Nominations After Presidential Transitions." *Presidential Studies Quarterly* Forthcoming.

Knudson, Jerry W. 1970. "The Jeffersonian Assault on the Federalist Judiciary, 1802–1805; Political Forces and Press Reaction." *American Journal of Legal History* 14: 55–75.

Koenig, Robert L. 1990. "No Rule on U.S. Attorney: Bush Didn't Order Dittmeier Ouster." *St. Louis Post-Dispatch* January 12, 1990.

Kramer, John, and Jeffrey Ulmer. 2002. "Downward Departures for Serious Violent Offenders: Local Court 'Corrections' to Pennsylvania's Sentencing Guidelines." *Criminology* 40: 897–932.

Krause, George A. 2009. "Organizational Complexity and Coordination Dilemmas in U.S. Executive Politics." *Presidential Studies Quarterly* 39: 74–88.

Krent, Harold J. 1989. "Executive Control over Criminal Law Enforcement: Some Lessons from History." *American University Law Review* 38: 275–312.

Krutz, Glen S., Richard Fleisher, and Jon R. Bond. 1998. "From Abe Fortas to Zoe Baird: Why Some Presidential Nominations Fail in the Senate." *American Political Science Review* 92 (4): 871–81.

Kuklinski, James H., and John E. Stanga. 1979. "Political Participation and Government Responsiveness: The Behavior of California Superior Courts." *American Political Science Review* 73: 1090–99.

LaFree, Gary D. 1980. "The Effect of Sexual Stratification by Race on Official Reactions to Rape." *American Sociological Review* 45: 842–54.

Lasswell, Harold. 1936. *Politics: Who Gets What, When, How.* Whittlesey House.

Lee, Frances E. 2016. *Insecure Majorities: Congress and the Perpetual Campaign.* University of Chicago Press.

Levenson, Laurie L. 1999. "Working Outside the Rules: The Undefined Responsibilities of Federal Prosecutors." *Fordham Urban Law Journal* 26: 553–72.

Levine, Samuel J. 2016. "The Potential Utility of Disciplinary Regulation as a Remedy for Abuses of Prosecutorial Discretion." *Duke Journal of Constitutional Law & Public Policy* 12: 1–12.

Levy, Leonard W. 1996. *A License to Steal: The Forfeiture of Property.* University of North Carolina Press.

Lewis, David E. 2003. *Presidents and the Politics of Agency Design: Political Insulation in the United States Government Bureaucracy, 1946–1997.* Stanford University Press.

Lewis, David E. 2008. *The Politics of Presidential Appointments: Political Control and Bureaucratic Performance.* Princeton University Press.

Lipset, Seymour Martin, and William Schneider. 1987. *The Confidence Gap: Business, Labor, and Government in the Public Mind.* Revised Edition. Johns Hopkins University Press.

Liptak, Adam. 2007. "For Federal Prosecutors, Politics Is Ever-Present." *New York Times* March 18, 2007.

Lochner, Todd. 2002. "Strategic Behavior and Prosecutorial Agenda Setting in United States Attorneys' Offices: The Role of U.S. Attorneys and Their Assistants." *The Justice System Journal* 23: 271–94.

Ma, Yue. 2002. "Prosecutorial Discretion and Plea Bargaining in the United States, France, Germany, and Italy: A Comparative Perspective." *International Criminal Justice Review* 12: 22–52.

MacDonald, Jason A. 2013. "Congressional Power over Executive Branch Policy Making: Limitations on Bureaucratic Regulations, 1989–2009." *Presidential Studies Quarterly* 43: 523–37.

Madonna, Anthony, and Ian Ostrander. 2017. "No Vacancy: Holdover Capacity and the Continued Staffing of Major Commissions." *Journal of Public Policy* 37: 341–61.

Malcolm, John G. 2013. "Civil Asset Forfeiture: Good Intentions Gone Awry and the Need for Reform." *The Heritage Foundation: Legal Memorandum* 151: 1–14.

Mansnerus, Laura. 2001. "New York's U.S. Attorneys Suddenly Lack Job Security." *New York Times* February 22, 2001.

Maor, Moshe. 2010. "Organizational Reputation and Jurisdictional Claims: The Case of the U.S. Food and Drug Administration." *Governance: An International Journal of Policy, Administration, and Institutions* 23: 133–59.

Marion, Nancy E., and Willard M. Oliver. 2012. "Going Symbolic: Presidential Use of Symbolic Rhetoric in Crime Control Policy." *Criminal Justice Policy Review* 24: 716–34.

Martineau, Kim. 2001a. "Bush Bucks State's Tradition." *Times Union* March 16, 2001.

Martineau, Kim. 2001b. "Federal Attorney to Leave in May." *Times Union* March 21, 2001.

Martinek, Wendy, Mark Kemper, and Steven R. Van Winkle. 2002. "To Advise and Consent: The Senate and Lower Federal Court Nominations, 1977–1998." *Journal of Politics* 64: 337–61.

Mather, Kate. 2016. "L.A. Police Chief Beck Backs Charges Against Officer Who Fatally Shot Venice Homeless Man." *Los Angeles Times* January 11, 2016.

Mather, Lynn. 1979. *Plea-Bargaining or Trial: The Process of Criminal-Case Disposition*. Lexington Books.

Maxfield, Linda Drazga, and John H. Kramer. 1998. "Substantial Assistance: An Empirical Yardstick Gauging Equity in Current Federal Policy and Practice." *United States Sentencing Commission* January: 1–25.

McCaffrey, Shannon. 2001. "Jockeying Begins over Appointment of U.S. Attorneys, Judges in New York." *Associated Press* February 8, 2001.

McCarthy, Justin. 2015. "More Americans Say Crime Is Rising in U.S." *Gallup* October 22, 2015. https://news.gallup.com/poll/186308/americans-say-crime-rising.aspx.

McCarty, Nolan, Keith T. Poole, and Howard Rosenthal. 2006. *Polarized America: The Dance of Ideology and Unequal Riches*. MIT Press.

McCarty, Nolan, and Rose Razaghian. 1999. "Advice and Consent: Senate Responses to Executive Branch Nominations 1885 - 1996." *American Journal of Political Science* 43: 1122–43.

McCubbins, Mathew D., Roger G. Noll, and Barry R. Weingast. 1987. "Administrative Procedures as Instruments of Policy Control." *Journal of Law, Economics, and Organization* 3: 243–77.

McMillion, Barry J. 2017. *The Blue Slip Process for U.S. Circuit and District Court Nominations: Frequently Asked Questions*. Congressional Research Service.

Melilli, Kenneth J. 1992. "Prosecutorial Discretion in an Adversary System." *BYU Law Review* 1992: 669–704.

Metcalfe, Christi, and Ted Chiricos. 2018. "Race, Plea, and Charge Reduction: An Assessment of Racial Disparities in the Plea Process." *Justice Quarterly* 35: 223–53.

Miller, Banks, and Brett Curry. 2019. *U.S. Attorneys, Political Control, and Career Ambition*. Oxford University Press.

Miller, Gary. 2000. "Above Politics: Credible Commitment and Efficiency in the Design of Public Agencies." *Journal of Public Administration, Theory, and Practice* 10: 289–327.

Miller, Gary J. 2005. "The Political Evolution of Principal-Agent Model." *Annual Review of Political Science* 8: 203–25.

Miller, Gary J., and Terry M. Moe. 1986. "The Positive Theory of Hierarchies" in *Political Science: The Science of Politics*, edited by Herbert F. Weisberg, 167–200. Agathon Press, Inc.

Miller, Lisa L. 2010. "The Invisible Black Victim: How American Federalism Perpetuates Racial Inequality in Criminal Justice." *Law & Society Review* 44: 805–42.

Miller, Marc L. 2004. "Domination & Dissatisfaction: Prosecutors as Sentencers." *Stanford Law Review* 56: 1211–69.

Miller, Marc L., and Samantha Caplinger. 2012. "Prosecution in Arizona: Practical Problems, Prosecutorial Accountability, and Local Solutions." *Crime and Justice* 41: 265–310.

Misner, Robert L. 1996. "Recasting Prosecutorial Discretion." *Journal of Criminal Law & Criminology* 86: 717–77.

Moe, Terry M. 1984. "The New Economics of Organization." *American Journal of Political Science* 28: 739–77.

Moe, Terry M. 1985. "Control and Feedback in Economic Regulation: The Case of the NLRB." *American Political Science Review* 79: 1094–1116.

Motivans, Mark. 2017. "Federal Justice Statistics, 2014—Statistical Tables."

Mustard, David B. 2001. "Racial, Ethnic, and Gender Disparities in Sentencing: Evidence from the U.S. Federal Courts." *Journal of Law and Economics* XLIV: 285–314.

Nagel, Ilene H., and Stephen J. Schulhofer. 1992. "A Tale of Three Cities: An Empirical Study of Charging and Bargaining Practices Under the Federal Sentencing Guidelines." *Southern California Law Review* 66: 501–66.

Nathan, Richard P. 1983. *The Administrative Presidency*. Wiley.

National Commission on Law Observance and Enforcement. 1931. *Report on Prosecution*. George W. Wickersham, Chairman. United States Government Printing Office.

Nelson, Jack, and James Gerstenzang. 1989. "Bush Fights Perception of a Floundering Start." *Los Angeles Times* March 8, 1989.

Nelson, Michael J. 2014. "Representative Justice? Public Opinion and the Criminal Justice System." *Journal of Law and Courts* 2: 117–52.

Nelson, Michael J., and Ian Ostrander. 2016. "Keeping Appointments: The Politics of Confirming United States Attorneys." *Justice System Journal* 37: 211–31.

Neuffer, Elizabeth, and Stephen Kurkjian. 1989. "McNamara Resigns as US Attorney; Prosecutor Cites Swirl of Controversy." *Boston Globe* January 31, 1989.

Neustadt, Richard. 2001. "The Presidential 'Hundred Days': An Overview." *Presidential Studies Quarterly* 31(1): 121–25.

Neustadt, Richard E. 1990. *Presidential Power and the Modern Presidents*. Revised Edition. Free Press.

New York Times. 1870. "A Department of Justice" July 10, 1870.

New York Times. 1985. "Conviction Clouding Future for Ohio Republican" March 10, 1985.

Nixon, David C. 2001. "Appointment Delay for Vacancies on the Federal Communications Commission." *Public Administration Review* 61: 483–92.

Nixon, David C. 2014. "Institutional Conflict and Perceived Property Rights in Appointment Politics." *Congress & the Presidency* 41: 223–47.

Nixon, Richard. 1968. "Address Accepting the Presidential Nomination at the Republican National Convention in Miami Beach, Florida." *The American Presidency Project* August 8, 1968.

Nokken, Timothy P., and Brian R. Sala. 2000. "Confirmation Dynamics: A Model of Presidential Appointments to Independent Agencies." *Journal of Theoretical Politics* 12: 91–112.

North, Douglas, and Barry Weingast. 1989. "Constitutions and Commitment: The Evolution of Institutions Governing Public Choice in Seventeenth-Century England." *The Journal of Economic History* 49(4): 803–32.

O'Connell, Anne Joseph. 2009. "Vacant Offices: Delays in Staffing Top Agency Positions." *Southern Californial Law Review* 82: 913–1000.

O'Connell, Anne Joseph. 2020. "Actings." *Columbia Law Review* 120: 613–728.

Office of Management and Budget. 2020. *Budget of the U.S. Government, Fiscal Year 2021: Historical Tables*. U.S. Office of Management; Budget.

O'Harrow Jr., Robert, Sari Horwitz, and Steven Rich. 2015. "Holder Limits Seized-Asset Sharing Process That Split Billions with Local, State Police." *Washington Post* January 16, 2015.

Oliver, Willard M. 1998. "Presidential Rhetoric on Crime and Public Opinion." *Criminal Justice Review* 23: 139–60.

Olson, Mary K. 1995. "Regulatory Agency Discretion Among Competing Industries: Inside the FDA." *Journal of Law, Economics, & Organization* 11: 379–405.

O'Neill, Michael Edmund. 2003. "When Prosecutors Don't: Trends in Federal Prosecutorial Declinations." *Notre Dame Law Review* 79: 221–90.

O'Neill, Michael Edmund. 2004. "Understanding Federal Prosecutorial Declinations: An Empirical Analysis of Predictive Factors." *American Criminal Law Review* 41: 1439–98.

Orden, Erica, Manu Raju, Evan Perez, and Kara Scannell. 2020. "Geoffrey Berman Is Leaving Office Immediately After Standoff with Trump Administration." *CNN* June 20, 2020.

Ostrander, Ian. 2015. "Powering down the Presidency: The Rise and Fall of Recess Appointments." *Presidential Studies Quarterly* 45: 558–72.

Ostrander, Ian. 2016. "The Logic of Collective Inaction: Senatorial Delay in Executive Nominations." *American Journal of Political Science* 60: 1063–76.

Ostrander, Ian. 2017. "The Politics of Executive Nominations in the Post Nuclear Senate." *Congress & the Presidency* 47: 752–76.

O'Toole, Thomas. 1981. "Lag in Selecting Prosecutors, Judges Take a Toll in Caseloads and Morale." *Washington Post* May 23, 1981.

Pear, Robert. 1981. "Senators to Select U.S. Attorneys." *New York Times* March 20, 1981.

Peffley, Mark, and Jon Hurwitz. 2010. *Justice in America: The Separate Realities of Blacks and Whites*. Cambridge University Press.

Peppers, Todd C. 2006. *Courtiers of the Marble Palace: The Rise and Influence of the Supreme Court Law Clerk*. Stanford University Press.

Perry, H. W. Jr. 1998. "United States Attorneys: Whom Shall They Serve?" *Law and Contemporary Problems* 61: 129–48.

Peters, Gerhard, and John T. Woolley. 2017. "The American Presidency Project."

Pfiffner, James. 1983. "The Carter-Reagan Transition: Hitting the Ground Running." *Presidential Studies Quarterly* 13: 623–45.

Pfiffner, James. 1996. *The Strategic Presidency: Hitting the Ground Running*. 2nd Edition. University of Kansas Press.

Pfiffner, James. 2018. "Organizing the Trump Presidency." *Presidential Studies Quarterly* 48: 153–67.

Piehl, Anne Morrison, and Shawn D. Bushway. 2007. "Measuring and Explaining Charge Bargaining." *Journal of Quantitative Criminology* 23: 105–25.

Pizzi, William T. 1978. "Prosecutorial Discretion, Plea Bargaining and the Supreme Court's Opinion in *Bordenkircher V. Hayes*." *Hastings Constitutional Law Quarterly* 6: 269–96.

Poole, Keith. 2009. "Common Space Scores" http://www.voteview.com/basic.htm.

Poole, Keith T. 1998. "Recovering a Basic Space from a Set of Issue Scales." *American Journal of Political Science* 42: 954–93.

Pound, Edward T. 1982. "U.S. Attorney in San Diego Dismissed." *New York Times* April 6, 1982.

Rakoff, Jed S. 2017. "Why Prosecutors Rule the Criminal Justice System—and What Can Be Done About It." *Northwestern University Law Review* 111: 1429–36.

Ramati, Phillip. 2009. "Interim U.S. Attorney Appointed in Midstate." *The Telegraph* July 31, 2009.

Randazzo, Kirk A. 2008. "Strategic Anticipation and the Hierarchy of Justice in U.S. District Courts." *American Politics Research* 36: 669–93.

Reagan, Ronald. 1988. *Remarks at a Republican Campaign Rally in Little Rock, Arkansas*. October 27, 1988.

Rich, Eric. 2007. "Justice Admits U.S. Attorney Was Forced Out." *Washington Post* March 7, 2007.

Rocque, Michael. 2011. "Racial Disparities in the Criminal Justice System and Perceptions of Legitimacy: A Theoretical Linkage." *Race and Justice* 1: 292–315.

Romer, Thomas, and Howard Rosenthal. 1978. "Political Resource Allocation, Controlled Agendas, and the Status Quo." *Public Choice* 33: 27–43.

Rosenbaum, David E. 1996. "Rostenkowski Pleads Guilty to Mail Fraud." *New York Times* April 10, 1996.

Rosenzweig, Paul. 2020. "Why Bill Barr Got Rid of Geoffrey Berman." *The Atlantic* June 21, 2020.

Rosica, James L. 2001. "Prosecutor Wants to Stay." *Tallahassee Democrat* Februrary 17, 2001.

Ruiz, Rebecca R., Robert Gebeloff, Steve Eder, and Ben Protess. 2020. "A Conservative Agenda Unleashed on the Federal Courts." *New York Times* March 14, 2020.

Saltzburg, Stephen A., and Daniel J. Capra. 1996. *American Criminal Procedure: Cases and Commentary*. West Publishing.

Sampson, Kyle. 2005a. "RE: Question from Karl Rove. Email Sent Sunday" Email message. January 9, 2005. 7:34 p.m.

Sampson, Kyle. 2005b. "U.S. Attorneys. Email to Harriet Miers" Email message. March 2, 2005. 5:42 p.m.

Savage, Charlie. 2020. "Who Can Fire a Court-Appointed U.S. Attorney? An Abrupt Legal Fight, Explained." *New York Times* June 20, 2020.

Savage, David G. 2007. "Replacing U.S. Attorneys Stretches Back to Reagan." *Los Angeles Times* March 23, 2007.

Scherer, Nancy, Brandon L. Bartels, and Amy Steigerwalt. 2008. "Sounding the Fire Alarm: The Role of Interest Groups in the Lower Federal Court Confirmation Process." *Journal of Politics* 70: 1026–39.

Schumer, Charles. 2020. "Schumer Statement Calling on Jay Clayton to Withdraw His Nomination & for the DOJ IG to Launch an Investigation into Trump Admin. Efforts to Interfere with SDNY Investigations" Press Release. June 20, 2020.

Scott, Kevin M. 2006. "Understanding Judicial Hierarchy: Reversals and the Behavior of Intermediate Appellate Judges." *Law & Society Review* 40: 163–92.

Scott, Kevin M. 2007. *U.S. Attorneys Who Have Served Less Than Full Four-Year Terms, 1981–2006*. Congressional Research Service.

Sen, Maya. 2014. "How Judicial Qualification Ratings May Disadvantage Minority and Female Candidates." *Journal of Law and Courts* 2: 33–65.

Senate Judiciary Committee. 2007. *Preserving Prosecutorial Independence: Is the Department of Justice Politicizing the Hiring and Firing of U.S. Attorneys?* Hearings before the Committee on the Judiciary United States Senate. March 6, March 29, May 15, June 5, July 11,; August 2, 2007. 110th Congress. 1st Session.

Senate Subcommittee on Criminal Justice. 1980. "Hearings on Forfeiture of Profits of Narcotics Traffickers."

Serrano, Richard A. 2007a. "Alarm Rises over Firing of U.S. Atty. In San Diego." *Los Angeles Times* March 19, 2007.

Serrano, Richard A. 2007b. "Border Policing Was a Trial for 3 U.S. Attorneys." *Los Angeles Times* April 15, 2007.

Sessions, Jefferson. 2017. "Department Charging and Sentencing Policy" U.S. Department of Justice. May 10, 2017.

Sessions, Jefferson. 2018a. "The Attorney General's Guidelines on the Asset Forfeiture Program."

Sessions, Jefferson. 2018b. "Zero-Tolerance for Offenses Under 8 U.S.C. §1325(a)." U.S. Department of Justice. April 6, 2018.

Seymour, Jr., Whitney North. 1975. *United States Attorney*. William Marrow.

Shapiro, Ari. 2009. "Obama Administration Poised to Pick U.S. Attorneys." *NPR Politics* January 27, 2009.

Shear, Michael D. 2017. "Months After Firing U.S. Attorneys, Trump Nominates Replacements." *New York Times* June 12, 2017.

Shear, Michael D., Mark Landler, Matt Apuzzo, and Eric Lichtblau. 2017. "Trump Fires Acting Attorney General Who Defied Him." *New York Times* January 30, 2017.

Shepsle, Kenneth. 2017. *Rule Breaking and Political Imagination*. University of Chicago Press.

Shermer, Lauren O'Neill, and Brian D. Johnson. 2010. "Criminal Prosecutions: Examining Prosecutorial Discretion and Charge Reductions in the U.S. Federal District Courts." *Justice Quarterly* 27: 394–430.

Shipan, Charles R. 2004. "Regulatory Regimes, Agency Actions, and the Conditional Nature of Congressional Influence." *American Political Science Review* 98: 467–80.

Shipan, Charles R., and Megan L. Shannon. 2003. "Delaying Justice(s): A Duration Analysis of Supreme Court Confirmations." *American Journal of Political Science* 47: 654–68.

Shortell, David, and Evan Perez. 2020. "Trump to Nominate New Top Prosecutor for Washington, DC." *CNN* May 18, 2020.

Shugerman, Jed Handelsman. 2014. "The Creation of the Department of Justice: Professionalization Without Civil Rights or Civil Service." *Stanford Law Review* 66: 121–72.

Smith, Chris. 2017. "Rod Rosenstein's Revenge—and What Comes Next." *Vanity Fair* May 18, 2017.

Smith, Steven S. 2014. *The Senate Syndrome: The Evolution of Procedural Warfare in the Modern Senate*. University of Oklahoma Press.

Sniffen, Michael J. 1981. "Smith Says Administration Will Continue Traditional Policy." *Associated Press* March 19, 1981.

Sollenberger, Mitchel A. 2003. *The History of the Blue Slip in the Senate Committee on the Judiciary, 1917–Present*. Congressional Research Service.

Solowiej, Lisa A., Wendy L. Martinek, and Thomas L. Brunell. 2005. "Partisan Politics: The Impact of Party in the Confirmation of Minority and Female Federal Court Nominees." *Party Politics* 11: 557–77.

Spaulding, Norman W. 2008. "Professional Independence in the Office of the Attorney General." *Stanford Law Review* 60: 1931–79.

Spohn, Cassia, Dawn Beichner, and Erika Davis-Frenzel. 2001. "Prosecutorial Justifications for Sexual Assault Case Rejection: Guarding the 'Gateway to Justice.'" *Social Problems* 48: 206–35.

Spohn, Cassia, and Robert Fornango. 2009. "U.S. Attorneys and Substantial Assistance Departures: Testing for Interprosecutor Disparity." *Criminology* 47: 813–46.

Spohn, Cassia, and David Holleran. 2001. "Prosecuting Sexual Assault: A Comparison of Charging Decisions in Sexual Assault Cases Involving Strangers, Acquaintances, and Intimate Partners." *Justice Quarterly* 18: 651–88.

Spohn, Cassia, and Jeffrey Spears. 1996. "The Effect of Offender and Victim Characteristics on Sexual Assault Case Processing Decisions." *Justice Quarterly* 13: 649–79.

Stefansky, Emma, and Kia Makarechi. 2017. "Trump's Firing of U.S. Attorneys Raises Eyebrows, Prompts Conflict." *Vanity Fair* March 11, 2017.

Steigerwalt, Amy. 2010. *Battle over the Bench: Senators, Interest Groups, and Lower Court Confirmations*. University of Virginia Press.

Stillman, Sarah. 2017. "Jeff Sessions and the Resurgence of Civil Asset Forfeiture." *The New Yorker* August 15, 2017.

Stolberg, Sheryl Gay. 2007. "Bush Criticizes Handling of Prosecutors' Dismissals." *New York Times* March 15, 2007.

Stras, David R. 2007. "Why Supreme Court Justices Should Ride Circuit Again." *Minnesota Law Review* 91: 1710–51.

Strohm, Chris. 2019. "Rod Rosenstein Resigns: A Look Back at His Controversial Tenure." *Fortune* April 29, 2019.

Stuntz, William J. 2004. "Plea Bargaining and Criminal Law's Disappearing Shadow." *Harvard Law Review* 117: 2548–69.

Subcommittee on Courts, Civil Liberties, and the Administration of Justice. 1978. *Selection and Removal of U.S. Attorneys*. U.S. House of Representatives. 95th Congress, 2nd Session. March 13; May 10–11.

Talbert, Jeffrey C., Bryan D. Jones, and Frank R. Baumgartner. 1995. "Nonlegislative Hearings and Policy Change in Congress." *American Journal of Political Science* 39: 383–405.

Task Force on the Federalization of Criminal Law. 1998. *The Federalization of Criminal Law*. American Bar Association, Criminal Justice Section.

Thomas, Pierre. 1994. "Rostenkowski Indicted on Charges He Defrauded the U.S. of $500,000." *Washington Post* June 1, 1994.

Tiede, Lydia Brashear. 2009. "The Impact of the Federal Sentencing Guidelines and Reform: A Comparative Analysis." *Justice System Journal* 30: 34–39.

Trump, Donald J. 2017. "Inaugural Address" from The American Presidency Project. January 20, 2017.

Tyler, Tom R., and Yuen J. Huo. 2002. *Trust in the Law: Encouraging Public Cooperation with the Police and Courts*. New York: Russell Sage Foundation.

Ulmer, Jeffrey T. 2012. "Recent Developments and New Directions in Sentencing Research." *Justice Quarterly* 29: 1–40.

U.S. Department of Justice. 1980. *Department of Justice Principles of Federal Prosecution*. U.S. Department of Justice.

U.S. Department of Justice. 2001. "White House and Justice Department Begin U.S. Attorney Transition" Press Release 01-107. March 14, 2001.

U.S. Department of Justice. 2008. *An Investigation into the Removal of Nine U.S. Attorneys in 2006*. U.S. Department of Justice.

U.S. Department of Justice. 2014. "Attorney General, Deputy and Associate." *Organization, Mission & Functions Manual* September 9, 2014 https://www.justice.gov/jmd/organization-mission-and-functions-manual-attorney-general.

U.S. Department of Justice. 2017. "Attorney General Sessions Issues Policy and Guidelines on Federal Adoptions of Assets Seized by State or Local Law Enforcement" Press Release 17-795. July 19, 2017.

U.S. Department of Justice. 2018a. *Department of Justice Organizational Chart*. https://www.justice.gov/file/1047436/download.

U.S. Department of Justice. 2018b. *Historical Timeline of U.S. Attorneys*. https://www.justice.gov/usao/timeline/history#event-556011.

U.S. Department of Justice. 2019a. "Asset Forfeiture Policy Manual."

U.S. Department of Justice. 2019b. "Former Attorney General Rod J. Rosenstein" May 13, 2019 https://www.justice.gov/archives/dag/staff-profile/former-deputy-attorney-general-rod-j-rosenstein.

U.S. Department of Justice. 2019c. *FY 2020 Budget Request at a Glance*. https://www.justice.gov/jmd/page/file/1142306/download.

U.S. Department of Justice. 2019d. *Asset Forfeiture Policy Manual*.

U.S. Department of Justice. 2020a. *150 Years of the Department of Justice*. https://www.justice.gov/history/timeline/150-years-department-justice#event-1267196.

U.S. Department of Justice. 2020b. "About DOJ" https://www.justice.gov/about.

U.S. Department of Justice. 2020c. "Attorney General William P. Barr on the Nomination of Jay Clayton to Serve as U.S. Attorney for the Southern District of New York" Press Release 20-570. June 19, 2020.

U.S. General Accounting Office. 1981. "Asset Forfeiture—a Seldom Used Tool in Combatting Drug Trafficking."

U.S. General Accounting Office. 2003. "Federal Drug Offenses: Departures from Sentencing Guidelines and Mandatory Minimum Sentences, Fiscal Years 1999–2001."

U.S. Senate. 2020. *Trump Cabinet Nominations*. United States Senate. https://www.senate.gov/legislative/nominations/Trump_cabinet.htm.

U.S. Sentencing Commission. 2018. "U.S. Sentencing Guidelines Manual."

Vecchi, Gregory, and Robert T. Sigler. 2001. *Assets Forfeiture: A Study of Policy and Its Practice*. University of North Carolina Press.

Vinegrad, Alan. 2017. "DOJ Charging and Sentencing Policies: From Civiletti to Sessions." *Federal Sentencing Reporter* 30: 3–8.

Vorenberg, James. 1981. "Decent Restraint of Prosecutorial Discretion." *Harvard Law Review* 94: 1521–73.

Wagner, Diane. 2009. "Georgia Attorney General Candidate Max Wood Has Ties to Rome." *Rome News-Tribune* October 8, 2009.

Warchol, Greg L., Dennis M. Payne, and Brian R. Johnson. 1996. "Criminal Forfeiture: An Effective Alternative to Civil and Administrative Proceedings." *Police Studies* 19: 51–66.

Warren, Charles. 1923. "New Light on the History of the Federal Judiciary Act of 1789." *Harvard Law Review* 37: 49–132.

Waxman, Seth P. 2000. "Twins at Birth: Civil Rights and the Role of the Solicitor General." *Indiana Law Journal* 75: 1297–1315.

Weber, Richard. 2007. "Asset Forfeiture: Introduction." *United States Attorneys' Bulletin* 55: 1–2.

Weingast, Barry R. 1984. "The Congressional Bureaucratic System: A Principal-Agent Perspective (with Applications to the Sec)." *Public Choice* 44: 147–91.

Weingast, Barry R., and Mark J. Moran. 1983. "Bureaucratic Discretion or Congressional Control: Regulatory Policymaking by the Federal Trade Commission." *The Journal of Political Economy* 91: 765–800.

Weiser, Benjamin. 2018. "With No Nomination from Trump, Judges Choose U.S. Attorney for Manhattan." *New York Times* April 25, 2018.

Weiser, Benjamin, William K. Rashbaum, Nicole Hong, Maggie Haberman, and Katie Benner. 2020. "Clash over U.S. Attorney Who Investigated Trump Associates Sets Off Crisis." *New York Times* June 19, 2020.

Weiss, David C. 2008. "Nothing Improper? Examining Constitutional Limits, Congressional Action, Partisan Motivation, and Pretextual Justification in the U.S. Attorney Removals." *Michigan Law Review* 107: 317–64.

Werner, Leslie Maitland. 1984. "U.S. Attorney in Cleveland Is Discharged by President." *New York Times* October 3, 1984.

Whelan, M. Edward. 2003. *Temporary Filling of Vacancies in the Office of United States Attorney*. U.S. Department of Justice.

The White House. 2009. "President Obama Nominates Michael Moore, Carmen Ortiz and Edward Tarver to Be US Attorneys" Press Release. September 18, 2009.

Whitford, Andrew. 2002. "Decentralization and Political Control of the Bureaucracy." *Journal of Theoretical Politics* 14: 167–93.

Whitford, Andrew B., and Jeff Yates. 2003. "Policy Signals and Executive Governance: Presidential Rhetoric in the 'War on Drugs.'" *Journal of Politics* 65: 995–1012.

Whitford, Andrew B., and Jeff Yates. 2009. *Presidential Rhetoric and the Public Agenda: Constructing the War on Drugs*. Johns Hopkins University Press.

Williams, Marian R. 2002. "Civil Asset Forfeiture: Where Does the Money Go?" *Criminal Justice Review* 27: 321–29.

Williams, Marian R., Jefferson E. Holcomb, Tomislav V. Kovandzic, and Scott Bullock. 2010. "Policing for Profit: The Abuse of Civil Asset Forfeiture." The Federalist Society.

Wilmot, Keith A., and Cassia Spohn. 2004. "Prosecutorial Discretion and Real-Offense Sentencing: An Analysis of Relevant Conduct Under the Federal Sentencing Guidelines." *Criminal Justice Policy Review* 15: 324–43.

Womack, Amy Leigh. 2011. "U.S. Attorney Moore Setting Priorities for Office." *The Telegraph* January 24, 2011.

Wood, B. Dan. 1988. "Principals, Bureaucrats, and Responsiveness in Clean Air Enforcements." *American Political Science Review* 82: 213–34.

Wood, B. Dan, and Richard W. Waterman. 1991. "The Dynamics of Political Control of the Bureaucracy." *American Political Science Review* 85: 801–28.

Wright, Ronald F. 2012. "Persistent Localism in the Prosecutor Services of North Carolina." *Crime and Justice* 41: 211–64.

Wright, Ronald F., and Rodney L. Engen. 2006. "The Effects of Depth and Distance in a Criminal Code on Charging, Sentencing, and Prosecutor Power." *North Carolina Law Review* 84: 1935–82.

Wright, Ronald, and Marc Miller. 2002. "The Screening/Bargaining Tradeoff." *Stanford Law Review* 55: 29–118.

Wright, Ronald, and Marc Miller. 2003. "Honesty and Opacity in Charge Bargains." *Stanford Law Review* 55: 1409–17.

Yates, Sally Quillian. 2015. "Individual Accountability for Corporate Wrongdoing" U.S. Department of Justice. September 9, 2015.

Ziner, Karen Lee. 2001. "Curran to Remain U.S. Attorney." *Providence Journal-Bulletin* March 19, 2001.

Index

For the benefit of digital users, indexed terms that span two pages (e.g., 52–53) may, on occasion, appear on only one of those pages.